Global Standards of Market Civilization

AF695998

Global standards call upon us to change the individual, the society, the state, and the international system. Global standards of market civilization have ramifications from the macro-level of international institutions to the micro-level of personal well-being.

This unique volume interrogates the way that civilizational standards are encouraging social, political and cultural conformity among states in an economically globalized world. Navigating the conceptual history of 'standards of civilization', a diverse range of authors investigate the idea of markets as civilizers of individuals, societies, states, and relations between states. The conceptual framework is brought to bear on empirical cases that discuss how the world's powerful international economic institutions generate policy standards (IMF, WTO, OECD and others), as well as the capacity of those on the receiving end to conform, resist and exploit them.

This book will be of interest to students and researchers of globalization; international political economy; comparative political economy; economic history; political theory; governance; international relations and international law.

Brett Bowden is Research Fellow in the Centre for the History of European Discourses at the University of Queensland.

Leonard Seabrooke is Associate Professor in the International Center for Business and Politics, Copenhagen Business School, and Adjunct Senior Fellow in the Department of International Relations, RSPAS, The Australian National University.

RIPE series in global political economy

Series Editors:

Louise Amoore	*University of Newcastle, UK*
Randall Germain	*Carleton University, Canada*
Rorden Wilkinson	*University of Manchester, UK*

Formerly edited by Otto Holman (University of Amsterdam), Marianne Marchand (Universidad de las Américas-Puebla), Henk Overbeek (Free University, Amsterdam) and Marianne Franklin (University of Amsterdam)

The RIPE series editorial board are:

Mathias Albert (Bielefeld University, Germany), Mark Beeson (University of Queensland, Australia), A. Claire Cutler (University of Victoria, Canada), Marianne Franklin (University of Amsterdam, the Netherlands), Stephen Gill (York University, Canada), Jeffrey Hart (Indiana University, USA), Eric Helleiner (Trent University, Canada), Otto Holman (University of Amsterdam, the Netherlands), Marianne H. Marchand (Universidad de las Américas-Puebla, Mexico), Craig N. Murphy (Wellesley College, USA), Robert O'Brien (McMaster University, Canada), Henk Overbeek (Vrije Universiteit, the Netherlands), Anthony Payne (University of Sheffield, UK) and V. Spike Peterson (University of Arizona, USA).

This series, published in association with the Review of International Political Economy, provides a forum for current debates in international political economy. The series aims to cover all the central topics in IPE and to present innovative analyses of emerging topics. The titles in the series seek to transcend a state-centred discourse and focus on three broad themes:

- the nature of the forces driving globalisation forward
- resistance to globalisation
- the transformation of the world order.

The series comprises two strands:

The RIPE Series in Global Political Economy aims to address the needs of students and teachers, and the titles will be published in hardback and paperback. Titles include:

Transnational Classes and International Relations
Kees van der Pijl

Gender and Global Restructuring
Sightings, Sites and Resistances
Edited by Marianne H. Marchand and Anne Sisson Runyan

Global Political Economy
Contemporary Theories
Edited by Ronen Palan

Ideologies of Globalization
Contending Visions of a New World Order
Mark Rupert

The Clash within Civilisations
Coming to Terms with Cultural Conflicts
Dieter Senghaas

Global Unions?
Theory and Strategies of Organized Labour in the Global Political Economy
Edited by Jeffrey Harrod and Robert O'Brien

Political Economy of a Plural World
Critical Reflections on Power, Morals and Civilizations
Robert Cox with Michael Schechter

A Critical Rewriting of Global Political Economy
Integrating Reproductive, Productive and Virtual Economies
V. Spike Peterson

Contesting Globalization
Space and Place in the World Economy
André C. Drainville

Global Institutions and Development
Framing the World?
Edited by Morten Bøås and Desmond McNeill

Global Institutions, Marginalization, and Development
Craig N. Murphy

Critical Theories, International Relations and 'the Anti-Globalisation Movement'
The Politics of Global Resistance
Edited by Catherine Eschle and Bice Maiguashca

Globalization, Governmentality, and Global Politics
Regulation for the Rest of Us?
Ronnie D. Lipschutz, with James K. Rowe

Routledge/RIPE Studies in Global Political Economy is a forum for innovative new research intended for a high-level specialist readership, and the titles will be available in hardback only. Titles include:

1. Globalization and Governance *
Edited by Aseem Prakash and Jeffrey A. Hart

2. Nation-States and Money
The Past, Present and Future of National Currencies
Edited by Emily Gilbert and Eric Helleiner

3. The Global Political Economy of Intellectual Property Rights
The New Enclosures?
Christopher May

4. Integrating Central Europe
EU expansion and Poland, Hungary and the Czech Republic
Otto Holman

5. Capitalist Restructuring, Globalisation and the Third Way
Lessons from the Swedish Model
J. Magnus Ryner

6. Transnational Capitalism and the Struggle over European Integration
Bastiaan van Apeldoorn

7. World Financial Orders
An Historical International Political Economy
Paul Langley

8. The Changing Politics of Finance in Korea and Thailand
From Deregulation to Debacle
Xiaoke Zhang

9. Anti-Immigrantism in Western Democracies
Statecraft, Desire and the Politics of Exclusion
Roxanne Lynn Doty

10. The Political Economy of European Employment
European Integration and the Transnationalization of the (Un)Employment Question
Edited by Henk Overbeek

11. Rethinking Global Political Economy
Emerging Issues, Unfolding Odysseys
Edited by Mary Ann Tétreault, Robert A. Denemark, Kenneth P. Thomas and Kurt Burch

12. Rediscovering International Relations Theory
Matthew Davies and Michael Niemann

13. International Trade and Developing Countries*
Bargaining Coalitions in the GATT & WTO
Amrita Narlikar

14. The Southern Cone Model
The Political Economy of Regional Capitalist Development in Latin America
Nicola Phillips

15. The Idea of Global Civil Society
Politics and Ethics of a Globalizing Era
Edited by Randall D. Germain and Michael Kenny

16. Governing Financial Globalization
International Political Economy and Multi-Level Governance
Edited by Andrew Baker, David Hudson and Richard Woodward

17. Resisting Intellectual Property
Debora J. Halbert

18. Neoliberal Hegemony
A Global Critique
Edited by Dieter Plehwe, Bernhard Walpen and Gisela Neunhöffer

19. Global Standards of Market Civilization
Edited by Brett Bowden and Leonard Seabrooke

20. Beyond Globalization
Capitalism, territoriality and the international relations of modernity
Hannes Lacher

21. Images of Gramsci
Connections and contentions in political theory and international relations
Edited by Andreas Bieler and Adam David Morton

* *Also available in paperback*

Global Standards of Market Civilization

Edited by Brett Bowden and Leonard Seabrooke

Routledge
Taylor & Francis Group
LONDON AND NEW YORK

First published 2006
by Routledge
2 Park Square, Milton Park, Abingdon, Oxon. OX14 4RN

Simultaneously published in the USA and Canada
by Routledge
270 Madison Avenue, New York, NY 10016

Routledge is an imprint of the Taylor & Francis Group, an informa business

Transferred to Digital Printing 2007

© 2006 Brett Bowden and Leonard Seabrooke for selection and editorial matter; individual contributors their contributions

Typeset in Baskerville by Taylor & Francis Books

All rights reserved. No part of this book may be reprinted or reproduced or utilized in any form or by any electronic, mechanical, or other means, now known or hereafter invented, including photocopying and recording, or in any information storage or retrieval system, without permission in writing from the publishers.

British Library Cataloguing in Publication Data
A catalogue record for this book is available from the British Library

Library of Congress Cataloging in Publication Data
Global standards of market civilization / edited by Brett Bowden and Leonard Seabrooke.

p. cm. -- (Routledge/RIPE studies in global political economy)

Includes bibliographical references and index.

ISBN 0-415-37545-2 (hardback : alk. paper) 1. International economic relations. 2. Globalization--Social aspects. 3. Comparative civilization. 4. Economic history. I. Bowden, Brett, 1968- II. Seabrooke, Leonard, 1974- III. Title. IV. Series.

HF1359.G5775 2006

303.48'2--dc22

2005029071

ISBN10: 0-415-37545-2 (hbk) ISBN13: 978-0-415-37545-0 (hbk)
ISBN10: 0-203-08620-1 (ebk) ISBN13: 978-0-203-08620-9 (ebk)
ISBN 10: 0-415-45985-0 (pbk) ISBN 13: 978-0-415-45985-3 (pbk)

Publisher's Note
The publisher has gone to great lengths to ensure the quality of this reprint but points out that some imperfections in the original may be apparent

Contents

Notes on Contributors

Jacqueline Best is Assistant Professor in the School of Political Studies at the University of Ottawa. Her publications include *The Limits of Transparency: Ambiguity and the History of International Finance* (Cornell 2005), as well as articles in the *Review of International Political Economy*, *New Political Economy*, and the *Review of International Studies.*

Brett Bowden is a Research Fellow in the Centre for the History of European Discourses at the University of Queensland. He has published in *Alternatives: Local, Global, Political*, *Citizenship Studies*, *National Identities*, *Critical Review of International Social and Political Philosophy*, and the *Journal of the History of International Law*. He is the co-editor (with Michael T. Davis) of *Terror: From Tyrannicide to Terrorism in Europe, 1605–2005* (UQP 2007).

André Broome is a Doctoral Candidate in the Department of International Relations, Research School of Pacific and Asian Studies, the Australian National University.

Mlada Bukovansky is Associate Professor of Government at Smith College. Her publications include *Legitimacy and Power Politics* (Princeton 2002), as well as articles in *International Organization*, *Review of International Political Economy* and *Review of International Studies.*

Jillian Clare Cohen is an Assistant Professor at the Leslie Dan Faculty of Pharmacy and Director of the Comparative Program on Health and Society, Munk Centre for International Studies, at the University of Toronto. She has worked as a pharmaceutical policy specialist for the World Bank and the WHO, as well as an adviser to governments on pharmaceutical policy issues, particularly Brazil, Bulgaria, and Ghana.

Barry Hindess is Professor of Political Science in the Research School of Social Sciences at the Australian National University. His recent works include *Discourses of Power* (Blackwell 1995), *Governing Australia* (with Mitchell Dean, Cambridge 1998), *Corruption and Democracy in Australia* (Democratic Audit 2004), and *Us and Them: Anti-elitism in Australia* (with Marian Sawer, API Network 2004), as well as numerous articles on democracy, liberalism and empire, and neo-liberalism.

John M. Hobson is Professor of Politics and International Relations at the University of Sheffield. His book publications comprise: Everyday *International Political Economy* (co-edited with Leonard Seabrooke, Cambridge 2007), *The Eastern Origins of Western Civilisation* (Cambridge 2004), *Historical Sociology of International Relations* (co-edited with Steve Hobden, Cambridge 2002), *The State and International Relations* (Cambridge 2000), *The Wealth of States* (Cambridge 1997), and *States and Economic Development* (with Linda Weiss, Polity 1995).

Gemma Kyle is an international taxation consultant. She has previously worked for the International Tax and Treaties Division in the Australian Treasury.

Peter Larmour is Reader in Public Policy and Governance in the Asia Pacific School of Economics and Government, the Australian National University. His publications include *Foreign Flowers: Institutional Transfer and Good Governance in the Pacific Islands* (Hawai'i 2005).

Michael J. Oliver is Professor of Economics at École Supérieure de Commerce de Rennes. He is the author of numerous articles, four books, and two edited volumes, including *Exchange Rate Regimes in the Twentieth Century* (with Derek H. Aldcroft, Edward Elgar 1998).

Geoffrey A. Pigman is a Lecturer in Political Economy at Bennington College and a Visiting Fellow at the Center for Global Change and Governance, Rutgers University. He is the author of *The Politics of the World Economic Forum* (Routledge 2006), and has published in *Review of International Political Economy*, *Review of International Studies*, *Global Society*, and *International Studies Perspectives*.

Leonard Seabrooke is Associate Professor in the International Center for Business and Politics at the Copenhagen Business School. His book publications comprise *US Power in International Finance* (Palgrave 2001), *The Social Sources of Financial Power* (Cornell 2006), and *Everyday International Political Economy* (co-edited with John M. Hobson, Cambridge 2007).

Matthew Watson is Senior Lecturer in Political Economy at the University of Birmingham. His publications include *Foundations of International Political Economy* (Palgrave 2005), as well as articles in, among others, *Review of International Political Economy*, *Economy and Society*, *Politics*, and *New Political Economy*.

Series Preface

Across the social sciences, teachers and researchers struggle daily to understand the motive springs of the world we live in. This intellectual (and practical) struggle can take inspiration from the 18th century Neapolitan philologist and philosopher Giambatista Vico, whose verum-factum principle states that only those who have made the world retain a capacity to understand it. The world that has recently been 'made' into a globalized, capitalist, market economy requires the kind of historically-sensitive, interpretive and hermeneutic approach to knowledge championed by Vico, and it is precisely such an approach that is offered by Brett Bowden and Leonard Seabrooke in their edited collection, *Global Standards of Market Civilization.*

This volume brings together a diverse group of scholars concerned with how standards of civilization have become constructed, used and abused by social and political forces. Attributing the veneer of 'civilization' to non-western societies has been an implicit yardstick by which western societies have judged others, and the authors in this volume want to assess how well this yardstick itself stands up to critical examination. Most importantly, they ask how the norms and practices of advanced capitalist market relations reflect and refine existing standards of civilization: or better yet, how such notions of civilization underpin and influence the supposedly technical and economic institutions of market society. In this way Bowden and Seabrooke have posed a quintessential question of political economy: how do normative values translate into and support material patterns of production, exchange, distribution and consumption.

In asking this question the editors of this volume have demonstrated yet again that political theory and international political economy are historical bedfellows rather than conspiratorial gladiators. Whether it is Matthew Watson's use of Adam Smith, or Barry Hindness's consideration of liberalism, asking how norms and values give rise to codes of conduct and standards of regulation enable us to more fully apprehend how the grip of market civilization is strengthening even as parts of the global economy become more fragile and unstable. 'Civilization' might well be a dangerous concept, as the editors remind us in the final chapter. But refusing to acknowledge and pursue the many intricate links between 'civilization' and the unfolding world order is equally dangerous, and surely foolhardy.

The Routledge/RIPE Series in Global Political Economy seeks to publish innovative and cutting edge scholarship that pushes forward our understanding of how the world is organized, why it is developing in particular directions, and how globalizing tendencies across a range of social relations are reinforcing or undermining these changes. Three important intellectual strands have permeated many of its titles: a curiosity and determination to bring together new and different literatures that offer the promise of better understanding how power and authority are organized within the global political economy; a focus on issues broadly associated with globalization and governance as key elements of such power and authority; and a concern with the way in which today's global political economy is changing and thereby forcing us to adapt our conceptual frameworks to take account of the changing nature of politics and political economy in a global context.

This volume exemplifies our mandate and makes links to a number of other volumes in the series, such as, among others, Randall Germain and Michael Kenny's *The Idea of Global Civil Society*, Catherine Eschle and Bice Maiguashca's Critical Theories, International Relations and the 'Anti-Globalisation Movement', and Dieter Senghaas's *The Clash within Civilisations*. It sets itself up as an interrogation of civilizational problematics which span different intellectual traditions; it works across a wide terrain that embraces the major institutional foundations of the global political economy; and it connects contemporary issues with their historical antecedents. *Global Standards of Market Civilization* will therefore command a readership interested in the diverse threads that support and undermine societies in an age of globalization, and we are pleased to include it in the series.

Louise Amoore, *University of Newcastle upon Tyne, UK*
Randall Germain, *Carleton University, Canada*
Rorden Wilkinson, *University of Manchester, UK*

Acknowledgements

The benefits of long casual walks through Australia's national parks can be intellectual as well as physical. This project emerged from our wanderings and wonderings on the relationship between the notion of a standard of civilization, which has reared its head again in political theory and international politics, and the idea of globalization generating policy homogeneity in political economy literature. The concept of 'global standards of market civilization' was the result of our meanderings from the park to the pub to publication, and we are very happy that the contributors to this volume have found it a useful framework to bring political theory and political economy together. As these fields often talk past each other, often while sitting back-to-back, making them talk to each other has been quite fun. The discussions that have emerged between the editors and contributors, both virtual and at conferences, have brought the framework to life and will, we hope, sustain debate for some time to come. We thank our contributors for providing original material and avoiding edited-collection re-hash.

Len thanks the Department of International Relations in the Research School of Pacific and Asian Studies at the Australian National University, where he was Research Fellow from 2003 until late 2005, and where work on the project was completed. Particular thanks go to Mary-Louise Hickey for her proofreading and comments that greatly improved the manuscript. Brett thanks the Centre for the History of European Discourses at the University of Queensland.

We thank the three anonymous reviewers for Routledge for their critical comments, which have improved the volume considerably. Our particular gratitude goes to Herman M. Schwartz for his extensive critical comments on many of the chapters in this volume. Randall Germain signaled early interest in the project and encouraged its development along with series editors Louise Amoore and Rorden Wilkinson – thank you all for your support. We also thank Heidi Bagtazo from Routledge for her support and professionalism – it has been a pleasure. Finally we thank our partners, Gerda Roelvink and Anna Carnerup, for their love, support, and patience.

Brett Bowden
Leonard Seabrooke

List of Abbreviations

AIDS	Acquired Immune Deficiency Syndrome
APEC	Asia-Pacific Economic Co-operation
ASEAN	Association of Southeast Asian Nations
BIS	Bank for International Settlements
BoE	Bank of England
C20	Committee of Twenty
CFATF	Caribbean Financial Action Task Force
CFB	Corporation for Foreign Bondholders
CPI	Corruption Perceptions Index
CRA	credit-rating agency
DSB	Dispute Settlement Body
DTA	double taxation agreement
EC	European Community
EMEs	emerging market economies
EMU	European Monetary Union
EU	European Union
FATF	Financial Action Task Force on Money Laundering
FDI	foreign direct investment
FSF	Financial Stability Forum
G10	Group of Ten
G20	Group of Twenty
G5	Group of Five
G7	Group of Seven
G8	Group of Eight
GATT	General Agreement on Tariffs and Trade
GDP	gross domestic product
HIPC	Highly Indebted Poor Countries
HIV	Human Immuno Deficiency Virus
HTPI	harmful tax practices initiative
IBF	International Banking Facility
ICAC	Independent Commission Against Corruption
ICU	International Clearing Union
IFIs	international financial institutions

IMC	Imperial Maritime Customs
IMF	International Monetary Fund
IMS	international monetary system
MAI	Multilateral Agreement on Investment
Mercosur	Mercado Común del Sur
MGE	modern global economy
MSF	Médecins Sans Frontières
NAFTA	North American Free Trade Agreement
NGOs	non-governmental organizations
NIS	National Integrity System
OECD	Organization for Economic Co-operation and Development
OED	Operations Evaluation Department, World Bank
OFC	offshore financial center
OPEC	Organization of Petroleum-Exporting Countries
PRGF	Poverty Reduction and Growth Facility
R&D	research and development
ROSCs	Reports on the Observance of Standards and Codes
S&P	Standard & Poor's
SAF	Structural Adjustment Facility
SAP	Structural Adjustment Program
TI	Transparency International
TIEA	Taxation Information Exchange Agreement
TRIPS	Trade Related Aspects of Intellectual Property Rights
UN	United Nations
UNDP	United Nations Development Programme
USAID	United States Agency for International Development
VER	Voluntary Export Restraint
WEF	World Economic Forum
WHO	World Health Organization
WTO	World Trade Organization

Introduction

1 Civilizing markets through global standards

Brett Bowden and Leonard Seabrooke

With the evolution of the modern states system there have existed 'standards of civilization' to which states must measure up to and conform if they are to fully participate as legitimate and sovereign members of international society. The capacity for a high level of social co-operation and self-government of any given society, including economic governance, has long represented a hallmark of 'civilization'. Historically a society required the organizational capacity to enter into and uphold mutually binding contracts under the law of nations; the principle of reciprocity being a key demand of relations among the society of states. And while the idea of 'uncivilized' societies is at odds with recent trends toward political correctness, today terms such as 'good governance' imply a similar logic whereby states and societies are required to conform to contemporary global standards of civilization. At the same time, as in the past, the workings of markets continue to be thought of as having a 'civilizing' effect on society; both internally amongst its members and in external relations with other societies. As Norbert Elias has argued, the pacification of domestic societies – 'the relatively peaceful life of large masses of people – is in good part based on' the state's monopolization of violence. However, not so long ago Elias observed that 'if the reduction of mutual physical danger or increased pacification is considered a decisive criterion for determining the degree of civilization, then humankind can be said to have reached a higher level of civilization within domestic affairs than on the international plane'. According to Elias, at the global 'level we are living today just as our so-called primitive ancestors did' – something akin to international anarchy (Elias1988: 180–1). As to whether this is the case or not is a matter of considerable debate, and is of more than just a peripheral concern of this book. The establishment and enforcement of global standards of market civilization are at the very heart of efforts to pacify international relations through expanding and normalizing the complex web of ties that bind states together – supposedly to their mutual advantage.

This brings us to the issue of globalization, economic globalization in particular. The concept of civilization and its relationship to globalization has received renewed attention in the wake of recent events in the conduct and study of international politics, including the realm of international political economy (e.g. Mozaffati 2002; Cox 2002; Gill 1995; Linklater 2004). While civilization is a term that is widely bandied about in modern political discourse (and the popular realm beyond), its meaning is generally poorly understood. As such the term is often misused, even abused. Our aim here is to set the record straight and to provide a more nuanced insight into how the term might more usefully be applied to the study of globalization. In particular we seek to demonstrate how the notion of a 'standard of civilization' as going hand-in-hand with the 'golden straitjacket' (Friedman 1999) of free-market capitalism has not been sufficiently thought through. The concept of a standard of civilization is necessary to the globalization debate because it provides the basis from which peoples and states are ranked according to their capacity to fit within market globalization. This book questions how this can be justified. While we are talking here about civilization – or the *ideal* of civilization – and standards of civilization in particular, we are not so much referring to *civilizations* in the Huntingtonian sense (Huntington 1996). Rather, our point of reference for discreet socio-political collectives is the state, for it is primarily through the state, its various apparatus, and its engagement with international and intergovernmental institutions that peoples are managed in the contemporary international system. In essence, then, this collection of essays deals with issues of globalization, governance, and the management of peoples in contemporary international political economy. It does so by using global standards of market civilization as the means to that ends.

Extant contributions to this emerging field by Robert W. Cox, Stephen Gill, Gerrit Gong, Samuel Huntington, Mehdi Mozaffari, and Susan Strange tend to focus on outright 'clashes', totalizing neo-liberalism, or legal international institutions. They do not sufficiently problematize the use of civilization within the globalization debate. It is here where there are some complementarities between the notion of a standard of civilization – externally established benchmarks for socio-political self-organization – and the notion of policy diffusion from international institutions to states. To date this literature has rarely talked to each other but there is much to be gained by doing so.

Within political economy literature the concept of policy diffusion has become increasingly popular, as has literature developed from organizational sociology on institutional isomorphism (DiMaggio and Powell 1991; Thomas *et al.* 1987). Much of the focus within political economy and international relations literature is on the processes through which global standards flow down to states, often attributing little agency to those on the receiving end of a standard. Typically a standard is introduced through policy diffusion via technical capacity building (Simmons and Elkins 2004), from the exercise of 'structural power' as authority shifts from states to markets under neo-liberal globalization (Strange 1996), by an international institution's use of 'intellectual technologies' (Barnett and Finnemore 2004), or through the inculcation of norms on what is appropriate behavior (Finnemore and Sikkink 1998). Most prevalent of studies on how states conform to a standard of civilization is early constructivist work in international relations. For this literature a norm may be spread through the creation of a 'civilizing' discourse. States willingly adopt the norm in order to demonstrate that they measure up to a standard of civilization, that they can be good members of international society (Finnemore 1996; Price 1997).

A key criticism of this earlier literature in political economy and international relations is that while it borrowed from sociological institutionalism there was not much that was sociological about it. More recently work in international relations, however, has problematized how a standard of civilization, and the notion of an international society, is 'Janus-faced', that its adoption by states generated different outcomes and is context dependent (Suzuki 2005). Here norm diffusion and socialization is not only how a 'logic of appropriateness' was extended to states wishing to be civilized, but how norms can constitute the meaning of behavior (Ruggie 1998).

Similarly, in political economy the literature on policy diffusion, particularly the notion of policy convergence, has been challenged by 'varieties of capitalism' scholarship that emphasizes how institutional change takes place along national path-dependent lines (Hall and Soskice 2001). Recent 'economic constructivist' work has also become sensitive to the inextricability of ideas from interests, and how the spread of ideas requires struggle and contestation among social groups within a polity (Blyth 2002; Seabrooke 2006). Finally, 'new institutionalist' literature has demonstrated that norms on policy change, particularly global standards, are not simply diffused but, rather, *translated* into domestic contexts (Kjær and Pedersen 2001; Jacobsson *et al.* 2004). All of this recent literature has great potential for understanding not only how global standards of market civilization are devised from the 'top-down', but also how 'bottom-up' processes influence their adoption or defiance. It also asks us to look at practices of global standards of market civilization rather than viewing institutions as providing always the same advice, or states passively adopting global standards. From this aspect market civilization becomes not simply the dominant political and economic power's benchmarks for technical capacity or 'world's best practice', leading us to assess others' need to civilize and adapt their capacity to meet the standards of modern capitalism. Such self-referential and functionalist analysis is certainly not what Elias (2000) had in mind in his studies of civilizing processes. Rather, if we question civilization as a framework for meaning, such as we should economic globalization or capitalism, we allow ourselves to understand non-functional and non-economic dynamics that inform what can be referred to as a global standard of market civilization (see also Kristensen 2005). Increasingly innovative work has questioned market-civilizing processes by tracing their practices through which they originate in the institutions promoting them, as well as how they are practiced within different national contexts and economic systems. This volume contributes to this growing body of literature.

Civilization, the civilizing ideal, and standards of civilization

In essence, the capacity for reasonably complex socio-political organization and self-government according to prevailing standards are widely thought of as central requirements of civilization. The presence, or otherwise, of the institutions of society that facilitate governance in accordance with established traditions – originally European but now more broadly Western – have long been regarded as the hallmark of the makings of, or potential for, civilization. Central to the ideal of civilization are its tripartite components: economic civilization, social civilization, and legal civilization (Collingwood 1992). What they amount to is socio-political civilization, or the capacity of a collective to organize and govern itself under some system of laws or constitution (see Bowden 2004b). The oft-overlooked implications of this value-laden conception of civilization led to the colonial-era legal 'standard of civilization'; and more recently its political successors, such as the global standards of market civilization explored herein.

Historically, the standard of civilization was a means used in international law to distinguish between civilized and uncivilized peoples in order to determine membership in the international society of states. The concept entered international legal texts and practice in the eighteenth and nineteenth centuries under the influence of anthropologists and ethnologists who drew distinctions between civilized, barbarian, and savage peoples based on their respective capacities for social co-operation and organization. Operating primarily during the European colonial period, and sometimes referred to as the classical standard of civilization, it was a legal mechanism designed to set the benchmark for the ascent of non-European nations to the ranks of the civilized society of states. Membership in international society conferred full sovereignty upon a state entitling it to full recognition and protection under international law. A civilized state required: 1) basic institutions of government and public bureaucracy; 2) organizational capacity for self-defense; 3) published legal code and adherence to the rule of law; 4) the capacity to honor contracts in commerce and capital exchange; and 5) recognition of international law and norms. If a nation could meet these requirements it was generally deemed to be a legitimate sovereign state entitled to full recognition as an international personality.

The inability of many non-European societies to meet these European-established criteria and the concomitant legal distinction that separated them from civilized societies led to the unequal treaty system of capitulations. The right of extraterritoriality, as it was also known, regulated relations between sovereign civilized states and quasi-sovereign uncivilized states in regard to their respective rights over, and obligations to, the citizens of civilized states living and operating in countries where capitulations were in force. In much of the uncivilized world this system of capitulations incrementally escalated to the point that it became the large-scale European civilizing missions that in turn became colonialism.

The formal standard of civilization was effectively rendered redundant at the close of the Second World War. The abrogation of the laws of war as seen in the nature of the totalitarian aggression perpetrated by members of the thought to be civilized world highlighted the anachronism of maintaining a legal distinction between civilized and uncivilized states. The use of nuclear weapons and the subsequent evolution of the concept of mutually assured destruction further undermined the notion of distinguishing between degrees of civility. The war also prompted a growing number of civilized states to recognize that the claims of anti-colonial movements in much of the Third World to their right of sovereign, independent self-government was increasingly justified and legitimate.

While it might be accurate to mark the post-Second World War demise of the formal standard of civilization that is not to say that something similar has not continued to serve much the same purpose in practice, at least in the conduct of international politics if not in international law. During much of the Cold War era, the Westphalian states system was effectively a two-tiered system divided along much the same lines as in the colonial era. It was a system whereby the superpowers and their allies abided by an understanding that peace in Europe should be maintained at any cost, while at the same time the contest for influence in the Third World was keenly pursued, often by means of violent proxy wars.

In the twenty-first century the world continues to be divided according to states' capacities for socio-political organization or systems of government, and still in accordance with Western standards of 'good governance'. Today states are not often explicitly characterized as civilized or uncivilized; rather, distinctions are now drawn between states that are increasingly referred to as well-ordered or not well-ordered; civic or predatory; post-modern, modern, or pre-modern; legitimate or rogue; and in the extreme, good or evil. The post-Cold War-cum-War on Terror(ism) order is generally more receptive to suggestions that liberal democracy and the values associated with it, such as human rights and free markets, are universal aspirations. Hence follows the argument that human rights and democracy combined with policies that promote neo-liberal economic globalization are the appropriate standard for the globalized and interdependent world of the twenty-first century.

As with the classical standard of civilization, the current measure of civilization revolves around non-Western states' capacity to self-govern in a manner that allows them to engage with the West (through trade etc.) in adherence to international law and custom. For some, the identification of different zones of civilization is nothing more than a description of existing or emergent political realities, but on another level its normative advocates see the West as the vanguard of global order. While there is a need to distinguish between different types of states on the basis of legitimacy, it generally goes unacknowledged that there are detrimental consequences to the enforcement of any standard of civilization. The theory of different shades of civilization necessarily requires differential treatment – that is, double standards – where the boundaries of those zones intersect; on the one hand privileging members of the international society of civilized sovereign states, and on the other setting high barriers to entry for the excluded. Moreover, just as the division of the world into civilized and uncivilized peoples and the enforcement of the classical standard of civilization led to colonialism, so too there are serious implications for how the thought to be less civilized world is intervened in by the supposedly more civilized world in the present era through global standards of market civilization.

Closely related to the ideal of civilization and its accomplice, standards of civilization, is the idea of progress. This idea has two related aspects: the first is that the human species universally progresses, albeit at different rates, from an original primitive or child-like condition, referred to as savagery, through barbarism, to civilization. The second is that all human experience, both individual and collective, is cumulative and directed toward the ongoing improvement of the individual, the society in which the individual lives, and the world in which the society must survive. Acceptance of both propositions leads to the notion that human history has a purpose or *telos*; that history is a story of universal linear progress toward a certain point or end. Or what Mozaffari refers to as the movement toward a 'global civilization' based on Western values and ideals (2001).

The idea of progress is said to represent the 'first theory of modernization' (Iggers 1982: 65). And Robert Nisbet has made the pertinent point that the 'abundance in the social sciences of foundations and government agencies dedicated to such concepts as "underdeveloped" "modernization" and "developed" is tribute to the persisting hold of the idea of progress in the West' (Nisbet 1980: 308). Probably the most well-known theory of modernization of the twentieth century is Walt Rostow's five stages of economic growth theory. At the height of the Cold War, and at a time when communism was perceived to pose its greatest threat to capitalist democracy, Rostow proposed what was explicitly a 'non-communist manifesto' for economic development. He identified in his manifesto five distinct stages of societal-economic progress, evolving in the following order: traditional society; the preconditions for take-off; take-off; the drive to maturity; and, finally, the age of high mass-consumption. Despite being labelled an economic theory, socio-political organization naturally plays a significant part. In elaborating his manifesto, Rostow argued that the stages he identified are 'not merely descriptive', nor are they 'merely a way of generalizing certain factual observations about the sequence of development in modern societies'. Rather, he maintained that they 'have an inner logic and continuity. They have an analytic bone-structure, rooted in a dynamic theory of production' (Rostow 1961: 4–13).

The relevance of modernization theory to this book is revealed in Gong's claim that 'one cannot speak of "modernization," or the "process of becoming modern," in historical perspective without referring to what an earlier age called "civilization" and the "process of becoming civilized"'. And Gong maintains that this conceptualization is 'Still relevant today', for 'there are no value-free models of development or economic and financial interaction' (Gong 1998; 2002: 80). This statement coolly implies an unabashed air of superiority in Western societies' catalogue of claims of achievements and having arrived at modernity. To put it another way, modernity is widely regarded as being the world in which Westerners of capitalist liberal democracies live, while the rest of the world – particularly the Third World – is thought of as somehow being 'backward' or 'pre-modern'. This process is not simply from the First World to the Third. In the nineteenth century during the classical standard of civilization some societies that were excluded from the first tier of civilized societies, such as Russia, referred to their need to overcome 'backwardness' through industrialization (Gerschenkron 1962; Kotsonis 1998). In modern parlance 'backwardness' is identified with underdevelopment. From this viewpoint modernization, or modernity, is achieved via development. This idea is quite clearly expressed by the then World Bank Senior Vice President and Chief Economist Joseph Stiglitz's account of what it means to be developed.

> Development represents a *transformation* of society, a movement from traditional relations, traditional ways of thinking, traditional ways of dealing with health and education, traditional methods of production, to more 'modern' ways. For instance, a characteristic of traditional societies is the acceptance of the world as it is; the modern perspective recognizes change, it recognizes that we, as individuals and societies, can take actions that, for instance, reduce infant mortality, extend lifespans, and increase productivity. Key to these changes is the movement to 'scientific' ways of thinking, identifying critical variables that affect outcomes, attempting to make inferences based on available data, recognizing what we know and what we do not know.
>
> (Stiglitz 1998)

Or in Richard Norgaard's more skeptical tone, 'Modernity, in short, promised to transform the heretofore slow and precarious course of human progress onto a fast track.... At mid-twentieth century, progress somehow still assured peace, equality, and happiness for all.' And further, that this 'confidence in the possibilities of progress was rallied in support of an international economic development that would transform the lives of even the most "obdurate" landlord and peasant in the most "backward" reaches of the globe' (Norgaard 1994: 1). As the following chapters outline, this process has not always been smooth sailing; all too often the fast-track option has been derailed, leaving considerable wreckage and the inevitable return to the drawing board. But there have also been some successes.

Should we equate success with the delineation of a superior way of doing things? In addition to the older discourse on 'backwardness' is the more recent propagation of how to transform institutions within 'transition' economies. Much of this literature carries the baggage of modernization theory described above, but it is imbued with a new verve drawn from the end of the Cold War and the triumph of liberal capitalism (e.g. Fukuyama 1989, 1992). Nowhere is this more evident than in post-communist 'transition' states where the 'shock therapy' reforms of the early-1990s sought to instil free-market capitalism (e.g. Sachs 1994). Here the initial aim was to change institutions to create market incentives. Institutional isomorphism across post-communist states established by international financial institutions (IFIs) would provide clear signals to the West that the Eastern bloc was trying to meet the new standards of market civilization. However, as political scientists and sociologists have been keen to point out, social change does not simply reply to changes in market incentive. Social re-engineering is not quite as straightforward as changing the formal structure of institutions. And in cases where 'shock therapy' institutional 'revolution' was successful it was highly dependent on a social evolution of attitudes that welcomed market capitalism as suitable behavior (Campbell and Pedersen 1996). Global standards may be imposed from above, but they can only be truly implemented with consent from below. Moreover, despite providing the 'right' formal institutions desired by IFIs or others, states may still not change their domestic social behavior. Such gaps between rhetoric and practice may be the case in many emerging market economies (EMEs) that formally adopt the IFIs' requests to reform institutions in line with global standards but not their practices. EMEs might be, in other words, learning to 'talk the talk' without 'walking the walk'. Following these themes this book not only outlines how global standards are imposed, but also how they are contested.

Structure of the book

The authors in this collection do not share one view of what civilization or a civilizing ideal comprises. Rather, the chapters provide not only different interpretations of global standards of market civilization, but also varied political views on how standards can be justified (contrast, for example, Michael Oliver's chapter with John Hobson's). All of the authors, however, do explore a set of common themes through different conceptual material and empirical cases. The key themes are:

- *Normalization*: global standards of market civilization are based on a global normalization of liberal positivism.
- *Contestation*: global standards of market civilization can be contested by recipient states and peoples through various strategies.
- *Market mechanisms*: global standards of market civilization view the mechanism of free capitalist markets as necessary for states to enhance their capacity for socio-political self-organization.
- *Self-inculcation*: global standards of market civilization demand moral inculcation of the self, particularly at the level of individual self-responsibility.
- *Ranking of peoples*: global standards of market civilization involve, implicitly or explicitly, the moral ranking of different peoples.

These themes cut across the book's two main parts: the first of which deals with the historical and theoretical aspects of global standards of market civilization. The second substantive section addresses the various component parts that constitute market civilization through a series of case studies. Accordingly, the book is organized into two parts: 'Conceptual history' and 'Contemporary cases'. The contribution of the history of primarily Western political thought is complemented by case studies on contemporary and historical examples of standards of market civilization at play. These are not uncontested issues, and it is important to note that the contributors herein represent both 'for' and 'anti' arguments on global standards of market civilization. An indispensable element of this book is its raising of awareness of the 'pros' and 'cons' through its promotion of internal debate around the key themes.

Part I, 'Conceptual history', begins with Brett Bowden's discussion of the ideal of civilization and its oft-neglected normative implications. Exploring further the key concepts and issues introduced above, he examines how the normative demands of civilization have historically led to the imposition of legal standards of civilization and concomitant civilizing missions; from the European colonial era down to the present. This is followed by a discussion of the idea that the workings of the marketplace serve to act as a civilizer of peoples and societies, both in their domestic relations among citizens and in the societies' external dealings and interactions, whether they be with allies, competitors, or adversaries.

In Chapter 3 Barry Hindess investigates how peoples are managed through the diffusion of the states system and its partnering concept of citizenship. He highlights tensions in the emerging international order as both an order of citizenship and democracy and an order of domination. The spread of neo-liberal conceptions of citizenship and the turn toward democracy as the norm have played important roles in preparing states for participation in global markets. Significant here is that neo-liberal citizenship requires individual self-responsibility and, for the state, discipline in socio-political organization and the meeting of contracts. A lack of discipline on either level sends the signal to other states in the system of a failure or incapacity to meet civilizational standards. Hindess highlights how post-colonial states in particular, and their citizens, have been urged to 'own' and therefore accept responsibility for the success, but more significantly the potential failure, of market reforms, whether they had much say in them in the first instance or not.

Chapter 4 is Matthew Watson's account of classical political economy and the emphasis on the conduct of the individual within systems of production, distribution, and exchange. Focusing on the work of Adam Smith, Watson argues that, contrary to the common view in which the workings of markets are part of the process through which standards of civilization are established, Smith operated with an alternative understanding of the causal relationship between the two. He suggests that Smith refused to take the workings of markets for granted, instead arguing that individuals had to bear a disposition toward 'civility' before a functioning market economy could be created. The Smithian ideal is the construction of a market economy in which all power relationships are dissolved, whereby no one person is able to engage in the overt exercise of power over any other person. This first requires the reconstruction of the individual in line with the principles of 'self-government', which Smith defines as the 'control of the passions'. Smith's idea of a flourishing market economy as the civilizational standard is portrayed as rooted in a particular type of human cognition, in which interpersonal relationships are guided by mutually constituted sentiments of propriety. Watson suggests that, for Smith, a true market economy is indivisible from a society that operates to the standards of 'sympathy', which establishes commutative justice as an unquestionable public good.

John M. Hobson forcefully argues in Chapter 5 that market-based standards of civilization have their origins in racism associated with European identity-formation from the eighteenth century on. He charts the construction of racist standards through which Europeans divided the world into a kind of 'intellectual apartheid' regime. Arguing that while materialists assume that by around 1780 Europe had attained world economic primacy, and that standards merely reflected this, Hobson suggests that, given that the major Eastern powers were still on approximate par with Europe, Europeans 'invented' this bipolar view of the world. He further considers how standards of civilization instructed British civilizing missions in the East, exploring how this entailed pacification, cultural conversion, and the plundering of resources. He concludes by arguing that, while standards of civilization have dropped out of legal discourse, market standards of civilization nevertheless continue informally and constitute the basis of contemporary American civilizing missions in much the same way that they did for colonial Europe.

Concluding Part I on 'Conceptual history' is Chapter 6 in which Mlada Bukovansky highlights some of the problems associated with the widespread promotion of anti-corruption as a standard of market civilization and an all-important safeguarding tool in this era of heightened economic globalization. She explores how anti-corruption rhetoric and campaigns, when couched in contemporary neo-liberal institutional and rationalist language, employ rhetorical tools ill-suited to the task. Bukovansky argues that analysis limited to instrumental rationality, when corrupt practices are themselves easily categorized as instrumentally rational, has inadequate critical thrust. Hence a thoroughgoing critique that deploys the concept of corruption needs to go beyond instrumentalism and bring to bear some sort of moral reference point with which to evaluate political institutions and political action. Her chapter explores documentary material pertaining to anti-corruption efforts to demonstrate its critical omissions, and suggests some ways in which the critical force of the corruption concept might be revitalized to address contemporary concerns.

Part II on 'Contemporary cases' explores and discusses how global standards of market civilization have emerged in the modern word. It begins in Chapter 7 with Peter Larmour's account of Transparency International (TI), an international non-government organization founded to combat corruption in international business activities. The chapter looks at TI as a standard setter and agent of market civilization, paying particular attention to some of the techniques it has developed, including: networking; the franchising of national chapters; the publication of an annual 'Corruption Perceptions Index'; the publication of a 'Source Book'; and the development of Business Principles for Countering Bribery. Larmour suggests that 'civilization' may well be a coercive process; as such his chapter is particularly concerned with the kinds of power deployed in 'civilizing' techniques. He analyzes these techniques as examples of 'policy transfer' and the results of processes of mimicry and professionalization that lead to institutional isomorphism.

In Chapter 8 Michael J. Oliver examines the evolution of the international monetary system over the past 150 years and its continuing role as a fundamental standard of market civilization. He assesses how private individuals and public institutions have rightfully provided a benchmark of civilization in international monetary relations. The chapter further considers why the market solutions of the Gold Standard were replaced by an unfounded belief that only national governments and a supra-national institution (the International Monetary Fund (IMF)) could bring civility to the system. Oliver outlines how with the Bretton Woods framework as the global standard setter, co-operation between members was desirable in order to stabilize exchange rates, to regulate capital flows, and to guarantee that international obligations did not override domestic policy objectives. He further shows how the central tenets of Bretton Woods were challenged, but the introduction of floating exchange rates did not herald a return to the ruinous nature and impasse of the interwar system. Moreover, he outlines how financial markets began to impose their own standards of civilization and discipline on countries that pursued wayward economic policies in the 1980s and 1990s. While the power and influence of financial markets have been criticized, Oliver's chapter concludes that the only way to extend civility across nations and to stabilize the international monetary system is through market solutions, bolstered by effective supra-national institutions.

Chapter 9 is André Broome's account of the imposition of a standard of market civilization that ushered in drastically changed labor standards in the successor states of the Soviet Union. As Central Asian governments formally adopted the objective of moving toward market economies, with some prompting, he notes that high among key recommendations for economic reform was the World Bank's emphasis on reforming labor institutions. The chapter highlights how the reform of formal labor institutions and their compliance, or otherwise, with global market standards must be substantively implemented in order to play a crucial role in determining a state's living standards. Substantive implementation, however, can be easily blocked by informal institutions within the economy, also blocking an evolutionary transition from a centrally planned to a market economy. Examining both the World Bank's official policy recommendations for labor reform and how Central Asian governments responded to them, Broome suggests that an institutional approach that emphasizes how governments *translate* international policy prescriptions into domestic contexts in order to facilitate institutional change is a more useful way of understanding the Bank's influence in specific domestic contexts than analytical perspectives that treat ideas like objects being diffused with little modification between countries.

Jacqueline Best notes in Chapter 10 that two very potent phrases have recently begun to appear in statements from the IMF: 'universal standards' and 'civilizing globalization'. This represents a significant departure from the neutral and technical language that we have come to associate with international financial governance, appealing instead to more explicitly moral conceptions of international order. Best states that the IMF invokes what it believes to be a more liberal and optimistic conception of civilization that is both inclusive and universal. But she questions whether such a conception is in fact possible. As such her chapter examines the parallels and discontinuities between these ideas in historical and more recent conceptualizations of standards of market civilization, with particular reference to the arena of international financial standards. She suggests that recent proposals for greater 'transparency' in international financial reform do in fact constitute an effort to impose a new set of standards of market civilization. Given this, Best argues that the parallels between nineteenth-century and contemporary ideas of civilization should be of serious concern. She contends that, while we may have formally rejected as racially discriminatory the shades of civilization distinctions that underpinned nineteenth-century standards of civilization, such implicit moral hierarchies continue to haunt current conceptions of economic civilization.

Chapter 11 provides a different take on market civilization and financial governance. Leonard Seabrooke outlines how a standard of civilization has changed in global capital markets during two periods of intense financial globalization, 1880–1915 and 1970–2005. In providing the historical context for these two periods Seabrooke illustrates how the creditworthiness of states has developed hand in hand with demonstrations of meeting a standard of civilization. In the late nineteenth century extremely high levels of capital flows from the First World to EMEs were due to intense personal public and private creditworthiness networks in England and an explicit idea that investment into EMEs was civilizing. In accordance with this presumed moral superiority was a view that EMEs who defaulted on investment could be justly punished, including through force. He then illustrates how, in the most recent period of financial globalization, creditworthiness within global capital markets has transformed to reflect the depersonalization of capital access in the US. Here private actors, such as credit rating agencies, have increased their power, just as international institutions have turned their attention to data dissemination and surveillance rather than direct coercion. The new global standard of market civilization requires EMEs to demonstrate a capacity for socio-political self-organization, but without the explicit moral content of the past and without the threat of force. As a consequence EMEs have a greater capacity to 'talk the talk' to actors in global finance while using the market to transform their societies in ways congruent with their own societal norms.

In Chapter 12, Gemma Kyle examines why the Organization for Economic Co-operation and Development (OECD) has been unsuccessful in institutionalizing global standards for tax co-operation through the harmful tax practices initiative (HTPI), despite increasing concerns with tax evasion, bank secrecy, and information exchange following the events of 11 September 2001. She suggests that neo-liberal institutional analyses alone cannot account for the OECD's apparent failure because of the tendency to emphasize a linear path to institutional development. Rather, Kyle demonstrates how tax havens have been able to contest the imposition of a global standard of market civilization by using the rhetoric of sovereign protection against the OECD. Policy diffusion and institutional change do not follow a linear path. Kyle concludes that resistance and contestation undermines the capacity of the OECD to generate consensus over the appropriateness of its policy ideas and renders the institutional development of global standards of tax co-operation under the current OECD harmful tax initiative highly unlikely.

Jillian Clare Cohen begins Chapter 13 by questioning the meaning of civility within markets. She argues that market civilization has a dual nature; civility calls for global laws for the protection of intellectual property rights, while the ideal of civilization implies the betterment of humankind. She examines this problem through a study of pharmaceutical policy within the global trade system, particularly the role of the World Trade Organization (WTO). Cohen's argument is based on the contention that pharmaceuticals have curative and therapeutic qualities, and as such they should not be considered as just another consumerable or commodity. Taking her case a step further, she argues that access to vital and good-quality medicines is now increasingly being considered a basic human right, particularly in view of the HIV/AIDS crisis, which has demonstrated in dramatic terms the importance of access to drugs. Cohen's chapter demonstrates the stark global inequities in access to all-important pharmaceuticals between the developed and the developing worlds, because of the failures of both markets and governments. But she warns things could get worse before they get better given the potentially adverse impact of the WTO's Trade Related Aspects of Intellectual Property Rights (TRIPS) Agreement on drug access. Cohen shows how the global market standards demanded by the TRIPS Agreement could exacerbate an already morally unsatisfactory global pharmaceutical market by creating further barriers to widespread drug access.

Part II concludes with Chapter 14, Geoffrey A. Pigman's examination of changing attitudes to the place of global trade, from its promotion as a civilizer through to more recent attempts to civilize global trade itself. Pigman suggests that the idea of civilizing world trade invokes a Janus face of dual meaning reminiscent of Karl Polanyi's (1944) 'double movement', wherein the relentless drive of self-regulating market mechanisms to span the globe and disembed from human social relations has been resisted by the efforts of governments and peoples to mitigate against what are often drastic social, economic, and political dislocations. The chapter outlines how nineteenth-century promoters of trade liberalization saw trade as part of the civilizing mission to bring wealth, profit, culture, and institutions of good governance to all corners of the globe. This is contrasted with the emergence of 'alterglobalization' resistance to the discourse of neo-liberal globalization at the end of the twentieth century, which indicates how the fruits of global trade itself have empowered effective strategies of resistance to the widening disparities of wealth and power that global markets have perpetuated. Pigman concludes that global social movements have challenged the various institutions regulating the global standards of the neo-liberal trade regime – the WTO, the IMF and World Bank, the OECD, the World Economic Forum – to 'civilize' world trade by re-embedding it within a sustainable global framework of human social relations.

In Chapter 15, Brett Bowden and Leonard Seabrooke revisit the collection's key themes and draw conclusions from the battery of arguments outlined in the preceding chapters. They also draw out the key policy implications for the management of international institutions and the prospects for policy homogeneity, translation, and diffusion. The book ends with a reflection on how global standards of market civilization should be regarded within academic literature and policy debates.

Concluding remarks

This volume is concerned with how global standards of market civilization can be conceptualized and how they work in an era of intense globalization.

International institutions have increasingly embraced, and are responding to, globalization by asserting the need for states in the developed and, especially, developing world to reform themselves in line with global standards. Such standards are evident across a number of crucial issue-areas that are both interrelated and intensifying. From financial crises to the HIV/AIDS pandemic, from the formation of 'national integrity systems' to fight corruption, to the role of reformation of the moral self, global standards demand us to change to successfully engage market civilization. Such changes have ramifications from the macro-level of international institutions to the micro-level of personal health and well-being. Bringing together political theory and political economy provides us with a more satisfactory lens to view and understand the origins and functions of global standards of market civilization, and whether they can be justified.

Part I

Conceptual history

2 Civilization, standards, and markets

Brett Bowden

This chapter elaborates on the key concepts, issues, and themes foreshadowed in the Introduction. Each of these concepts and issues are unique in their own way but they are also necessarily interrelated; and each serves as an all-important foundation stone of the very nature of this collection. I will begin by outlining the ideal of civilization, giving some background to its origins and exploring its contested meanings and (mis)usages. Following this is an account of the concept of standard of civilization; a concept that in good part arises out of the very nature of the term civilization and the ideals it invokes. Finally, the chapter looks at the historical and contemporary relations between the ideal of civilization and markets, paying particular attention to the notion that markets play a civilizing role in and between societies.

The ideal of civilization

In recent years the terms 'civilization' and 'civilizations' have regained some of their lost prominence as tools for describing and explaining the workings of various fields of the social sciences. Both of these terms continue to be interpreted and applied in a variety of manners and different contexts; or, in some cases, misinterpreted and misapplied. Throughout its history the ideal of civilization has been imbued with a normative component, whereby self-governing socio-political collectives – civilized society – are established as the standard to which less civilized societies should aspire if they are to join the ranks of the civilized 'family of nations'. This is an aspect that is often overlooked or goes unacknowledged in the contemporary – and sometimes confused – use of both terms. Also unacknowledged in many recent appeals to 'civilization' are the consequences that stem from its promotion as 'ideal type': to be an uncivilized society is to be a less than fully sovereign society, which brings with it the increased likelihood of external intervention by fully sovereign, civilized societies. And this is precisely what this book is about: how modern states are intervened in, either directly or indirectly, through modern market-based standards of civilization.

The first task here is to give a brief review of the circumstances under which the word *civilization* entered into French, English, and German usage. These languages are the most significant for a number of reasons, not the least of which is that they are the three languages that dominated European diplomacy in the eighteenth and nineteenth centuries when *civilization* entered European thought. The significance of civilization as both a word and an idea, and the key role the three prominent Western European languages played in shaping both, are captured in Emile Benveniste's statement: 'The whole history of modern thought and the principal intellectual achievements in the western world are connected with the creation and handling of a few dozen essential words which are all the common possession of the western European languages' (Benveniste 1971: 289). *Civilization* is one of the words.

For much of the twentieth century, a century in which two world wars, the Great Depression, and the Holocaust all served to undermine the very *idea* of civilization, it seemed as though it was more the case that it *was* one of those words. Despite this, the middle years of the century did produce a number of comprehensive studies of the rise and fall of major civilizations. The 1980s also saw the publishing of a major study on the standard of civilization in international society (Gong 1984), but this too was a largely historical study and by century's end these styles of investigation had become scarce. One of the contemporary works that has captured imaginations in the revival of 'civilization studies' as a legitimate or worthwhile field of study is Samuel Huntington's 'clash of civilizations' thesis (Huntington 1993, 1996). The airing of this thesis and the post-Cold War-cum-war on terrorism international political climate into which it was born has generated extensive and ongoing debates that have helped to re-popularize the term civilization(s); nowhere is this more so than in the study of international politics. Despite being a noted contributor to this revival, Huntington offers an oversimplified history and definition of the term, stating that the 'idea of civilization was developed by eighteenth-century French thinkers as the opposite of "barbarism"'. Simply put, 'To be civilized was good, to be uncivilized was bad.' Huntington does acknowledge that out of its origins evolved a distinction between the usages of civilization in the singular and 'civilizations in the plural'. But this development is also oversimplified to the point that the arrival of the latter merely marks the 'renunciation of a civilization defined as an ideal, or rather as the ideal' (Huntington 1993: 40–1). The study of the plural variant, or 'civilizations as fact', however, is not as readily divorced from a concern with 'civilization as ideal' as Huntington suggests. Rather, as Fernand Braudel notes, the triumph of one over the other 'does not spell disaster' for it, because out of necessity they are tied together in 'dialogue' (Braudel 1980: 213).

French origins

In late eighteenth-century France, the term civilization was imbued with a plurality of meanings. Serving as something of a 'synthetic' or 'unifying concept', civilization was used to describe both a process through which individual human beings and nations became civilized, and the cumulative outcome of that process. As Jean Starobinski states, 'The crucial part is that the use of the term, *civilization*, to describe both the fundamental process of history and the end result of that process established an antithesis between civilization and a hypothetical primordial state (whether it be called nature, savagery, or barbarism)' (Starobinski 1993: 5; emphasis in original).

Apart from the distinction between civilization as process and the condition resulting from that process, there is a further distinction between civilization as '*fact*' and civilization as '*value*' or '*ideal*'. In the former sense it is largely a descriptive term used to identify what are thought to be quantifiable values held in common by a distinct group of peoples. In the latter sense civilization is a 'normative concept on the basis of which it was possible to discriminate the civilized from the uncivilized'.

(Starobinski 1993: 7–8).

What is elsewhere described as civilization as fact is referred to by Lucien Febvre as its 'ethnographic' usage:

> In the first case civilization simply refers to all the features that can be observed in the collective life of one human group, embracing their material, intellectual, moral and political life and, there is unfortunately no other word for it, their social life. It has been suggested that this should be called the 'ethnographical' conception of civilization. It does not imply any value judgement on the detail or the overall pattern of the facets examined. Neither does it have any bearing on the individual in the group taken separately, or their personal reactions or individual behaviour. It is above all a conception which refers to a group.
>
> (Febvre 1973: 220)

But even this definition is more than just descriptive. It too has an (unacknowledged) normative component. Civilization is not usually used to describe the collective life of just any group, as culture sometimes is; rather it is reserved for collectives that demonstrate a degree of co-operation, urbanization, and organization. This normative assumption is evident in the fact that Febvre's ethnographic markers all relate, either directly or indirectly, to a group's sociopolitical organization. Following this 'ethnographic' account of civilization Febvre gives a definition of civilization as an ideal or value:

> In the second case, when we are talking about the progress, failures, greatness and weakness of civilization we do have a value judgement in mind. We have the idea that the civilization we are talking about – ours – is itself something great and beautiful; something too which is nobler, more comfortable and better, both morally and materially speaking, than anything outside it – savagery, barbarity or semi-civilization. Finally, we are confident that such civilization, in which we participate, which we propagate, benefit from and popularize, bestows on us all a certain value, prestige, and dignity. For it is a collective asset enjoyed by all civilized societies. It is

> also an individual privilege which each of us proudly boasts that he possesses.
>
> (Febvre 1973: 220)

Clearly, the former usage is used to describe distinctive *civilizations* across time and place, while the latter signifies a benchmark for *the* civilization – that is, it represents the *ideal of civilization* – by which all other societies or collectives are compared to and measured against. While the former have been subject to much comparative historical analysis, it is the conception of civilization as ideal that is more the concern here. The reason for focusing on the value-laden dimension of civilization begins to reveal itself when looking into further accounts of civilization, such as that of Comte de Volney's in *Éclaircissements sur les États-Unis*, published in 1803 after his travels in the United States. Reflecting the general principles of social contract theory, but, just as importantly here, the criteria of requiring a capacity for self-government, Volney wrote:

> By civilization we should understand an assembly of the men in a town, that is to say in an enclosure of dwellings equipped with a common defence system to protect themselves from pillage from outside and disorder within . . . the assembly implied the concepts of voluntary consent by the members, maintenance of their right to security, personal freedom and property: . . . thus civilization is nothing other than a social condition for the preservation and protection of persons and property etc.
>
> (quoted in Febvre 1973: 252)

The demand for a nation or people to have the capacity to organize into a co-operative society with the capacity for self-government is central to the very idea of civilization. The identification of different collectives as *civilizations* on the basis of their capacity for social co-operation and self-government has really only served to distinguish them from other human collectives. Noteworthy is that it is not just about a people organizing and governing in any fashion that counts. Rather, it is about governing in accordance with certain standards – first set by Europe and later by the West more generally – that determines a society's approximation to the idealized standard of civilization.

English origins

Adam Ferguson's declaration in *An Essay on the History of Civil Society* that 'Not only the individual advances from infancy to manhood, but the species itself from rudeness to civilization' (Ferguson 1966: 1) is thought to be the first use of 'civilization' in English. As Duncan Forbes states in his introduction to the 1966 edition of the *Essay*, what Ferguson was looking for was a 'true criterion of civilization' (1966: xx). And as Ferguson clearly states in the *Principles of Moral and Political Science*, that criterion was some degree of socio-political organization. He writes in the *Principles* that:

> success of commercial arts . . . requires a certain order to be preserved by those who practice them, and implies a certain security of the person and property, to which we give the name civilization, although this distinction, both in the nature of the thing, and derivation of the word, belongs rather to the effects of law and political establishment, on the forms of society, than to any state merely of lucrative possession or wealth.
>
> (Ferguson 1975, Vol. I: 252)

From these passages and from the general theme of Ferguson's *Essay* it is apparent that, like the French, he too uses the term civilization to describe both a process and a condition.

As indicated by both Volney's and Ferguson's respective accounts of civilization, it becomes increasingly the case that socio-political-legal organization is inherently and inextricably linked to the ideal of civilization. An example of this is John Stuart Mill's essay of 1836 titled 'Civilization'. Mill, like others before him, notes that 'The word civilization . . . is a word of double meaning', sometimes standing 'for *human improvement* in general, and sometimes for *certain kinds* of improvement in particular' (Mill 1962: 51). For the purposes of his essay, however, Mill is referring to civilization as an ideal condition, or what he calls 'civilization in the narrow sense: not that in which it is synonymous with improvement, but that in which it is the direct converse or contrary of rudeness or barbarism'. And he is not talking here just about the condition of the individual, but 'the best characteristics of Man and Society' (Mill 1962: 51–2).

The presence, or otherwise, of the institutions of society that facilitate governance in accordance with established (Western) European traditions was widely believed to be a hallmark of the makings of, or potential for, civilization. Mill was representative of this belief in his assertion that 'In savage life there is little or no law, or administration of justice; no systematic employment of the collective strength of society, to protect individuals against injury from one another.' Despite the fact that similar institutions performed similar functions in the non-European world, the absence of institutions that resembled those of the 'civilized' nations of Europe meant that much of the world beyond its borders was deemed by 'civilized' Europe to fall short of meeting Mill's necessary 'ingredients of civilization'. For as Mill stated, 'We accordingly call a people civilized, where the arrangements of society, for protecting the persons and property of its members, are sufficiently perfect to maintain peace among them' (Mill 1962: 52–3).

The requirement of a capacity for socio-political organization and the role of society are reaffirmed in Mill's declaration that 'There is not a more accurate test of the progress of civilization than the progress of the power of co-operation.' For it was widely held that 'It is only civilized beings who can combine', and 'none but civilized nations have ever been capable of forming an alliance', whereas savages on the other hand are characterized by an 'incapacity of organized combination'. The reasoning behind this belief was that 'All combination is compromise: it is the sacrifice of some portion of individual will, for a common purpose', and as such it was argued that 'the whole course of advancing civilization is a series of such training' (Mill 1962: 55–6).

For Mill, civilization was marked by the 'sufficient knowledge of the arts of life'; the 'diffusion of property and intelligence'; the 'sufficient security of property and person'; and the 'power of co-operation' in society so as to 'render the progressive increase of wealth and population possible' (Mill 1962: 53–7). But the maintenance of civilization did not come cheaply, for Adam Smith argued that increase in wealth and population was in fact a prerequisite for the discharge of the 'first duty of the sovereign' of civilized societies, that of protecting the society from external 'violence and injustice'. And according to Smith it was 'only by means of a standing army . . . that the civilization of any country can be perpetuated', an exercise that becomes increasingly expensive the larger a society grows and the more a 'society advances in civilization' (Smith 1910, Vol. II: 196–7). Here we have the makings of a concept of market civilization; based on the notion that those who can self-organize politically and not be a burden on others – including the defense of property rights and contracts – are able to create continuous growth.

German origins: Kultur *versus* Zivilisation

While the evolution of the word civilization ran along roughly parallel lines of thought in French and English, in German language and usage *Zivilisation* stood for something quite different and was altogether subordinate to the concept of *Kultur*. While still useful, *Zivilisation* is a term of 'second rank' that really only deals with superficialities such as external appearances; *Kultur* on the other hand is a term that is said to be representative of Germany's self-understanding of national pride and sense of achievement – its sense of being. Furthermore, the French and English conceptions of civilization generally refer to political, social, economic, religious, scientific, and/or moral issues; the German term *Kultur* on the other hand is essentially reserved for expounding intellectual, artistic, and religious facts or values. Moreover, the German concept of *Kultur* is inclined to include a distinct divide between these more valued concerns on the one side, and subordinate political, social, and economic issues on the other (Elias 2000; Schäfer 2001).

Some of the reasons behind the distinctions between the French/English concept of civilization and its German counterpart *Kultur* have been set out by Norbert Elias in *The Civilizing Process*. In short, Elias argues that the differences are attributable to the contrasting roles played by the respective intellectual classes that gave birth to and shaped the meanings of the concepts. In France, for instance, the concept of *civilization* – and French civilization itself – was born at court and in Paris cafés where it took shape amidst ongoing intellectual exchanges between a politicized and politically engaged French intelligentsia. In contrast, German *Kultur* was generated by a more widely dispersed, less interactive middle-class German intelligentsia that Elias describes as 'far removed from political activity, scarcely thinking in political terms and only tentatively in national ones, whose legitimation consists primarily in its intellectual, scientific or artistic *accomplishments*' (Elias 2000: 10; emphasis in original). Given the late development and tenuous unity of the German state, the intellectual middle class was highly individualized and said to be 'floating in the air to some extent', distinctly different from the 'closed circle' or 'society' that was the French court. The space it occupied was *das rein Geistige* (the purely spiritual), where a preoccupation with scholarship and the development of the mind or intellect (*Bildung*) was both a refuge and source of pride. Politics, commerce, and the economy on the other hand were peripheral concerns in which there was little scope or prospect for engagement (Elias 2000: 24).

In speaking of a time long before the word civilization had come into being, in 1958 the German historian G. Kuhn characterized the victory of the barbarian hordes of Germany over the armies of Imperial Rome as 'the victory of peasants over warriors, of country over town, of culture over civilization' (quoted in Braudel 1980: 182). But according to Victor Hugo, even when the 'barbarism' of German *Kultur* defeated the 'light' that was French civilization, it still lost out because of what it was not. Addressing the French National Assembly in 1871 following defeat in the Franco-Prussian War at the hands of Germany, Hugo proclaimed:

> And while the victorious nation, Germany, the slave horde, will bend its brow beneath its heavy helmet, France, the sublime vanquished nation, will wear the crown of a sovereign people.
>
> And civilization, once again set face to face with barbarism, will seek its way between these two nations, one of which has been the light of Europe, and the other of which will be the night.
>
> (quoted in Starobinski 1993: 20–1)

The key point here is Hugo's proclamation that, despite its defeat, the French nation was still considered superior to a less than unified Germany precisely because, unlike Germany up to that point, it was, and had long been, a sovereign, centrally and self-governed nation. As stated, a nation's capacity for socio-political organization and self-government, and hence its claims to sovereignty, have a significant bearing on whether or not it is said to be 'civilized', thus meeting a requisite standard of civilization.

Standards of civilization

Arising in good measure out of the normative nature of the ideal of civilization, not so long ago it was thought that our world was reasonably neatly divided between 'savage', 'barbarian', and 'civilized' peoples. For instance, in 1877 in the opening pages of *Ancient Society*, Lewis Henry Morgan wrote, 'It can now be asserted upon convincing evidence that savagery preceded barbarism in all tribes of mankind, as barbarism is known to have preceded civilization' (Morgan 1964 [1877]: 5). And that the 'three distinct conditions are connected with each other in a natural as well as necessary sequence of progress'. Morgan also maintained that 'The idea of property has undergone a similar growth and development. Commencing at zero in savagery, the passion for the possession of property, as the representative of accumulated subsistence, has now become dominant over the human mind in civilized races' (Morgan 1964 [1877]: 11).

The distinction drawn between 'civilized' and 'barbarous' states led to what became known as the system of capitulations or the right of extraterritoriality. As the Italian jurist Pasquale Fiore pointed out,

> The object of the Capitulations is to determine and to regulate the relations between civilized and uncivilized states, as regards the exercise of their respective sovereign rights with respect to the citizens of civilized states who reside in the countries where Capitulations are in force.
>
> (Fiore 1918: 362; see also Part 2 of John M. Hobson in this volume)

That is, Europeans residing in 'uncivilized' states.

Another consequence of, or perhaps more accurately a major component of, the legal distinction between 'civilized' and 'uncivilized' peoples is what Georg Schwarzenberger termed the 'standard of civilisation in international law' (1955); or what Gerrit Gong later called 'the standard of "civilization" in international society' (1984). Operating during the European colonial period, the standard of civilization was a legal mechanism designed to set the benchmark for the ascent of non-European states to the ranks of the civilized 'Family of Nations', and, with it, their full recognition under international law. Reflecting the requirement of a capacity for self-government, Schwarzenberger summarizes the legal standard as follows:

> The test whether a State was civilised and, thus, entitled to full recognition as an international personality was, as a rule, merely whether its government was sufficiently stable to undertake binding commitments under international law and whether it was able and willing to protect adequately the life, liberty and property of foreigners.
>
> (Schwarzenberger 1955: 220)

Naturally, the protection afforded to 'foreigners' was limited to citizens of civilized states; that is, Europeans.

In his study of the standard of civilization, Gong expounds a more extensive set of criteria for determining whether a state is civilized or not. In order to be deemed civilized a state had to conform to the following requirements:

1. a 'civilized' state guarantees basic rights (i.e., life, dignity, and property; freedom of travel, commerce, and religion), especially those of foreign nationals;
2. a 'civilized' state exists as an organized political bureaucracy with some efficiency in running the state machinery, and with some capacity to organize for self-defense;

3. a 'civilized' state adheres to generally accepted international law, including the laws of war; it also maintains a domestic system of courts, codes, and published laws which guarantee legal justice for all within its jurisdiction, foreigners and native citizens alike;
4. a 'civilized state' fulfills the obligations of the international systems by maintaining adequate and permanent avenues for diplomatic interchange and communication.

The standard of 'civilization' also included a more subjective requirement:

> 5. a 'civilized' state by and large conforms to the accepted norms and practices of the 'civilized' international society, e.g., suttee, polygamy, and slavery were considered 'uncivilized' and therefore unacceptable.
>
> (Gong 1984: 14–15)

The legal standard became redundant upon the settlement of the Second World War. In large part the abrogation of the laws of war as witnessed by the nature of the totalitarian aggression perpetrated by members of the thought-to-be 'civilized' world put paid to maintaining a legal distinction. The principle was further undermined by the use of nuclear weapons and the subsequent evolution of the concept of mutually assured destruction. Even prior to the Second World War, leading jurists recognized that adhering to a standard of civilization was something of a political and legal anachronism. For example, Hersh Lauterpacht declared, 'Modern international law knows of no distinction, for the purposes of recognition, between civilized and uncivilized States or between States within and outside the international community of civilized States' (Lauterpacht 1947: 31). Commenting on this development, Schwarzenberger misses the irony in his statement that 'At this point doctrine reaches the other extreme. The standard of civilisation has vanished, and States are supposed to be under a legal duty to recognise even non-civilised States and their governments' (Schwarzenberger1955: 227).

As this passage suggests, while the legal standard of civilization might have been superseded in the annals of international law, that is not to say that something similar did not continue to serve the same purpose in the conduct of international politics. As Martin Wight noted, during the Cold War the states system remained 'divided still concentrically between the world city and the world rural district'. And out of this two tiered states system came 'One of the unwritten understandings of the Cold War . . . that the peace of Europe shall be warily preserved while the struggle is pursued for influence and position throughout the Third World' (Wight 1977: 125).

Since Wight made these observations, the collapse of communism and the break-up of the Soviet Union have brought the Cold War to an end. Nevertheless, the notion that there exists a hierarchy of states has outlived the Cold War and has its fair share of adherents. Whilst it is interpreted and described in a range of ways, its 'key theme is that disparities in capability are reflected, more or less formally, in the [membership and] decision making of the society of states' (Clark 1989: 2).

In his account of the classical standard of civilization, Gong points to the possibility that 'at least two possible successors may have arisen as new standards in contemporary international society'. The first is a 'standard of non-discrimination or standard of human rights' (Gong 1984: 90–3). The second is a 'standard of modernity', and takes two possible forms: one 'vindicates the nineteenth-century assumption that the laws of science, being universal, undergirded a rational cosmology which would bring the "blessings of civilization" to all'. Its primary significance is related in terms of the 'standard of living' and 'quality of life' that can be achieved universally via the application of science and technology to issues of health, nutrition, and general well-being. The other shape it might take is in the guise of a 'contemporary cosmopolitan culture' reflecting the 'shared values, moral norms, and experiences' given popular expression in terms like the 'global village' and 'global city' (Gong 1984: 92–3). But, like Wight, Gong made these observations in the midst of a world divided by the tensions of the Cold War – there was no agreement on universally shared values and norms, let alone experiences. On the contrary, the Cold War divide engendered an environment that inhibited the formation of a universal international society based on shared ideological values and norms that some advocated. Rather, given the opposing camps desperation to woo allies at virtually any cost and willingness to bring them into the fold regardless of the nature of the regime, the Cold War made for some odd alliances of convenience. But as noted, the end of the Cold War was seen by many in the West as a triumphant turning point that ushered in a 'new world order' in which capitalist liberal democracy had defeated all-comers. Post-Cold War international politics are now conducted in an environment in which the concepts of individual rights, participation in government, and unhindered access to the goods and services available in the marketplace, are widely thought to be the universal aspirational norm.

The 'triumph of the West', or, possibly as significantly, the triumphalism of the now dominant West, has allowed it to set the agenda in terms of defining a 'standard of civilization' for the twenty-first century. Mehdi Mozaffari makes the point that the 'role of formulating' and setting the principles which constitute the standard of civilization 'is incumbent upon the predominant civilization'. Thus, in the present era the 'global standard of civilization is therefore defined – primarily – by the dominant Western civilization, which happens to be democratic', liberal, and economically globalized (Mozaffari 2001: 253–4). In essence then, it is argued that a variation of the 'might equals right' or realist brand of logic prevails; seeing it is the West that dominates, it is the West that sets the standard.

Markets as civilizers

John Darwin makes the pertinent point that 'So long as colonialism was identified as with the task of "civilization" – the diffusion of civility – commerce must be its *Doppelgänger*' (Darwin 2000: 325). On this general point, commerce and economic interdependence have long been seen as having a civilizing effect on both discreet political communities, and neighboring societies with which they interact. Around the time of Christ, Philo of Alexandria argued that commerce was an expression of the 'natural desire to maintain a social relationship', while the first-century historian Lucius Annaeus Florus claimed, 'If you destroy commerce, you sunder the alliance which binds together the human race' (cited in Pagden 2000: 8). In the eighteenth century Montesquieu testified that 'Commerce is a cure for the most destructive [of] prejudices' and serves to 'unite nations' (1949 [1748]: 316). More recently, David Ricardo stressed that 'Under a system of perfectly free commerce' between nations, the 'pursuit of individual advantage is admirably connected with the universal good of the whole'; thus, 'it diffuses general benefit, and binds together by one common tie of interest and intercourse, the universal society of nations throughout the civilized world' (Ricardo 1891: 114). The link between commerce and peace is an important idea that still has considerable influence in the pursuit of a peaceful international political order based on Immanuel Kant's claim that the 'spirit of commerce' is 'incompatible with war', and 'sooner or later' just such a spirit 'gains the upper hand in every state'. Why? Because despite other uncertainties, 'the power of money is perhaps the most dependable of all the powers (means) included under the state power'. Therefore, given that trade is said to be beneficial to all contracting parties, in the name of continuing economic prosperity, 'states see themselves forced, without any moral urge, to promote honourable peace and by mediation to prevent war wherever it threatens to break out' (Kant 1963 [1795]: 114).

More recently, the link between commerce, democracy, and peace has been outlined in terms of pacific 'democratic values' arising from the 'norms of contract that are endemic in prosperous market socioeconomies' (Mosseau 2000: 473). Aspects of this argument are not too dissimilar from ideas outlined by Elias in his account of the civilizing of domestic society. In *The Civilizing Process* Elias writes of the expanding 'web of human relationships' and 'the lengthening of the chains of social action and interdependence', such that 'more and more people must attune their conduct to that of others' (Elias 2000: 445–8). This is essentially the same argument to that used by democratic peace theorists who extrapolate these same principles to the global arena. They maintain that states with a complex web of interdependent relations of trade and foreign investment, states that are also constrained in the range of actions at their disposal in their international relations by domestic popular public opinion, are more likely to seek peaceful mediation, negotiation, or compromise over the resort to the threat or use of violent force. In short, capitalist democratic states are said to have too much to lose by resorting to violent and expensive conflicts. While this theory has its committed adherents, democratic polities are not necessarily inherently peaceful when it comes to dealing with non-democratic societies. Furthermore, as a counterpoint to the general argument that commerce promotes interdependence and therefore reduces the likelihood of recourse to war, one need only recall that the Spanish used infractions of their supposed right to trade as a justification for waging war against the Amerindians of the New World.

The issue of economic development brings us to David Fidler's promotion of an economically liberal standard of civilization that also incorporates a conflation of human rights-democracy-cum-economically globalized liberal modernity. The direction that Fidler sees the standard as heading toward, if not already at, is what he refers to as a 'standard of liberal, globalized civilization' (Fidler 2000: 389). This standard comes about by what he identifies as parallel or concurrent 'standards of civilization and globalization'. While the 'historical contexts' of the classical standard of civilization and the new standard of globalization might be 'dramatically different', he claims that 'the substance of the two standards is not'. Just as the classical 'standard of civilization required the creation and maintenance of certain conditions that would allow Westerners to conduct commerce and trade safely and effectively in non-Western countries', so does the standard of globalization. Fidler suggests the 'standards of civilization and globalization share the central objective of improving the conditions of economic interaction between the West and the rest' (Fidler 2000: 400). Furthermore, Fidler sees the classical standard and the standard of globalization as sharing the same origins: the former reflecting the norms of European civilization of an earlier era, the latter reflecting 'the norms of the same civilization now expanded beyond the confines of Europe and North America' (Fidler 2000: 401).

In a nutshell, Fidler contends that the 'confluence of the standards of civilization and globalization at the end of the twentieth century produces the composite *standard of liberal, globalized, civilization*'. The defining characteristics of the new standard of civilization are:

> (1) respect for basic civil and political human rights; (2) respect for the importance of civil society in domestic and international politics; (3) commitment to democratic governance; (4) commitment to the 'rule of law' domestically and internationally; (5) commitment to free market economics domestically and free trade and investment internationally; and (6) commitment to developing and applying science and technology to political, legal, economic, and social challenges.
>
> (Fidler 2000: 409)

The commitment to economic liberalism and the application of science and technology to virtually all facets of social policy have become a cornerstone of international public policy. They are promoted in various intergovernmental forums and by the key international financial and trade institutions, such as the World Bank, the International Monetary Fund, the Bank for International Settlements, and the World Trade Organization (WTO). But not only are they promoted by these institutions and regimes, membership or participation in most of them actually requires the adoption of and commitment to such policy measures. In this regard these organizations all play key roles in setting and enforcing international standards of civilization as they relate to areas such as governmental transparency and corruption, fiscal and monetary policy, trade, and arbitration and dispute settlement, just to name a few (some of which are the focus of following chapters). Particularly since the financial crises that hit Asia, Latin America, and Russia in the mid- to late 1990s, and lingered on into the following century, a kind of 'standard of financial modernity' now regulates actors and transactions in the international financial system. The primary objective of the standard is to guarantee offshore investments and property, including against nationalization or expropriation, through the quarantining of domestic operations against corruption and arbitrary interference by promoting transparency and the free exchange of information. As with other standards, the standard of financial modernity distinguishes between what are routinely referred to as 'developed economies', 'emerging economies', and 'non-market economies' in the contemporary international financial system. Gong describes the function of the 'standard of financial modernity' thus: if states wish to attract trade and foreign investment, or maintain credit, then to be full members of the modern financial and trading system they 'must adapt and adhere to a new standard increasingly ensconced in the international system' (Gong 1998).

Taking China's recent accession to the WTO as an example of the workings of the system, before being granted membership China had to make concessions on a raft of what were once largely sovereign domestic economic policy issues. Just a few being: anti-dumping and countervailing measures; industrial policy, including subsidies; judicial review, uniform administration, and transparency; product-specific safeguards; quantitative import restrictions, including prohibitions and quotas; sanitary and phytosanitary measures; trade-related aspects of intellectual property rights; and transitional review mechanisms.

It is not a straightforward process; there are a lot of hoops to jump through before a country can be said to measure up to the requisite standards of economic and market civilization. In a similar manner, international credit rating agencies such as Standard and Poor's, and Moody's play a significant role in setting internationally accepted standards of economic governance. Some ratings agencies even issue country sovereign ratings; a poor rating or a rating downgrade can have a significant impact on a country's capacity to attract foreign direct investment or source commercial loans (see Leonard Seabrooke's chapter in this volume). At the same time, matters of economics and trade cannot be divorced from other arenas of societal activity. As Anthony Pagden notes, 'the world economy, which has come to constitute a new kind of human environment', is also a creation of Western cosmopolitan culture, therefore, 'belonging to that environment demands signing up to its political and social values as well'. Furthermore, it is difficult to separate it from its imperial moorings when one considers that 'the entire development project', as carried out by the West in the 'underdeveloped' non-Western world, continues to be motivated by the notions of 'humanity' and 'benevolence' that were in large part justifications for the civilizing missions of old (Pagden 1998: 14).

Along similar lines to Fidler, Mozaffari argues that 'the rise of a "global standard of civilization" reflects the transformation of the world' that is currently taking place as part of the 'ongoing process of globalization'. He further claims that 'globalization has considerably reduced the differences between various [competing] world visions' (Mozaffari 2001: 247–51). Globalization is said to have prompted a 'global convergence' in the nature of states, which in turn impacts on the nature of 'inter-state relations'. This convergence, he contends, is a result of shifts in the 'orientation of states', whereby contemporary state orientation is said to be shifting in the general 'direction of capitalism and liberalism'. Mozaffari acknowledges that not all 'countries share the same ideas and values'; however, he insists 'it is undeniable that the gap between different world visions is now as narrow as it has ever been historically', as non-Western states begin to 'internalize' Western values and norms. To this end, he asserts that the dual 'pillars of our current mega-civilization remain unchallenged'; that is, 'adherence to liberalism and capitalism (in all their variety and nuance) . . . are on the increase'. As a result of this 'convergence', Mozaffari concludes that if

> we accept globalization as a fact and an inescapable reality, and if we accept that in a single global world, multiple, concurrent and contradictory civilizations cannot coexist, then we have to acknowledge the existence, or at least the emergence, of a global civilization.
>
> (Mozaffari 2001: 250–1)

In a nutshell, 'capitalism and liberalism = global civilization' (Mozaffari 2001: 259).

As to whether we have to accept these premises, let alone the conclusion, is highly questionable, but herein lies the general problem. In offering this interpretation, Mozaffari either does not realize or does not think it necessary to point out that the range of cultural and ideological points of view are not necessarily coming together as such. Rather, it is the case that one pole remains firmly planted while others are being drawn or coaxed toward it. The foundations of the case for a global civilization are rather shaky given that, in reviewing the historical process of globalization and its impact on international law, Mozaffari concludes that 'since the beginning of the *Renaissance*, and particularly after the Peace of Westphalia in 1648, only European civilization has succeeded in producing a set of norms and creating various institutions and organizations with a global/universal scope and dimension'. By contrast, he claims that the 'old civilizations' – which presumably means archaic or pre-modern civilizations, for they continue to survive – 'be they Chinese, Islamic, Indian and so on' have failed to make 'any successful attempts at elaborating an alternative "international law"'. In an effort to explain his conclusions, Mozaffari attributes the non-Western world's 'weak contribution to the improvement and correction of dominant norms' to the overall 'lack of democracy and the weakness of civil society' (Mozaffari 2001: 257–8). But this criticism seems to be little more than Western triumphalism of the worst kind and a rehashing of the might-equals-right logic when it comes to setting norms and standards. And it also does not explain the implication that Western-style democracy and civil society are supposed to have been contributing factors to the establishment of international law, particularly given that the foundations of modern international law are rooted in a Europe in which democracy was largely unknown and civil society nascent at best (cf. Bowden 2005).

The general nature of the problem for non-Western societies in their endeavor to measure up to contemporary standards of market civilization is captured in Paul Ricoeur's question: 'In order to get onto the road toward modernization, is it necessary to jettison the old cultural past which has been the *raison d'être* of a nation?' The problem is generally one of 'unearth[ing] a country's profound personality', a personality that for many has been suppressed and denied under the yolk of colonialism by the imposition of a foreign personality. For non-Western peoples or states, arising out of this situation is a paradox Ricoeur explains thus:

> [O]n the one hand, it has to root itself in the soil of its past, forge a national spirit, and unfurl this spiritual and cultural revindication before the colonialist's personality. But in order to take part in modern civilization, it is necessary at the same time to take part in scientific, technical, and political rationality, something which very often requires the pure and simple abandon of a whole cultural past. It is a fact: every culture cannot sustain and absorb the shock of modern civilization. There is the paradox: how to become modern and to return to sources; how to revive an old, dormant civilization and take part in universal civilization.
>
> (Ricoeur 1965: 277)

But are non-Western states permitted to pursue an alternative development path even if they wish to? Do not global standards of market civilization effectively prevent them from doing so? The limitations on their options (and the nature of the threat) are explicit in Fidler's insistence that the 'Western standard of civilization prevailed in the clash of civilizations because the Western countries were the builders of the new international society and exercised their superior power to ensure that the society was built in their image' (Fidler 2000: 406). Today that image is one of a society increasingly economically globalized and committed to 'free' markets and 'free' trade. The following chapters will give us a better indication of how states conform to and resist the pressures of globalizing and universalizing market standards of civilization in a range of key sectors and international institutions.

3 Civilizing peoples through state citizenship and democracy

Barry Hindess

The entire Western world, it now seems, is intent on spreading democracy across the globe. Many Western states have established agencies specifically devoted to the promotion of representative government elsewhere, the American National Endowment for Democracy being the largest and best-known example. This objective, albeit tempered by other policy considerations, has long been a central plank of US foreign policy (Robinson 1996). It has even been cited, after the event, as a rationalization for the American and British invasion of Iraq in 2003. The European Union insists that all candidates for membership must satisfy its standards of democracy and human rights. Democracy is also promoted by the United Nations (UN), and it is seen by international financial institutions and the major development agencies as an integral part of good governance. The emerging global order of market civilization thus appears to involve a global standard of citizenship and democracy, and of the individual liberties that they require. Yet critics present this emerging order in a very different light. Stephen Gill writes of a disciplinary neo-liberalism that grants 'privileged rights of citizenship and recognition to corporate capital and large investors' (Gill 1998: 23). Walden Bello (1994) argues that we are witnessing the colonization – the recolonization in many cases – of much of the non-Western world. Michael Hardt and Antonio Negri make a closely related claim. 'Empire', they tell us, 'is materializing before our very eyes. . . . It is a decentered and deterritorializing apparatus of rule that progressively incorporates the entire global realm' (Hardt and Negri 2000: xi, xii).

The emerging international order is seen, then, both as an order of citizenship and democracy and as an order of domination, a novel version of imperialism. There is much to be said for both perceptions and therefore, also, much to be said against them. To focus only on the former is to ignore the realities of Western exploitation, yet to focus only on the latter is to deny the commitment of the international agencies and the major Western powers to the expansion of democracy and human rights. Anthony Pagden's discussion of the links between the modern discourse of good governance and Enlightenment conceptions of world order suggests a way in which these seemingly opposed perceptions might be brought together and even, to some degree, reconciled. Pagden notes that the discourse of 'good governance' is most commonly associated with development within post-colonial states. Yet it can also be seen as advancing a vision of international order that involves 'not only states, but also non-statal and avowedly non-political bodies, particularly the international financial agencies and multinational corporations' (Pagden 1998: 7). Here, the government that takes place within states and the government of the international arena are seen as intimately connected, as they have been throughout the modern period. If we are to grasp how a global standard of citizenship and democracy can also be seen as a standard of domination, we should take both levels of government into account. My discussion of this point leads, first, to a brief history of the modern system of states, second, to an account of liberalism as a project of government emerging within that system, and, third, to an examination of how this project has responded to twentieth-century changes in the system of states. This last issue brings us, finally, to the contemporary standard of citizenship and democracy.

Citizenship in the system of states

If citizenship is a matter of relations between individuals and the state to which they belong and between these individuals themselves, it is also one of the markers used by states in their attempts to regulate the movement of people within and across their borders. Citizenship operates within states, but it is central also to an international regime that divides humanity into the citizens of numerous states and assigns to states the right and the obligation to manage their own internal affairs, including the regulation of entry and exit. The most immediately disturbing effect of this arrangement is that states are encouraged to look after their own and to be correspondingly less concerned about the condition of those whose citizenship lies elsewhere. The UN Declaration of Human Rights, for example, claims to be universal in scope, but it places responsibility for the implementation of the rights it identifies squarely on the states in which individuals have their citizenship, leaving other states with only limited responsibilities in this respect. States that manifestly fail to satisfy their obligations to manage their own internal affairs are often seen as posing a threat to other states and therefore as being legitimate objects of outside intervention.

To understand the place of citizenship, and later of democracy, within this supra-national regime, it is useful to begin with a brief history of the modern states system. The 1648 Peace of Westphalia and other agreements that brought the Thirty Years War to an end are conventionally taken to mark the emergence of a new European order of independent sovereign states (see Held 1995; Inayatullah and Blaney 2004; Keene 2002; Schmitt 1996; and Walker 1993). Political arrangements designed to pacify warring religious communities replaced conditions in which populations were subject to a variety of overlapping and conflicting sources of authority into conditions in which states were acknowledged as having the primary responsibility for the government of the populations within their territories. Three features of this states system are particularly important for our understanding of later developments. First, the sovereignty of a state is a function of its recognition as a state by other members of the system of states (Bierstecker and Weber 1995). This relational understanding of sovereignty is in marked contrast to the contractarian view set out by Thomas Hobbes, John Locke and Jean-Jacques Rousseau in the early modern period and again, more recently, by John Rawls. Contract theory invites us to think of states as if they had arisen out of formal or informal agreements amongst numerous individuals, who then became citizens of the states resulting from those agreements. This perspective suggests that sovereignty is essentially a matter of the internal relations between a state and its citizens on the one hand and of the capacity of a state to defend itself on the other. It also suggests that, in contrast to the order imposed by an overarching authority within a state, the system of relations between states is one of anarchy or disorder (Bull 1977).

Second, effective government within the member states of the Westphalian system is predicated on political conditions secured by the system itself. The principle of non-interference in the internal affairs of a sovereign state, for example, served as part of this regime of pacification by restricting the rights of supporters of one religion from intervening in the religious affairs of other participating states. At least for its more successful members, the European system of states secured a degree of freedom from outside interference without which it would hardly have been possible for them to practice and develop modern arts of governing the populations under their control. Finally, the Westphalian states system was, at least in its early stages, specifically European, covering territories and populations in parts of Europe by means of treaties and understandings between participating states. It imposed few constraints on states' interference in the affairs of those who inhabited territories not covered by these agreements and in which no truly sovereign states were thought to exist (Schmitt, 1996). States experienced little difficulty in deploying natural law and the Roman *jus gentium* to secure what they saw as lawful grounds for territorial expansion elsewhere (see Locke 1988 [1698]; Vitoria 1995 [1557]; and the discussions in Armitage 2004 and Anghie 1996 for influential early examples of such tendentious reasoning).

This last feature of the European states system allows us to identify two fundamental stages in the spread of that system to other parts of the world. First, European imperial adventures brought new territories and populations into the remit of the Westphalian system (Strang 1995). This, together with the use by Western states of a discriminatory 'standard of civilization' in their dealings with non-state entities and states (China, Japan, Russia, the Ottoman Empire, Thailand) that were not accepted as full members of the system of states (Gong, 1984), eventually resulted in the subordination of the greater part of humanity to direct or indirect rule by Western states. Imperial domination was the form in which the European states system first became global in scope. It divided humanity in a number of ways, one of which was the distinction between those who were citizens (of Western states) and those who were not.

This process of incorporating non-European populations into the European system of states was followed, first in the Americas and, somewhat later elsewhere, by the widespread achievement or imposition of independent statehood.

This is the second stage in the globalization of the European states system. It expanded the membership of the system of states, and established a new way of bringing non-Western populations under the rule of the states system (Seth 2000). The state, Hardt and Negri insist, 'is the poisoned gift of national liberation' (Hardt and Negri 2000: 135). Non-European populations now found themselves governed both by modern states of their own and by the overarching system of states within which their own independent states had been incorporated. This is the point at which citizenship, if not yet democracy, became an almost universal human condition.

To say that a state is sovereign is to say that it is subject to no legal superior. In this sense, the members of the international states system engage with each other as equals. Yet, as with other regimes of government that operate with no controlling center – we might think, for example, of the workings of an established market or of civil society – some members are clearly far more equal than others. Many sovereign states in Francophone Africa and Central Asia are dominated by what was once the imperial power. Others remain highly dependent on external assistance, having inherited poorly developed infrastructures along with governmental agencies and practices originally designed to serve a system of rule by outsiders. This condition leaves them vulnerable to regulation by international financial agencies that are clearly dominated by Western interests. Recently established states have been recognized as members of the international system of states, but few have been admitted to its more exclusive inner circle. Most are subject to updated versions of the European 'standard of civilization' that require them to demonstrate their fitness to participate in various international arrangements (the Organization for Economic Co-operation and Development (OECD), the General Agreement on Tariffs and Trade (GATT) and its successor, the World Trade Organization (WTO), providing the most obvious examples) and leave them vulnerable to the risk of intervention by other states (see Bowden 2004a).

Liberalism as a governmental project

Liberalism is often regarded as a normative political doctrine or ideology organized around a commitment to individual liberty, and especially to protecting that liberty against the state. One important limitation of this view is suggested by the observation that the subject peoples of European imperial possessions experienced liberal government as authoritarian rule. The liberal ideal may be for the state to rule over, and to rule through, the free activities of autonomous individuals, but liberals have traditionally taken the view that substantial parts of humanity do not, as a matter of fact, possess the minimal capacities for autonomous action that would enable them to be governed in this way. This tension between liberal ideal and liberal practice often involved a significant degree of hypocrisy, as many commentators have noted (Said, 1992; Guha 1997). Yet it was also a matter of liberal attempts to deal with a reality that, in their view, did not satisfy the conditions required for the operation of their preferred form of rule (Hindess 2001).

This disjunction between liberal ideal and practical reality suggested to liberal political reason, first, that populations may be ranked according to their level of improvement and, second, that the less improved were in need of reform. Some people, the more cultivated inhabitants of civilized states, were seen as approximating the desired condition of individual autonomy, and the remainder as being still some way from that condition. The project of reform suggested by this perception is the civilizing mission of government, a project of improving, by force if necessary, the condition and the character of subject populations. (In a well-known passage John Stuart Mill argues that 'even personal slavery, by giving a commencement to industrial life, and enforcing it as an exclusive occupation of the most numerous portion of the community, may accelerate the transition to a better freedom than that of fighting and rapine' (Mill 1977 [1865]: 394–5). Mill's point is not so much to endorse the practice of slavery – to which he was in fact opposed – as to emphasize how far some people had to go before they could be ready for individual liberty.) While the civilizing mission did not appear as a distinct budget item in imperial administration, it nevertheless served as a major organizing principle of imperial rule (see, for example Conklin 1997). Together with closely related imperial practices of divide and rule, it generated systematic patterns of discrimination between populations and sub-populations within them on the basis of what was thought to be their existing level of civilization or 'improvement'.

The move from direct imperial rule to independence left the liberal ranking of populations more or less in place, but it radically transformed the conditions under which the liberal project of improvement could be pursued. However, before turning to the consequences of that change, we need to consider a second important respect in which standard accounts of liberalism should be corrected. I began this section by noting that liberalism is often seen as a normative political doctrine or ideology. Yet, as Michel Foucault and others have argued, it can also be seen as a project of government concerned with addressing the severely practical problems involved in the government of states and their populations. This latter perception has been elaborated by the 'governmentality' school of social analysis, whose work has resulted in many valuable explorations of the diverse ways in which individual choice and self-regulation have been deployed as instruments of liberal government (e.g. Burchell *et al.* 1991; Barry *et al.* 1996; Dean 1999; Rose 1999). However, as my earlier remarks in this section may have suggested, this focus on the liberal government of freedom offers an unduly restricted account of the productive capacities of liberal political reason. Nevertheless, without denying the importance of liberal authoritarianism, it is its governmental use of liberty that I wish to focus on here.

Many observers have noted that the image of the market as a realm in which the activities of numerous individuals may be regulated and co-ordinated without direction from a single controlling center occupies an important place in liberal political thought. This image suggests first that individuals are governed in part by the reactions of others with whom they interact and that, at least among more civilized peoples, their interactions can normally be expected to take a peaceful form. This view suggests, in turn, that, while the promotion of suitable forms of free interaction may be an effective way of governing civilized populations, it may not be so successful in other cases. The market shows, second, that interaction with others can influence the internal standards that individuals use to regulate their own behavior – their sense of good and bad conduct, of what is acceptable or unacceptable in particular contexts, and so on. Market interaction can be seen, in other words, as a powerful instrument of civilization, inculcating such virtues as prudence, diligence, punctuality, self-control, etc. (Hirschman 1978; Holmes 1995). It follows that, if only market-friendly forms of property can be set securely in place, then market interaction itself may function as a means of improving the character of less civilized peoples. 'Light taxes and good laws', James Mill insisted in his *History of British India*, 'nothing more is wanted for national and individual prosperity all over the globe' (Mill 1975: 578). Authoritarian state intervention to reform property relations, and thus enable widespread market interaction to take off, has sometimes been seen as a liberal move towards a situation in which individuals may be governed through their free interactions.

The ideal image of the market, in effect, provides liberal political reason with a model of the governmental uses of freedom. Foucault observes that the market plays 'the role of a "test", a locus of privileged experience where one can identify the effects of excessive governmentality' (Foucault 1997: 76). Foucault's own account of liberalism and the governmentality accounts that have followed his lead have focused on the rationality of the government of the state, and of the population and territory over which the state claims authority, and they have accordingly pitched their analysis of the governmental usage of markets at this intra-state level. However, this liberal perception of the governmental utility of markets relates to the conduct of states as much as it does to that of human individuals (Howard 1978; Burchell and Linklater 1996). Liberals have seen international trade in goods and services as promoting the wealth of nations but also, and perhaps more importantly, they have regarded it as a decentralized means of regulating the conduct of states. The same applies, of course, to trade in financial instruments. It is well known that the freedom of action of national governments is often severely constrained by international financial markets but it is not sufficiently recognized that these markets have been promoted, as a matter of deliberate policy, by a number of powerful states and supra-national agencies (Helleiner 1994).

This last point brings us back to my earlier observation that liberalism should be seen as a governmental project, developing initially within the conditions provided by the European system of states. If the Westphalian system addressed the problem of pacifying warring populations by assigning those populations to the exclusive rule of discrete sovereign states, this did not entirely resolve and may even have exacerbated the related problem of pacifying rulers themselves. Indeed, the problem of civilizing states was a major concern of eighteenth-century political thought, and it has remained a central theme in liberal discussions of international order ever since. In this respect, Rawls's (1999) account of liberalism as primarily a matter of intra-state relations, which presents liberal discussion of international order as a derivative, secondary development, is seriously misleading. Liberalism is more properly seen as a positive project of government, concerned with governing the larger human population covered by the system of states. It has addressed this problem not only by incorporating humanity within the modern system of states, as the regimes of modern imperialism and post-colonial independence have each done in their own way, but also by using market interactions and other devices to civilize and to regulate the conduct of states themselves and the particular populations under their authority.

A standard of citizenship and democracy

How does this sketch of the liberal project of government relate to the contemporary standard of citizenship and democracy? I began this chapter by noting that, in order to understand the place of citizenship and democracy in the modern world, it is necessary to locate them as elements within a supra-national governmental regime. I then suggested that the sovereignty of states should be seen as an artifact of the system of states, and thus that it is misleading to regard states as constituted essentially on the basis of formal or informal agreements among their citizens. This means that the government of a state is never simply a matter of internal relations between the state and its own citizens or subjects, however democratic it might appear to be.

The suggestion that modern democratic states are not really controlled by their citizens is hardly new. Many commentators have argued that the institutions of representative government ensure that citizens play a strictly circumscribed role in the government of the state to which they belong (Hindess 2000). This is the substantive empirical foundation of the 'realist' theory of democracy, one of the most influential doctrines in twentieth-century political science (the classic account is Schumpeter 1976; Sartori 1987 presents a forceful recent variation). Modern democracies, realism tells us, are governed by a combination of elected officials and professional state bureaucracies. At most, the people decide who is to rule, not the substantive policies that their government is to pursue. The significance of this account for the liberal project of government lies in its suggestion that democracy, in the predominant modern sense of the term, brings together three different sources of political legitimacy: the charismatic element of leadership, participation in the appointment of elected officials, and the rationality of professional bureaucracy. The second is expected to promote among participants a sense of responsibility for the decisions made by their leaders, even if their influence on those decisions is actually very small. The third seems to ensure that the state is administered by suitably qualified personnel and its practices governed by the relevant expertise, thus providing a kind of quality assurance.

What most distinguishes democracy from other regimes, on this view, is not so much the overall sense of legitimacy that it promotes as its capacity, in Talcott Parsons's words, to mediate 'consensus in [the exercise of power] by particular persons and groups, and in the formation of particular binding policy decisions' (Parsons 1967: 516). It thus secures for the detailed activities of the state and its various functionaries a level of acceptance and compliance that non-democratic regimes are simply unable to match. It is this supposed capacity of modern democracy, not its rhetorical gestures towards popular control, that particularly appeals to the development agencies and financial institutions involved in promoting 'good governance' in the developing world, just as it does to those engaged in the government of Western states themselves. In both cases democracy is now thought to provide the most effective means of ensuring that the people will 'own', or at least that they will not actively resist, the package of political and economic reforms that their governments choose or are required to implement. The language of 'ownership' now plays an important part in development discourse (see Jacqueline Best and Leonard Seabrooke chapters in this volume). Joseph Stiglitz, then Vice-President of the World Bank, described the Bank's proposed Comprehensive Development Framework as involving 'a new set of relationships, not only between the Bank and the country, but within the country itself. . . . Central is the notion that the country (not just the government) must be in the driver's seat' (Stiglitz 1999: 22–3; see also the discussion in Cammack 2004). Several commentators (e.g. Williams 1998; Jayasuriya 2000) have suggested that the promotion of democracy may expose these political and economic reforms to popular resistance. The potential is certainly there, but its significance is tempered by the strictly circumscribed role that this form of democracy allows to citizens.

The fact that the conduct of contemporary states is subject to significant external constraints is not in itself a cause for concern – quite the contrary in fact. What should concern us, rather, is the grossly unequal character of the international order from which these constraints derive. All contemporary states, even the most powerful, are subject to a variety of international conventions, treaties, and a developing framework of international law on the one hand and the 'civilizing' effects of international trade on the other. Yet a clear majority of the new states that emerged from the end of empire, along with many non-Western states that had never been colonized, are also subject to the more specific regulatory mechanisms of the international development regime. Some of these states (with help from their powerful friends) have played the development game successfully while others have tried to play by radically different rules, usually with unhappy results, but most have fallen somewhere between these extremes.

The condition of citizenship and democracy in post-colonial states is also seriously constrained by governmental institutions and practices inherited from the colonial period, most of which were predicated on a view of the subject population as considerably less civilized than their rulers. While members of the political/administrative class in all modern states are likely to be tempted by such a view of the people they govern, it was more pronounced, and more freely expressed, in the case of imperial rule. This involved a clear distinction between citizens and subjects, and a systematic development of what eventually became known, in the case of Britain's African possessions, as indirect rule: that is, of a practice of government that worked through institutions that relied on what were thought to be indigenous customs and structures of authority (on British rule see Lugard 1923; on Western imperial administration more generally see Malinowski 1929; Mamdani 1996). Precisely because they were, at least in intention, based on indigenous practices, the detailed character of these ersatz governmental arrangements varied from one population to another. Yet their overall effect was to institutionalize what Mahmood Mamdani (1996) has called a regime of 'decentralized despotism' that promoted localized authoritarian rule within different sections of the population and reinforced, or even created, communal divisions. One of the most striking legacies of indirect rule in many post-colonial successor states is the continuing presence of a set of governmental routines and practices that seriously undercut what might seem to be the common condition of citizenship.

Starting from T.H. Marshall's (1950) pioneering discussion, the sociological theory of citizenship has routinely described it as involving three sets of rights: the *civil* rights to liberty and equality before the law; the *political* right to vote and to participate in the political process; and the *social* right to participate fully in a way of life that is shared by the citizens as a whole. Marshall argued that the state had a responsibility to ensure that these rights are in fact secured for all citizens. A closely related claim informs the aspirations set out in the UN Declaration of Human Rights – which might, in fact, be regarded as a declaration in favor of a universal right to citizenship. The import of Mamdani's argument, then, is that, while independence displaces the colonial distinction between citizen and subject, the legacy of indirect rule nevertheless continues to subvert many of the civil and political rights of citizenship.

With regard to social rights in particular, Marshall, followed by many social policy analysts, argued that the role of the state's social policy was to ensure that citizens were not in fact excluded from participation in the life of their society by reason of poverty, ill-health, or lack of education (see Bulmer and Rees 1996). While this sociological literature focuses on the prosperous states of the OECD, it is worth noting here since its insistence on the role of the state in securing the social rights of citizenship serves to mark another significant difference between citizenship in these states and citizenship elsewhere. Social rights are comparatively well developed in most Western states, although they are now under considerable neo-liberal pressure, but in the majority of other states they have barely had a chance to develop.

Another imperial legacy concerns the liberal ranking of populations, noted earlier, and thus of the need for a civilizing mission to bring about the improvement of the less advanced. While many of its practices have been adapted by post-colonial successor states, this mission can no longer be pursued in its familiar imperial guise. Instead, the liberal project of improvement is now pursued by two very different parties, with both overlapping and competing visions of what it might involve. It is pursued first, as it was in the colonial period, by significant minorities in the ex-imperial domains themselves, many of whom are also concerned to reaffirm (and thus to reinvent) elements of their own cultural heritage. The formation of such liberal minorities was one of the intended effects of imperial rule but, as Homi K. Bhabha (1994) observes, the mimicry that it involves invariably cuts both ways: while it serves the purposes of the colonial power in some respects it works against them in others. The affirmation of their own tradition – of Asian values, for example – by members of such minorities is also a kind of mimicry, and one that can be no less ambiguous in its effects. Like Western colonial officials before them, members of such liberal minorities can be expected to combine a civilized distaste for the dirty work of governing their less advanced compatriots with a reluctant acknowledgment of its necessity. But, since they have also taken over governmental functions that would once have been performed by officers of the imperial state, they do so under radically different circumstances. On the one hand, because of their local connections, the rulers and public officials of the successor states tend to be seen (and perhaps to see each other) as more vulnerable to corruption even than Western officials had been during the colonial period (Rose-Ackerman 1999). On the other, the positive affirmation of non-Western values provides them with a local, culturally specific variant of the patronizing liberal view that the people of these domains lack the capacity to govern themselves.

The liberal project of improvement is also pursued by Western states themselves working through a more distant set of indirect means: national and international aid programs that assist, advise, and constrain the conduct of post-colonial states; international financial institutions; and that fundamental liberal instrument of civilization, the market – including the internal markets of multinational corporations. In fact, the use of markets in regulating the conduct of states and in the conduct of government within them has become increasingly prominent as we move further away from the decolonizations of the mid-twentieth century. In liberal eyes, as noted earlier, the market appears to perform a variety of desirable functions: not only in promoting prosperity overall but also in regulating the conduct of states and fostering civilized attitudes and patterns of conduct among both their rulers and their inhabitants.

Where it could once rely on the decentralized despotism of indirect rule over the subjects of Western imperial possessions, liberal political reason now has no alternative but to treat those who it sees as most in need of improvement as autonomous agents. The old imperial divisions between citizens, subjects, and non-citizen others has been displaced by the post-imperial globalization of citizenship, and indirect rule within imperial possessions superseded by an even less direct form of decentralized rule, in which the inhabitants of post-colonial successor states are governed through sovereign states of their own. This is not to say that the new form of indirect rule is likely to be more successful than its imperial predecessors in imposing its will on target populations. My point, rather, is that it provides the global political context in which the promotion of 'good governance' has to be understood. Good governance is now seen as involving democracy, in the sense not only that the governments of states are expected to be minimally responsive to the wishes of their citizens but also that the citizens are expected to own, or at least to go along with, the policies of their government. Yet it is also seen as ensuring that the freedom of action of these governments, and therefore the ability of their citizens to determine what those actions will be, is severely constrained by internal and international markets.

These last points bring us, finally, to the modern standard of citizenship and democracy. I noted earlier that the image of the market as a means of regulating and co-ordinating the activities of numerous actors without direction from a single controlling center has always played a central role in liberal political thought. If there is a common thread linking the many late twentieth-century projects of neo-liberal reform, within particular states and in the international arena, it lies in the attempt to introduce market and quasi-market arrangements into areas of social life that had hitherto been organized in other ways: the corporatization and privatization of state agencies, the promotion of competition and individual choice in health, education, and other areas of what Marshall regarded as the proper sphere of social policy, the use of financial markets (and credit-rating agencies) to regulate the conduct of states, etc. These developments have striking consequences for both the political and the social aspects of citizenship: the political rights (such as they are) may remain but their scope is restricted as market regulation takes over from direct regulation by state agencies and the judgment of the market is brought to bear on the conduct of states, while the social rights of citizenship (where they exist) are pared back as provision through the market replaces provision directly or indirectly through the state.

It seems, in fact, that the advance of citizenship and democracy in the post-colonial world is to be secured under neo-liberal political conditions. Neo-liberal policies have become increasingly familiar to the populations of Western states in recent years, and this process will be intensified if the proposed constitution of the European Union is ratified by its members (led in part, almost paradoxically, by so-called 'New Europe'; the 'Baltic Tigers' in particular). There are interesting parallels between the rise of neo-liberalism and the associated collapse of social democracy in Western states and developments in post-colonial successor states (Low 1996). Both have gone some way down the path of privatization and corporatization, and both are subject to regulation by the international system of states, but the latter are subject to the further rigors of the international development regime. With regard to both the social rights of citizenship and the subordination of democracy to external constraint, through the implementation of global standards of market civilization, then, the neo-liberal project has advanced further in other parts of the world than it has in the West itself.

4 Civilizing market standards and the moral self

Matthew Watson

The debate about standards of civilization tends to treat states as ontological givens of the international system. Such standards imply a framework of action, consistent with international law, whereby states prove their eligibility to be considered a legitimate member of international society. Only those states that abide by the standards of civilization are deemed worthy of such membership. Any other state remains outside the boundaries of international society, and its existence as a state is qualified by insiders through the use of a variety of prefixes, such as 'pariah', 'predatory', or 'rogue'. The debate about standards of civilization therefore reifies a particular type of state as the ideal, and passes judgment on other states relative to their attempts to meet this ideal. A deliberate process of 'othering' takes place, such that the standards of civilization are determined by those who deem themselves already to be civilized, and these standards are then used as a mechanism by which to induce reform from those who organize their societies on a different basis. From the perspective of 'the civilized', they are an invitation for those 'not like us' to become ever more 'like us'.

There is an important economic dimension to contemporary standards of civilization. As the underlying theme of this volume suggests, these are, specifically, standards of *market* civilization. It is not enough for a state simply to affirm political principles that are enshrined in international law. For full status as a member of international society today, a state must assert its willingness to engage economically with others in a non-discriminatory manner, protecting and enhancing the development of a potentially global sphere of private property rights. It must provide a rule of law that defends the value of foreign-owned assets, it must commodify its labor force to make workers attractive to overseas investors, and it must accept that the circulation of goods within the economy is determined by market power and not state decree. In short, given contemporary standards of market civilization, a civilized nation has to be a trading nation, fully immersed in and reflecting the traditions of a commercial society.

Within modern ideologies of everyday life, trade is no longer merely an economic phenomenon. It is also assumed to be a mechanism for introducing and normalizing the values on which a good society is constructed. Membership of the World Trade Organization (WTO) and, therefore, membership of an international market economy, is considered a necessary prerequisite for entry into the club of civilized states (see Jillian Cohen and Geoffrey A. Pigman's chapters in this volume). A liberal trading environment is assumed to inculcate states with behavioral characteristics that are suitable, not only for success within commercial society, but also for a civilized life. A knock-on effect is assumed to operate, whereby values socialized through the economy are transferred into the political arena, subsequently coming to set the terms of the relationship between the state and the individual.

This, then, is the starting point for my discussion in this chapter. My aim is to situate contemporary debates about standards of market civilization within the context of much older debates, those associated with the classical tradition of political economy. More precisely, I use the work of the most influential of the classical political economists, Adam Smith, in order to shed a different light on what we understand by standards of market civilization. Re-read from a Smithian perspective, there are a number of obvious ironies in the contemporary debate.

For a start, the contemporary debate about standards of market civilization locates the discussion squarely at the level of the state. It is the state that is socialized, through the commercial way of life, to treat the individual in a just and prudent manner. In other words, the existence of a market society is taken as a given; at the very least, the formation of a commercial way of life precedes the process through which states are socialized in line with standards of market civilization. It is then the task of the state to demonstrate that it can act according to those standards in its treatment of the individual. For Smith, the line of causation is entirely reversed. The existence of a market society cannot be assumed a priori. Neither is it solely the context in which the state learns to act in a civilized manner toward the individual. Instead, the market society, as well as the commercial way of life that sustains such a society, is the product of interactions between individuals who are *already* conscious of the need to treat one another in a civil and equitable fashion. Market society does not create just individuals. For Smith, just individuals create market society. Moreover, in Smith's world, the state has little, almost no, role to play in that process, except perhaps in providing the basic education through which the individual learns to distinguish between a just and an unjust action. Indeed, the 'man of prudence', whom Smith holds in the highest regard (Fitzgibbons 1995: 58–74), forsakes public life for more virtuous employment (Smith 1982 [1759]: VI.i.1-16). Acting on behalf of the state is considered an unnecessary diversion from more meaningful and more useful activities that serve to sustain the commercial way of life.

In order to show how Smith reverses the line of causation evident in the contemporary debate about standards of market civilization, the chapter proceeds in three stages. In section one, I focus on Smith's account of the way in which individual actions propel the development of commercial society. I highlight the potential contradiction between Smith's obvious disdain for overt displays of material wealth and his view that the attempt to satisfy increasingly conspicuous consumption desires was the motive force for the commercial society he so admired. In section two, I focus on the mechanism through which the individual learns to temper what he called their imaginary wants, so that they may act with propriety and civility. Smith posits the existence of an 'impartial spectator' as an innate part of the self, who regulates behavior and imposes self-command. In section three, I focus on Smith's assertion of the stoic principles on which self-command rests. Smith's standards of market civilization arise very much from within the self, which stands in stark contrast to attempts to impose contemporary standards of market civilization through the development programs of international institutions. I conclude by reviewing this contrast, in particular in relation to the World Bank, suggesting that contemporary standards of market civilization are, from a Smithian perspective at least, an illusion.

My case is constructed on an assessment of the major themes of Smith's *The Theory of Moral Sentiments*. Perhaps understandably given the current dominance of both market-based institutions and market ideology, most people today focus their analysis of Smith on *The Wealth of Nations*, choosing to leave *The Theory of Moral Sentiments* unread. To my mind, this is a mistake. For a start, the popular conception of *The Wealth of Nations* is that it represents a populist defense of the market economy. However, as this was no part of Smith's intention, the popular conception demonstrates the superficial nature of most readings of *The Wealth of Nations*. It not only fails to adequately reflect the text, which actually reveals Smith to have anything but a utopian image of social life constructed on market norms. It is also entirely inattentive to his broader system of thought, which at all times emphasizes the moral dimension of economic life. It is this that constitutes the focus of *The Theory of Moral Sentiments* and, as a consequence, the content of *The Wealth of Nations* simply cannot be understood unless it is within the context of the arguments contained in *The Theory of Moral Sentiments*. If one is interested in Smith's most profound commentary on the moral dimension of economic life, then one must turn to his analysis in *The Theory of Moral Sentiments*.

Smith on the individual within market society

Adam Smith is widely acknowledged as the most influential theorist of the moral basis of market society. His *The Theory of Moral Sentiments*, published in its first edition almost twenty years before *The Wealth of Nations*, provides a systematic attempt to explain the moral bonds on which the commercial way of life is predicated. Smith's analysis is part description and part aspiration. His focus moves between the society that he sees around him and a more idealized view of the society that he believes could be created. Smith's concerns for understanding the condition of man – and it is the autonomous male who features throughout the book as the moral agent under study (see Justman 1993) – exhibits similar shifts. At times, man is presented with his faults laid bare: it is a dispassionate analysis of what happens when the individual fails to meet the standards of propriety that the good society demands. At other times, Smith concentrates on the state of man when he is cleansed of his faults: it then becomes an impassioned plea for society to model itself on the pristine individual.

Smith works simultaneously with three different conceptions of man: the man who acts, and whose actions are readily observable; what he calls 'the man within the breast', who operates as the conscience for the man who acts; and the idealized man, he that the man who acts could be if he becomes the perfect embodiment of the 'man within the breast'. Smith has a complex conception of the self, in which the individual subject is a contingent combination of these three different 'men'. It is this individual, who is in effect three 'men' at once, that Smith attempts to understand in relation to the developing market society of his day. The individuals who drive the market society through their consumption do so through their choice of actions, but equally those actions are restrained by the activation of each individual's conscience and their sense of the pristine subject they could become. The three elements of the individual subject place Smithian man in a potentially contradictory situation whenever he contemplates action. Such contradictions are evident throughout Smith's analysis of the individual within market society.

According to Smith, everyday life is dogged by the false perception that personal acquisitiveness, as an end in itself, is meaningful, worthwhile, even noble (Hill 2001: 21). It is within our capacity to see gratuitous wealth, and, much more so, displays thereof, as frivolous utility. However, the normal inclination of the mind is not to do so, but to fall under the spell of imagining what it must be like to have possession of those things that are currently out of reach (Verburg 2000: 36–7). Immediately, then, we are introduced to two of Smith's three states of manhood. On the one hand, we have the man who acts, the actual man, who strives to emulate those with riches for no reason other than acquisitiveness for its own sake. On the other hand, that man always has the potential to become the idealized version of himself, such that he sees acquisitiveness for what it really is: the vain pursuit of the unattainable masquerading as a short-cut to happiness.

In order to juxtapose those two states of manhood, Smith tells the tale of the 'poor man's son'. In doing so, he challenges much that is fundamental to the operation of commercial society, such as the worth of the possessions that participation in the commercial way of life allows the individual to enjoy. The poor man's son is the man who would be rich, but the man who would be rich is one who must first disable that other man, the one 'within the breast', who urges restraint when faced with the false promise of superficial possessions. It is only in the absence of 'the man within the breast' that: 'He [the poor man's son] is enchanted with the distant idea of this felicity [i.e. the comfort of richness that facilitates conspicuous consumption]' (Smith 1982 [1759]: IV.1.8). 'It appears', Smith continues, 'like the life of some superior rank of beings, and, in order to arrive at it, he devotes himself for ever to the pursuit of wealth and greatness' (Smith 1982 [1759]: IV.1.8). In time, however, the poor man's son comes to realize that this pursuit is ill-founded. It requires sacrifice: of the body (through a life of toil devoted to someone else's advantage – Smith 1998 [1776]: 429); of the spirit (through the subjection of the self to the 'mental mutilation' of the division of labor – Smith 1998 [1776]: 435); and of the mind (through subordinating virtue to the desire for wealth – Smith 1982 [1759]: VI.i.3). Yet, the material rewards that accrue to the poor man's son for all this sacrifice are finally revealed to him as 'mere trinkets'. 'He thinks [before he begins his quest for wealth] if he had attained all these, he would sit still contentedly, and be quiet, enjoying himself in the thought of the happiness and tranquillity of his situation' (1982 [1759]: IV.1.8). It is only once his quest is complete that he discovers that it was a mirage all along. In the meantime, he is depicted by Smith as a man who has sold his soul by prioritizing the pursuit of wealth over the pursuit of virtue.

It is difficult not to read into this tale the conclusion that, for Smith, the poor man's son should have remained poor. As Louis Schneider suggests, Smith saw no virtue in personal wealth *per se*: 'He writes readily of "the sober and industrious poor", but he has no parallel phrase suggestive of sympathy or compassion for the rich' (Schneider 1979: 57). Smith's concern is that the only way open for the poor man's son to leave his poverty behind is for him to dismiss from his presence 'the man within the breast'. The man who adapts his role within a market society, in order to chase the riches that such a society makes possible, is a man who denies himself fundamental elements of his own being. He can only ever be a fraction of the man that he has it within himself to become. He is destined to give himself to 'the most unrelenting industry' (Smith 1982 [1759]: IV.1.8), but all to achieve entirely empty goals.

Interestingly, for Smith, the attainment of such goals renders the male of market society increasingly effeminate. He works hard so that he may be able to adopt characteristics that, to Smith's mind, take him further away from being the idealized man that he might otherwise be. The man who enjoys the successes of market society does so by adorning himself and his home with goods that were in essence no different from those that earlier eighteenth-century critics had pointed to as evidence of the unseemliness of women's conspicuous consumption. The derision that Smith reserves for 'the frivolous accomplishments of that impertinent and foolish thing called a man of fashion' (Smith 1982 [1759]: I.iii.3.6) surfaces in his description of those accomplishments: he calls them 'baubles', 'trinkets', 'trifles', and 'toys'. As Stewart Justman suggests, all such descriptions are designed to highlight the effeminacy of the modern man, made manifest in the poor man's son, who cannot resist the temptations of a market society. 'The reader of *The Theory of Moral Sentiments* finds . . . that the men of commercial society are impelled by the faulty reason and wandering desire, the vanity and love of ornament that moralists of all persuasions censured in women' (Justman 1993: 4).

The cautionary elements of the tale of the poor man's son take on a whole new dimension when it is realized that, for Smith, the poor man's son is no exception, differentiated from the rest of society by the singularity of his lifestyle choice. He is the archetypal subject of a commercial way of life. Indeed, in the absence of such people, continuously in thrall to the possibility of satisfying ever expanding consumption desires, the commercial way of life would be a non-starter. Throughout all of Smith's economic writings, consumption is the sole end of investing in both fixed and circulating capitals (Jeck 1994: 557–8). For Smith, the growth of commerce and the growth of luxury are indivisible (Skinner 1993: 30). A market society stimulates imaginary wants, because without such wants there is nothing in which to embed the institutional support structure for that society (Baum 1996: 48). Smith's 'man of fashion' may be an object of disdain when viewed as an individual. However, the commercial way of life that drew Smith's admiration is wholly conditional upon the presence of multiple men of fashion.

Smith's cautionary tale of the poor man's son therefore turns into an equally cautionary tale for those who today would impose market society as a new standard of civilization. Reading *The Theory of Moral Sentiments*, we are confronted with Smith's concerns for the type of person we might become if we follow the most basic acquisitive tenets of market society. Perhaps more importantly, Smith laments the type of person that we are destined *not* to become if we allow ourselves to be enveloped by the alluring images and the limitless wants of the commercial way of life. Smith's idealized man, who remains in pristine condition as the perfect embodiment of 'the man within the breast', is not by necessity a participant within market society. Market society, with its spectacle of riches and its constant appeal to desires that might be satisfied, has a potentially corrupting influence on the individual and on the way in which human subjects understand their relationships with other people.

One constant theme running through Smith's work is the fallibility of the individual. For him, the most potent symbol of that fallibility was the desire to flatter oneself by supposing that one had more in common with the fortunate than the unfortunate (Smith 1982 [1759]: I.iii.3.1–8). While this corruption of the self arises in conjunction with a particular stage of economic development, it is not determined at the level of the economic. The self is corrupted from within, as it is an act of will to use the imagination to identify oneself in aspiration with the wealthiest members of society. Obsessive admiration for wealth was indeed a constant feature of the world that Smith observed around him and, as a consequence of that obsession, he complained that the virtuous sentiments were considered secondary to those that led merely to self-aggrandizement (West 1976: 112–16; Peil 1999: 103–6). A corrupted society emerges from this corruption of the individual – but, then again, so does a vibrant and dynamic economy (see Mlada Bukovansky and Peter Larmour's chapters in this volume). The struggle to emulate the wealthy is a manifestation of the desire for esteem; if we esteem the wealthy, we too can expect to be the recipients of similar esteem when we reach that state of life. Such struggles are based on attempts to accumulate wealth, and the accumulationist logic thus set in motion in turn provides the momentum for market society (Levine 1998: 41–2).

Hence, we come to the paradox with which Smith wrestled throughout *The Theory of Moral Sentiments*. In seeking to stipulate the moral basis of a functioning market society, Smith begins with the premise that the commercial way of life operates most smoothly in the presence of his idealized man – in other words, when it is populated by individuals in a pristine condition, each concerned to treat all others with nothing but propriety and respect. However, this cannot explain how the market society becomes a way of life in the first place. Its origins are intimately linked to the factors that provide its economic dynamism, and these in turn serve to normalize an accumulationist logic. Yet, this is the very same logic that is rooted in the demise of the pristine individual and the tendency to submit to the spectacle of a lifestyle of conspicuous consumption. The reproduction of the commercial way of life requires that one of Smith's three states of manhood be dominant (the idealized man), but the source of that way of life requires that another be dominant (the actual man, with all his faults and false desires). This leaves Smith in something of a quandary. In the following section I review his attempt to think his way out of the paradox he presents.

The impartial spectator and the condition of market society

Smith's dilemma is to explain how the man who provides the motive force for market society, with all his faults embodied in his desire for morally worthless material possessions, can be turned into the idealized man who enables market society to become a self-perpetuating entity, but who has no such faults. He suggests that the potential to effect such a change lies in the relationship between the man without and the man within. Throughout his reflections on the moral basis of market society, Smith alludes to the presence of the 'man within the breast'. In many ways, this is the key metaphorical device in Smith's theory of human agency. The man without is a manifestation of innate human fallibility. As such, he is prone to act in a manner that the man within would not condone, by giving in to the temptations of the selfish passions. For Smith, however, the true exercise of agency comes only when the individual acts as an autonomous moral agent, and this in turn requires the man within to impose himself on the man without. The 'man within the breast' is the conscience of the human agent.

The man without is able to take on the persona of the man within through his capacity to temporarily leave himself to see his experiences as others would view them (Smith 1982 [1759]: I.i.4.6–7). Smithian man does not live alone. Indeed, he cannot even comprehend what it truly means to be a man unless he is in the company of others (Smith 1982 [1759]: II.iii.2.1). On more than one occasion, Smith refers to life lived in 'some solitary state'. However, such references are prefixed by the clauses, 'were it possible' and 'if it was possible', showing that he believed that living life alone was a purely hypothetical state of being (Smith 1982 [1759]: III.i.3; IV.2.12). For Smith, the essence of the individual's social existence lies in the ability of that individual to imaginatively reconstruct the sentiments of other people. Smith calls this 'fellow-feeling' or 'sympathy': 'As we have no immediate experience of what other men feel, we can form no idea of the manner in which they are affected, but by conceiving what we ourselves should feel in the like situation' (Smith 1982 [1759]: I.i.1.2).

These social bonds, activated through the complex process of always being ourselves but always having the capacity to use our feelings to imagine how others are impacted upon by the life that they lead, are set within the context of continuous attempts by individuals to display their moral worth by acting conscionably. As such, the social bonds that tie people together, out of which society forms, are also the moral bonds that create the good society. 'Fellow-feeling', and the process through which individuals temporarily leave themselves to experience the sentiments of other people, is therefore the bedrock of the functioning market society.

For Smith, the reproduction of a market society cannot precede the constitution of the individual as a moral agent who acts with propriety. As a consequence, market society cannot be used as a civilizing force designed to create such individuals. The individual comes first, and it is out of particular types of individuals that market society arises as a self-perpetuating entity. To suggest that this happens the other way around is, from a Smithian perspective at least, very much to put the cart before the horse. Moreover, according to Smith, the social bonds out of which a functioning market order is produced are a distinctly localized phenomenon. To talk, as international institutions routinely do today, of a *global* market as a civilizing force is therefore to commit a double fallacy. The scope of 'fellow-feeling' has spatial limits and so, also, does the constitution of the moral agent who acts with propriety (Smith 1982 [1759]: III.3.4; VI.ii.1.16–17). The 'man within the breast' may impose himself fully to regulate behavior in circumstances in which the effects of that behavior are condensed within local-level community life. But he is likely to be quietened when social relations stretch across space and leave the intimacy of local surroundings.

Smith argues that we perceive the full social significance of events with much greater clarity when the implications of actions are manifest within our midst. In other words, we see things much better when we have direct experience of observing them than when that experience is relayed to us by others (Levy 1995: 302). In the absence of direct observation, we are likely to be a distinctly partial spectator of events. We see them through our own perspective only, and we fail to imaginatively reconstruct events through the perspective – and the emotions – of other people. We thus fail to act upon the moral principles on which the good and civilized society is founded. In Smith's words, 'The propriety of our moral sentiments is never so apt to be corrupted, as when the indulgent and partial spectator is at hand' (Smith 1982 [1759]: III.3.41).

The pristine state of man is much harder to achieve in circumstances in which social relations are played out at a distance, because the relative anonymity of those relations is an impediment to the 'other-directed' action that Smith believed was the basis of market order (Fusfeld 2002: 24). Given the tendency for current conditions of globalization to be conceptualized as 'action at a distance' (see Giddens 1991; Scholte 2000), this should be a chastening conclusion for those who would seek to build contemporary standards of civilization on a global market. From a Smithian perspective, the existence of a global market makes social relations anonymous to such an extent that it is likely to undermine the moral basis of market order. It induces the distinctly partial observation of events that are of concern to unknown others and, as a consequence, it elicits activities that are the antithesis of a civilized society.

In order to correct the self-serving characteristics of the partial spectator, Smith posits the existence of an impartial spectator within every one of us. It is the impartial spectator who acts as the 'man within the breast', and it is the impartial spectator who is activated every time we temporarily leave ourselves to judge the propriety of our sentiments. The impartial spectator will not approve of individually motivated actions unless those actions also serve to promote the wider ends of society (West 1976: 116). Smithian man therefore carries society within himself (Schneider 1979: 58). He internalizes an image of the good society, under the restraining influence of the impartial spectator, in order to ensure that he lives within the bounds of acceptable social behavior. As the whole of society is never physically present to witness and pass judgment on an individual's intentions, the impartial spectator acts as a substitute for society by doing so (Justman 1993: 86).

The partial spectator is therefore juxtaposed with the impartial spectator: the fallibility of man is balanced by restraint of the selfish passions. Such restraint, when it comes from within, is called 'self-command' by Smith. As David D. Raphael and Alec L. Macfie suggest, command of the self dominates the whole of the Smithian notion of virtue (in Smith 1982: 6). Smith prioritizes the virtues of acting justly, because it is justice that represents 'the main pillar that upholds the whole edifice [of] the great, the immense fabric of human society' (Smith 1982 [1759]: II.ii.3.4). Justice requires restraint (Verburg 2000: 25), and it falls to the impartial spectator to issue the edicts of self-command so as to preserve the basis of society. The impartial spectator thus demands what Andrew Skinner calls 'a certain mediocrity of expression' (Skinner 1979: 51), in the absence of which the very maintenance of society is placed in jeopardy. Yet, the motive force for the commercial way of life is precisely to dispense with the mediocrity of expression, especially when such expression takes the form of the trappings of wealth. The question remains, then, of the extent to which the impartial spectator is present within, even compatible with, the modern commercial way of life.

It is certainly true that the impartial spectator sets exacting standards of conduct for Smithian man. Smith talks openly of the 'prodigious effort' that is required before the man without begins to pass the tests of moderation set by the man within (Smith 1982 [1759]: I.iii.1.6). At the instigation of the impartial spectator, we may well attempt the imaginative transposition of place with other people, such that we become, in effect, the observers of our own behavior (Campbell and Skinner 1982: 104). However, before we can change places with the impartial spectator itself, there must be a perfect symmetry of intention between partial actor and impartial spectator. The partial actor must in fact be cleansed of all aspects of partiality, in order to appear in the pristine state of manhood.

Smith does not comment on whether the promptings of the impartial spectator should be seen as attempts either to impose courses of action that we would anyway wish to follow, or to repress our natural inclinations in the interests of a worthier cause. For him, the issue is not whether it is human nature to be originally benevolent or originally selfish (Rizvi 2002: 247). Rather, it is from the urgings of our conscience that we derive our incentives to act in a particular way. In turn, our conscience, when it appears to us as the impartial spectator, is a substitute for society. As such, the standard against which we measure our conduct is the aggregation of the influences upon us that arise from within society.

Adopting a Smithian perspective on the question of global standards of market civilization, the next task is to assess the extent to which the influences that arise from contemporary global consumer society are compatible with Smith's conception of a civilized way of life. Much has been written recently, in the context of discussions of consumer lifestyles, of the subjugation of individual identity to the consumption of the brand (see, for instance, Klein 2000; Hertz 2001). The global advertising industry is big business in its own right, and it both spends and makes huge amounts of money seeking to create and sustain the imaginary wants that propel the global economy. What Smith termed the 'deception' and 'vanity' of worthless desires (Smith 1982 [1759]: IV.1.9) is a principal driver of economic globalization. Moreover, in the attempt to satisfy such desires. Smith believed that an essential element of the self had to be sacrificed, which would lead subsequently to the loss of moral autonomy and the corruption of the good society (Smith 1982 [1759]: I.iii.3.1). Smith's standards for civility within market society therefore look very different from what is currently being offered as new standards of market civilization. I examine this difference in the following section, contrasting World Bank strategies for integrating developing countries into the global economy with the Smithian ideal.

Embedding standards of market civilization: the stoic tradition versus the World Bank

Smith did not expect the influences of society to always lead to conduct that is consistent with the standards of propriety. Indeed, society can disarm the impartial spectator by legitimating forms of behavior that are solely self-serving: how else would the 'deception' and 'vanity' that drive the commercial way of life be established as common character traits? He suggests that unseemly behavior arises most often when it is possible to point to other people engaging in exactly the same sort of behavior. Other people's indiscretions are a convenient excuse for placing the impartial spectator at arm's length. As Smith puts it, 'Such a thing, we hear men every day saying, is commonly done, and they seem to think this a sufficient apology for what, in itself, is the most unjust and unreasonable conduct' (Smith 1982 [1759]: V.2.15). The impartial spectator has little, if any, comeback in such circumstances. It is a representative of society, a substitute for society. As such, if society legitimates certain forms of behavior by failing to censure those who engage in them, the promptings of the impartial spectator are effectively deactivated. Turning to the specific issue at hand, if society is willing to condone lifestyles based on the most conspicuous forms of global consumerism, then it is difficult to see how global standards of market civilization could conform to Smithian standards of moral propriety.

Another mechanism is necessary, then, in addition to the existence of the impartial spectator, if we are to explain how civil standards of conduct become the norm. Without such a mechanism, Smith's theory of human agency collapses on the potential for society to disarm the impartial spectator. The irony of such a situation is clear. For, the impartial spectator only exists in the first place as a reminder to the individual that his or her interests are less important than those of society as a whole. As such, the individual is stripped of virtue when the impartial spectator is disarmed. However, Smith's whole purpose in *The Theory of Moral Sentiments* is to explain 'wherein does virtue consist' (Smith 1982 [1759]: VII.i.2). He therefore requires some means of instilling virtue back into the human agent.

He does this through appeal to the traditions of stoic philosophy, whereby the interests of the individual are clearly subordinate to the interests of society. As such, the will of the individual is to be used to act upon the precepts of self-command, in order to ensure that the interests of society are prioritized. It is from stoic philosophy that Smith takes the argument, not only that self-command is virtuous itself, but also that it is the basis of all other virtues (Smith 1982 [1759]: VI.iii.11).

However, the intimation from much of Smith's work suggests that we should not expect Smithian man to evolve into the pristine stoic. Stoicism teaches restraint, but to such an extent as to endanger the dynamism of the commercial way of life. A key principle of stoic philosophy is deference to established social hierarchies (West 1976: 107–9) and, in this way, Smith writes in not altogether condemnatory terms of '[o]ur obsequiousness to our superiors' (Smith 1982 [1759]: I.ii.2.3), as a means of protecting the 'distinction of ranks'. However, the commercial way of life requires not so much deference to established social hierarchies, but a desire to emulate the acquisitiveness of the higher ranks in order to subvert those hierarchies and to change station.

The pristine stoic acts with resolve to preserve the dignity that is embedded within established forms of living. In so far as Smithian man can be made to resemble the pristine stoic, he cannot bring himself to think of the pursuit of wealth as a good thing in its own terms, because the successful pursuit of wealth undermines established forms of living (Song 1997: 33). Stoicism exorcises desires, then, but the vitality of the commercial way of life depends entirely upon expanding desires to incorporate the false wants of material possessions. Smithian man may have to learn how to be virtuous, but market society, which itself relies on the existence of such virtue for its stability, appears to be a poor learning environment for stoic principles.

This returns the argument to the tensions embedded within market society, which once again causes us to question whether Smith is ever fully able to demonstrate how the moral basis of market society is regulated in line with standards of civility. Another explanation seems to be required, beyond the dissemination of stoic principles, if it is to be shown how Smithian man becomes sufficiently civil for life within a stable commercial society. In what is perhaps a somewhat circular manner, Smith locates that explanation in commerce itself. This suggestion was not novel to *The Theory of Moral Sentiments*. As long ago as 1630, Baptist Goodall declared that, in the modern world, 'traffick [by which he meant trade] breeds affection' (cited in Landa 1980: 212). Moreover, neither was this view unique to the modern world, as similar intimations can be traced all the way back to the first century AD. Smith extended such themes, whereby Smithian man is developed through the social effects of engaging in trade. The commercial way of life may be adorned with essentially meaningless material possessions, which persuade Smithian man to luxuriate in the trappings of 'taste' and 'fashion' (Smith 1982 [1759]: V.1.4). But the act of commerce makes him more interdependent and. as a consequence, also more sociable and attentive to the needs of others. As Ralph Lindgren argues, 'One of the principal reasons Smith favored the expansion of commerce was that by exposing men to the constant scrutiny of his neighbors [the] habit of subordinating the impulse of passion to the sentiments of others would be enhanced' (Lindgren 1973: 107). The benign effects of mutual dependence therefore introduce civilizing dynamics into the learning environment that Smithian man inhabits. By learning the commercial way of life, Smithian man may not come to embody the pristine stoic, but he does learn a certain civility.

Let me now bring the argument up to date, by way of a contemporary comparison. The current activities of the World Bank also serve to promote a commercial way of life, but there are important differences between this and what Smith had in mind in relation to the same issue. For the World Bank, incorporation into a global trading structure is treated very much as an end in itself, rather than as a means of introducing civility into the relationship between individuals. Indeed, within World Bank progams, individuals are actively encouraged to forsake the interdependence of a civilized society, so that they may understand themselves as being competitively aligned one against another (see André Broome's chapter in this volume). The commercial way of life today is set within a markedly different ideological context from that of Adam Smith's day (Fitzgibbons 1995: 69–70). Smith assumed that market society had to be populated with individuals whose first instinct was towards civil co-operation and mutual sympathy. In Justman's words, 'the commercial way of life improves men by polishing their manners and winning them away from uncivil passions. Trade smooths away the roughness of men as pebbles shaken in a bag lose their "sharp angles"' (Justman 1993: 45). By contrast, World Bank progams today attempt to put that roughness back. At the very least, they seek to toughen people up, to instill within them a survivalist instinct that enables them to withstand the rigors of global competition.

One of the most controversial of all World Bank activities is its attempt to refashion individual rationalities through its development progams. It is a standard position within the academic literature that the international institutions have long attempted to model all development strategies on the particular experience of Western industrialization (see, for instance, Mehmet 1999). The World Bank has pushed ahead with its reform proposals, whilst ignoring potential problems relating to the embeddedness of the new economic activities it is seeking to institutionalize. It continues to emphasize the cognitive practices that it deems to have been essential to the process of Western industrialization. In particular, it has tried to instill a utility-maximizing mindset within the developing world (Williams 1999).

However, this is fundamentally to misread the dynamics of Western industrialization – certainly if Smith's account of that process is anything to go by.

Smithian man, with his concern for protecting the moral basis of the market society, has been turned by the World Bank into 'economic man', whose sole concern is for his own material position. This represents a conscious effort to make people think of themselves first and foremost as individuals: not as people who make a contribution on behalf of society *to* the economy, but as people who act on their own behalf to take rewards *from* the economy. It is only once individuals have been reconstituted in their own minds in this way, and it is only once they have had their subject–object relationship with the economy redefined in this way, that it is possible for them to display the character traits of a utility-maximizing agent.

But what will this do for the maintenance of market society as a stable way of life? Smith argued that the unseemly scramble for personal gain was a threat to market society, because it replaced the civilized and the prudent individual with the conceited and the vain. He refers to 'place', by which he means social standing founded upon personal gain, as 'the cause of all the tumult and bustle, all the rapine and injustice, which avarice and ambition have introduced into this world' (Smith 1982 [1759]: I.iii.2.8). Yet, to covet 'place' is precisely the character trait that World Bank progams have attempted to establish in developing countries.

To this end, let me finish by drawing a direct comparison between Smithian standards of civility and World Bank attempts to impose global standards of market civilization. I have no reason to presume that World Bank officials are anything other than genuine in their stated intentions to bring both new sources of wealth and accompanying levels of civilization to less developed countries. However, their attempts to do so look to be entirely self-defeating from a Smithian perspective. For a start, Smith's standard of civility is founded directly upon encouraging the 'man within the breast' to exert influence over the man who acts within the context of society. Yet, World Bank progams seek positively to constrain the 'man within the breast', at least to the extent that the man who acts is being persuaded to act on a purely individualistic basis, with little or no regard for society as a whole. Whilst the 'man within the breast' reminds individuals to be aware of the needs of those around them, World Bank-inspired education reforms are designed to make individuals treat those around them as potential competitors. World Bank progams therefore act upon the individual in order to deactivate the 'man within the breast', thus operating in defiance of Smithian standards of civility.

World Bank progams are set within a normative context that provides a largely unthinking endorsement of market ideology. There is no link here with the work of Smith, except perhaps via the most superficial and selective reading of *The Wealth of Nations*. For Smith, the test of whether a society conformed to the market ideal lay in the extent to which the members of that society were an active embodiment of their own impartial spectators. For the World Bank, by contrast, the test of whether a society conforms to the market ideal reduces to how much of the World Bank's own preferred institutional framework that society has managed to put in place.

It is as if there is a checklist of regulatory measures that can simply be ticked off as evidence of progress toward a global standard of market civilization: the more that can be ticked off, the closer the society comes to being civilized. Under the terms of current World Bank progams, such measures include the presence of regulatory institutions founded upon the defense of private property rights, exposure of the capital account to the disciplining effects of international financial flows, the attempt to subject all clashes of economic interest to contractual resolution within private markets, as well as membership of the WTO and other formal guarantors that international law is to be respected. Nowhere in World Bank progams is there any recognition that standards of market civilization might in any way reflect, let alone be built upon, the moral constitution of the individual market actor. If this is to be believed, then standards of market civilization are apparently capable of being parachuted onto society from the outside, rather than being anything that grows organically from within the individual members of that society.

The World Bank conception of standards of market civilization therefore turns Adam Smith's view of the world on its head. For Smith, it is the moral constitution of the individual that is at the heart of a civilized way of life. For the World Bank, on the other hand, the moral constitution of the individual is not an issue: it is a government's willingness to construct the formal institutions of a market economy that determine whether or not it meets the standards of civilization. World Bank officials may be completely genuine in their conviction that exposure to global markets acts as a civilizing force for individuals. However, from a Smithian perspective, this is to view the problem entirely the wrong way around. It is the individual that is ontologically prior according to Smith, for the fairly obvious reason that the individual is formed before the market.

Conclusion

The recent history of World Bank progams suggests that they have been self-defeating; they have failed in their own narrow terms of bringing growth to the developing world. But maybe we should not be too surprised by this. From a Smithian perspective, it is impossible simply to impose standards of market civilization from the 'outside', unless the 'man within the breast' has first fully inculcated the human agent with the moral standards of propriety deemed necessary for life within market society.

Contemporary standards of market civilization tend to be presented as if they refer solely to the economic conditions by which a state must abide if it is to be treated as civilized by other states. There is rich irony when Adam Smith is enlisted, as the court philosopher of market society, to lend intellectual legitimacy to such a view. When the World Bank expresses the lineage of its development progams in terms of Smithian economics (on which, see Williams 1999), we have little choice but to ask which Smith it is talking about. For the Adam Smith who wrote *The Theory of Moral Sentiments* was as aware as anyone that the ability to maintain a stable market society was not solely, even mostly, a matter of economics.

Nowhere in Smith's preferred method of explanation is there a categorical distinction between economic and moral questions. The political economy of Smith is the practical application of moral philosophy (Dow *et al.* 1997). Contemporary standards of market civilization may have their legitimating ideology in free-market economics but, set in this context, such legitimation counts for little in the absence of prior philosophical reflection about the type of individual who is to inhabit the market system. For Smith, the individual had to be able to resist the superficial trappings of material gain, in order to respond to the promptings of the impartial spectator. Yet, the particular type of free-market economics that legitimates today's market system positively thrives upon the superficiality and instant gratification of consumer culture. As such, it is set up deliberately to distance the impartial spectator from the immediacy of human judgment. Adam Smith was ever the optimist when it came to the issue of human nature. However, from a Smithian perspective, it is difficult to be similarly optimistic about the likely success of current attempts to impose standards of market civilization.

5 Civilizing the global economy

Racism and the continuity of Anglo-Saxon imperialism

John M. Hobson

This chapter argues that the United States, like its British predecessor, has invoked a racist imperial project that seeks to promote a 'superior' Anglo-Saxon identity in the world. In contrast to mainstream materialist analyses of Anglo-Saxon imperialism or hegemony (e.g. Gilpin 1987; Cox 1987; Wallerstein 1984), I produce a culturalist approach. My claim is that in the last two centuries imperial Great Power politics and the modern global economy (MGE) have been constructed by Western racism. Radical materialist analysis assumes that to the extent that racism is important it is merely epiphenomenal to both the MGE and hegemony. But I argue that racism constitutes not so much the 'superstructure' of the MGE but enters the very 'base' or foundation that informs its reproduction – as it does with respect to the practice of hegemony in the world economy.

The main conceptual avenue into my approach lies with the racist notion of the 'market standard of civilization'. This concept complements but is not reducible to the notion of the *standard of civilization*, which formed the base of international law prior to 1945. While most scholars recognize that the standard was founded on racism, nevertheless because the standard was dropped from international law after the Second World War, so it is assumed that racism no longer informs either Great Power politics or the reproduction of the MGE (e.g. Gong 1984). By contrast, I argue that the racist market standard continued on down to the present day informing the basis of the American 'civilizing mission'.

The chapter is divided into three parts. Part 1 analyzes the construction of the racist discourse that in turn led to the market standard of civilization which lay at the base of the British civilizing mission. Part 2 examines how the standard was applied through British imperialism, while Part 3 reveals the continuity of racist power politics after 1945 as the imperialist market standard has been applied by the United States.

1 The racist origins of the imperial market standard of civilization, 1700–1850

The racist origins of British imperialism and the global economy

Today we often imagine the MGE as comprising three worlds: the First World (the Northern Core), the Second World (the communist/post-communist semiperiphery), and the Third World (the Southern periphery). And for some, it is allegedly in the nature of global capitalism that the Northern winners expand and develop at the expense of the Southern losers (e.g. Wallerstein 1984). Accordingly, it is assumed that only when capitalism ends will the unequal distribution of economic resources be redressed. Here I suggest that the three worlds of the MGE are not simply a product of capitalism but are also significantly informed by Western racist power politics. That is, the MGE comprises a fundamental cultural or *civilizational* East–West divide rather than a pure *economic* North–South divide. Taken to its logical extreme, this suggests that were we to get rid of racism, capitalism might be truly civilized for the betterment of global humanity.

The notion of the First, Second, and Third Worlds first emerged, albeit in informal terms, during the eighteenth and nineteenth centuries as the British invented a kind of 'civilizational league table' (see Table 5.1).

This classification derived from a series of racist ideas that were invented in Europe after 1700/1750. Racism takes two forms: implicit and explicit. Explicit (or Scientific) racism emerged in Britain after 1840, and locates difference according to genetic characteristics (see below). Beginning during the Enlightenment after 1700, implicit racism locates difference through environment and institutions. It might also be called cultural racism. Regarding the importance of climate/environment, thinkers such as Montesquieu and William Falconer argued that those peoples who live in temperate climates are inevitably hard-working and are characterized by an 'increased activity of the brain'. Conversely those living in arid climates are naturally phlegmatic or lazy. As Philip Curtin aptly noted: 'the conclusion is [that] . . . in Falconer's opinion, the best possible balance of human qualities is to be found near the northern edge of the temperate zone – in short in Britain' (Curtin 1964: 65–6). In this conception the whites lived in the most temperate zone (First World), the blacks in the most arid (Third World), with the yellows lying in between (Second World). More significantly, implicit racism emphasizes *institutional* difference. This focus rested in turn on two imaginary theoretical constructs: the Peter Pan theory of the East and the theory of Oriental Despotism.

The theory of Oriental Despotism asserted that Europe represented 'advanced civilization' because it supposedly had superior rational and liberal political institutions. It asserted that Europe was the birthplace of democracy, which in turn led to the rise of a strong civil society and the flourishing individual, whose rational economic actions propelled Europe through to advanced capitalism. Conversely, Asia was dismissed as the home of despotic states, which stifled the emergence of a strong civil society and thereby prevented the development of the rational individual. Accordingly, all economic progress was choked by the tentacles of the despotic state, thereby 'explaining' why Asia was backward and governed only by regressive cycles of stagnation. This was an imaginary construct because Europe only became democratic in the twentieth century and Eastern states had long enabled considerable economic progress (Hobson 2004).

Table 5.1: Inventing the civilizational league table and the three worlds of modern capitalism

Civilizational classification	**'Civilized'** (Premier league and Division 1) the First World	**'Barbaric'** (Division 2) the Second World	**'Savage'** (Division 3) the Third World
Corresponding Countries	Britain in the Premier League; Western Europe in Division 1	E.g., Ottoman Empire, Japan, China, Siam	E.g., Africa, Australia and New Zealand
Racial Colour	White	Yellow	Black
Temperament	Disciplined/ Hard-Working	Melancholic/Rigid	Phlegmatic/Lax
Climatic Character	Cold and Wet	Arid and Tropical	High Aridity
Human Character	Christian	Pagan	Atheistic/Pagan
Theory of Oriental Despotism	Liberal-democracy, Freedom, Individualism, Rationality	Despotism, Slavery, Collectivism, Irrationality	Despotism or Absence of Government, Collectivism/ Tribalism, Irrationality
Peter Pan Theory	Paternal/Masculine, Independent, Innovative, Rational	Adolescent/ Feminine, Imitative, Irrational	Child-like, Dependent, Imitative or Indifferent, Irrational
Social Legitimating Principles	The British as the Chosen People or Master-Race	The Fallen People	Natural 'Man' in the State of Nature
Political Legitimating Principles	Sovereign (Bordered Populated Space)	Non-sovereign/ Indirect Imperial Rule (Borderless Populated Space)	*Terra Nullius*/ Direct Colonial Rule (Vacant- or Waste-Space)
Resulting civilizational status	Normal	Deviant	Deviant

This idea was complemented by the construction of the Peter Pan theory of the East. This theory gave rise to various binary categories, which were dreamed up in order to differentiate the West from the East. Thus the West was imagined as: inventive, proactive, scientific, disciplined, self-controlled, practical, mind-oriented, independent, and paternal. This was indeed an imaginary construction given that between 500–1850 the West had been significantly dependent upon the superior Eastern technologies and ideas that had diffused across the global economy (Hobson 2004). By contrast, the East was imagined as the West's inferior opposite Other: imitative, passive, superstitious, lazy, spontaneous, exotic, body-oriented, dependent, and adolescent or child-like. And for precisely the same reason this too was no less an imaginary construct. More specifically, the Third World was imagined as that of black *child-like* savagery, while the Second World was conceived as yellow *adolescent* barbarism. Importantly, the discourse of East and West was synonymous with the patriarchal discourse. Thus we could replace the terms West and East with 'masculinity' and 'femininity' respectively, and end up with precisely the same set of binary opposites.

Enlightenment thinking placed all peoples along a mental continuum. Western man was privileged as fully rational in a mental and mature sense, whereas Eastern 'man' was irrational – i.e. immature and psychically undeveloped. Thus:

> given the [assumption of the] psychic unity of mankind, non-Europeans could of course be brought to adulthood, to rationality, to modernity, through a set of learning experiences. (The phrase 'colonial tutelage' was a signature of the doctrine, and this conception is encountered in most history and geography textbooks of the time.)
>
> (Blaut 1993: 96)

Indeed, the depiction of the West as a rational and paternal man juxtaposed against the East as an irrational and helpless child/adolescent was crucial in promoting the idea of the imperial civilizing mission as a moral duty. For it was axiomatic that only the paternal West could and *should* emancipate or redeem the child-like East, much like a father sees it as his duty to raise his child. Moreover, depicting the East as a seductive and exotic woman constituted a further drive for the patriarchal West to achieve imperial conquest, penetration, control and gratification.

Nowhere was the link between the Peter Pan theory, the theory of Oriental Despotism, and imperialism more clearly represented than in Rudyard Kipling's famous 1899 poem, 'The White Man's Burden'. For it was there that he described the Eastern peoples as 'half-devil and half-child'. The burden constituted a moral duty to 'relieve the sickness' of Eastern depravity and deprivation. Nevertheless it was also a burden given that the imperialists should expect no gratitude for their services to mankind. Rather the 'reward', Kipling warned his American audience, would be nothing more than: 'The blame of those ye better, The hate of those ye guard'.

Finally, a further important factor in the rise of implicit racism was the Protestant revival that occurred in Britain in the late eighteenth century.

> Missionaries, possibly more than members of other branches of the colonial establishment, aimed at the radical transformation of indigenous society. . . . They therefore sought, whether consciously or unconsciously, the destruction of pre-colonial societies and their replacement by new . . . societies in the image of Europe.
>
> (Christopher 1984: 83)

Indeed, once they had settled in various parts of the empire the missionaries 'pressed vigorously for government intervention to facilitate the civilizing mission' (Abernethy 2000: 222). For in addition to racism, 'the harsh contempt for the Chinese [and others] . . . was a product of missionary Protestantism and the disgust it could barely conceal for civilizations other than that of the West' (Edwardes 1971: 110). In general, Protestantism was a vital ideational component in prompting imperialism because it furnished the British with the self-conception of Britons as the Chosen People. This was epitomized in William Blake's famous poem 'Jerusalem', which instructed the British to never cease until they had 'built Jerusalem in England's green and pleasant land' (Colley 1992: 29–30). Thus from the conception of the British as God's Chosen People it was but a short step to view imperialism and the Anglicization of the world as Britain's Manifest Destiny.

By the 1840s implicit racism was complemented by the emergence of explicit or scientific racism. Books such as Robert Knox's *The Races of Man*, Benjamin Kidd's *Social Evolution* or Benjamin Disraeli's novel, *Tancred*, constructed a tripartite hierarchical division or civilizational scale of races based on skin colour: white, yellow and black. And scientific racism was blended with implicit racism to form the foundation of the idea of the moral necessity of imperialism conceived of as a 'civilizing mission'. This concoction found its expression in countless statements issued by prominent politicians and imperial bureaucrats. Typical was Joseph Chamberlain:

> I believe in this race, the greatest governing race the world has ever seen; in this Anglo-Saxon race, so proud, so tenacious, self-confident and determined, this race which neither climate nor change can degenerate, which will infallibly be the predominant force of future history and universal civilization.
>
> (cited in Hobson 2004: 237)

And Lord Curzon exclaimed that 'In empire, we have found not merely the key to glory and wealth, but the call to duty, and the means of service to mankind' (cited in Thornton 1966: 72).

Constructing the imperial 'market standard of civilization': containment versus cultural conversion

The result of the civilizational league table was the notion that the White Europeans were 'normal', the Easterners 'deviant'. And what made imperialism inevitable was that in this construction the British could not tolerate the Other either for the so-called despotic threat that it posed, or the deviance that it displayed. Accordingly, having constructed the Eastern Other as a deviant threat to Western identity, it had to be punished and disciplined through imperialism (Said 1991). Importantly, the place that the backward peoples occupied on the imaginary scale of civilization dictated the 'imperial form' that would be applied. Some Division Three countries, notably Australia, were branded with the legal concept of '*terra nullius*'. The lands of the savages were thought of as empty or waste spaces that had to be filled up by, or converted to, Western practices that accorded with advanced civilization. As Lord Carnarvon put it, 'the mission of England' invoked 'a spirit of adventure to fill up waste places of the Earth' (cited in Hyam 1976: 105). It was as if the savage peoples did not exist and were therefore discounted as the owners of the land that they occupied. Accordingly this mental deterritorialization meant that sovereignty could not be granted and that full formal-colonial takeover was entirely appropriate. By contrast, although the yellow barbaric peoples were undeserving of colonial rule, their countries were thought of as 'borderless spaces' that would be transcended through *informal* imperialism in order to 'correct' or discipline the yellow 'recalcitrants' along Western lines.

But there was a logical contradiction in the discourse of empire. For while the civilizing mission entailed the means for imposing *cultural conversion* (i.e. converting Eastern societies along Western lines in order to 'raise them up'), nevertheless this went hand-in-hand with *containment*, which sought to 'keep the backward peoples down'. There were two reasons for this. First, the ultimate rationale for cultural conversion was to eradicate the identity threat that the Other posed so that the British Self could feel superior. But in order to remain superior it was vital that the Other be prevented from reaching the level of British economic power since that would enable the East to pose a challenge to British supremacy (hence containment). Moreover, an identity gap had to be preserved so as to maintain Britain's sense of superiority. Or put differently, imperialism was designed to both civilize the Other (or reduce the Eastern Other to the Western Self) while simultaneously fixing the East as an eternal Other. And second, both strategies entailed the repression of the East. For while cultural conversion was sold or imagined as helping the East, it was in fact a strategy of ethnocide through which the target group's culture would be undermined or obliterated. Moreover, viewing the Eastern peoples as so decidedly inferior meant that they could be utilized or exploited to service the economic needs of the British given that they did not enjoy 'human rights'. Put differently, had the British viewed them as equals (i.e. as civilized human beings) in the first place, the civilizing mission might not have occurred.

Racism was enshrined in the notion of the 'market standard of civilization' that in turn was the measure against which all civilizations would be judged. Those that failed to meet the standard would be converted along Western liberal lines. Hence the standard directly implied cultural conversion. Accordingly, the colonies were to be granted liberal capitalism, a rational bureaucratic state, the rule of law and rational-legal systems (Gong 1984). Only once this had all been achieved could they finally be granted civilized status and hence sovereignty. One of the key disciplinary strategies was the imposition of free trade. For it was allegedly a 'civilizing process' because free trade would supposedly ensure that the Eastern peoples intensively develop their economies through specialization, individualistic self-help and hard work – the *leitmotif* of advanced civilization. The next section examines how the twin strategies of cultural conversion and containment that lay at the base of the racist market standard of civilization played out in terms of British imperial free trade policy.

2 The British civilizing mission: disciplining and punishing the East

Nowhere was the racist contradiction of British imperialism clearer than in the imperial policy of free trade. For while the policy was sold as a means of raising the Eastern economies up through cultural conversion, it simultaneously served to hold them down through containment. The clearest example of this was found in the case of India. In the seventeenth century the British economy had been heavily reliant upon superior imported Indian cotton textile manufactures (the Indian textile industry was the global leader). But by imposing free trade in India while relying on protectionism at home the situation was reversed, with the British textile industry coming to lead the world while the Indian industry was undermined or de-industrialized.

The hypocritical treatment of India was striking. Having held the Indian cotton manufacturing industry down with one boot (through very high domestic British tariffs), the other boot kicked British manufactures into India unimpeded. It was one of the most unfair free kicks the British awarded themselves. Thus while in the seventeenth century the British economy was a net importer of Indian textiles, by 1873 no less than 40–45 per cent of all British cotton textile exports went to India. And by the mid-nineteenth century India had been transformed into a raw cotton supplier for the Lancashire industry, which in turn exported the finished product back to India. In short, the social cost of the advancement of the British textiles industry was the de-industrialization of the Indian industry (Dutt 1943). As one nineteenth-century Briton, Horace Wilson, explained:

> Had not such prohibitory duties and decrees existed, the mills of Paisley and of Manchester would have been stopped. . . . They were created by the sacrifice of the Indian manufacturer. . . . The foreign manufacturer employed the arm of political injustice to keep down and ultimately strangle a competitor with whom he could not have contended on equal terms.
>
> (cited in Fryer 1988: 12)

Much the same story applied to the iron industry in which India had been one of the world's foremost producers. And as Friedrich List pointed out, this 'free' trading relationship between Britain and India ultimately constituted one of 'unequal exchange' in that it condemned the latter to rely on an agricultural/raw materials stage of production, thereby stymieing its industrial developmental prospects. Put differently, the policy of free trade in effect constituted a strategy whereby the British 'kicked away the ladder' in order to contain or hold down the Eastern economies (List 1885: 189, 368; Chang 2002). But *contra* List this strategy was not designed to maintain Britain's lead over other Continental countries, given that successive British governments did little to promote or maintain European free trade throughout the nineteenth century (Hobson 2002). It was rather designed to maintain Britain's lead over the Eastern economies since the British imposed free trade only *outside* of Europe.

While the Indian situation was the most extreme example, largely because the Indian iron/steel and cotton textile industries had been the leading global sectors, a similar situation played out in many other colonies. List's concept of unequal exchange applied to all the colonies, in so far as they were reorganized so as to supply raw materials and agricultural goods to feed British industrialization. As Alec Hargreaves aptly noted of the European colonies, despite the rationale for cultural conversion (the 'civilizing mission') the British

> did not, however, produce carbon copies of Europe's industrial economies. On the contrary, the colonies remained predominantly agricultural. They were to support, but not to compete with, Europe's industrial system by supplying foodstuffs and raw materials and providing markets for manufactured goods.
> (Hargreaves 1982: 167)

But there were a number of further racist double standards that underpinned British imperial free-trade policy. Within the Division Two countries free trade was spread through the imposition of Unequal Treaties. These allegedly constituted the vehicle through which the British would spread the 'gift of civilization'. They were 'granted' to many 'non-Western' countries including Brazil (1810), China (1842–60), Japan (1858), Siam (between 1824–55), Persia (1836, 1857), and the Ottoman Empire (1838, 1861). In each case, the country was stripped of tariff autonomy and tariffs were limited to a maximum of 5 per cent. The first racist double standard here is that, during the so-called free-trade era of the mid-nineteenth century, European states were subject to 'reciprocity-treaties' that were freely negotiated between 'contracting partners'. This clearly contrasted with the 'Open Door' treaties that were *imposed* upon the East. Moreover, British indifference to proactively spreading free trade across Europe contrasted starkly to her forceful imposition of free trade in the 'non-White' world. And more generally, Britain's *passive* military posture *vis-à-vis* Continental Europe after 1815 contrasted no less strikingly with Britain's frequent recourse to violence in the East (Hobson 2002: 307–14).

A second racist double standard here was that while the European economies industrialized through tariff protectionism – indeed Britain industrialized on the back of an average tariff of 32 per cent between 1700–1850 – the Eastern economies were forced to move straight to free trade or near free trade. Note that it would be only as late as 1980 when Western countries would finally match the levels of free trade that were imposed on the East in the nineteenth century. And many Eastern economies had lower tariffs than those found in the mid-nineteenth century heyday of European 'free trade'. Naturally this served to *contain* the Eastern economies because in contrast to the actual experience of Britain (and Europe more generally) it denied them the chance of building up their infant industries.

For all this, though, yet more contradictions or racist double standards emerged through imperial free trade. It is especially important to note here that the imposition of the Unequal Treaties was based not on a purely economic rationale but was also a means to undermine the cultural autonomy of many Eastern states and societies. And often the negative cultural impact was more onerous than that of economic containment. China provides an excellent example. The Opium Wars and subsequent imposed treaties proved to be a wedge to open China up to Britain's cultural assault on her identity.

There were three basic aspects concerning the negative cultural and political impact of British imperialism in China. First, through the Unequal Treaties, Chinese political autonomy was fundamentally assaulted by the enforcement at gunpoint of 'extraterritoriality' – the notion that *all* foreign residents, not just foreign diplomats, may live in China but would be subject only to their own Western laws. To this end a number of 'Concessions' were established (i.e. areas of land designated for foreigners who were subject to British law). And this was justified through European/Western international law because China was assessed as uncivilized and was, therefore, unworthy of sovereignty. As the Duke of Argyll declared at the time of the Second Opium War:

> It is supreme nonsense to talk as if we were bound to the Chinese by the same rules which regulate international relations in Europe. . . . It would be madness to be bound on our side by that code with a barbarous people, to whom it is unknown, and if known, would not be followed.
>
> (cited in Hyam 1976: 66)

Here it is also noteworthy that extraterritoriality was enforced against the Ottoman Empire, Thailand and many other countries, on the basis that they too failed to pass the 'civilization test'.

Second, Chinese sovereignty was assaulted through the Unequal Treaties by the British policy of forcing the Chinese into accepting foreign administration of key bureaucratic agencies such as the Postal Services, Imperial Maritime Customs (IMC) and taxing agencies (e.g. the Gabelle or salt tax). In particular, in 1863 Robert Hart became Head of the IMC, thereby amounting to a full British takeover. Clearly, the inability of the Chinese government to set its own foreign trade or tax policy constituted a major affront to its sovereignty and autonomy.

The third affront to Chinese cultural autonomy lay in the British insistence upon the abolition of the kowtow in 1873. While this had no economic consequences, of all the demands that the British made *this* was the most humiliating and consequential. Its effect was to shatter the whole social and discursive structure upon which the Chinese state and society had been founded, given that its legitimacy had historically rested on the practice of the kowtow, especially as conducted by foreign emissaries from 'vassal states'. Moreover, cultural humiliation was effected in a whole variety of ways, perhaps the most notorious example being when the British erected signs outside the Recreation Ground in Shanghai (now Huangpu Park) stating: 'No dogs or Chinese allowed'. One can only imagine how the British would have reacted had the Chinese taken over St James's Park (just down the road from Buckingham Palace) only to erect signs stating: 'No dogs or Britons allowed'.

All in all, imperial free trade was only in part about strengthening the British economy at the expense of the Eastern economies. Most importantly it enabled the British to convert the cultures of Eastern societies along Western lines. And what lay at the base of this strategy was the disciplinary power of the racist market standard of civilization to which all Eastern economies were forced to conform.

3 The American civilizing mission: disciplining and punishing the East

American identity and the continuity of the racist market standard of civilization

It is assumed that the post-1945 world came to be founded on an entirely new set of principles. Human rights would replace racism, the racist legal concept of the standard of civilization was replaced by the international law of co-operation, and colonialism was terminated. Furthermore, the beggar-thy-neighbour politics that had destroyed the League of Nations would be prevented by a new set of multilateral institutions, especially the General Agreement on Tariffs and Trade (GATT) and the International Monetary Fund (IMF). And all of this would be held in place by the benign actions of the US hegemon or the *Pax Americana*. But despite this commonly received view, the post-1945 era has in many crucial respects demonstrated a remarkable degree of continuity with the old racist-colonial era.

To the extent that others have noted a certain continuity between the *Pax Britannica* and the *Pax Americana* (especially Marxists and realists), this is usually ascribed to materialist factors: that the US and Britain have been the leading global capitalist great powers (e.g. Wallerstein 1984; Cox 1987; Gilpin 1987). Here I suggest that the continuity derives at least as much from their similar national identities. Both have been dominated by the Anglo-Saxon race, both embraced Protestantism, and both defined themselves negatively against a 'deviant' 'non-white' race. But for a variety of reasons, the American identity became a more extreme version. How so?

First and foremost, Puritanism was a more extreme form of Protestantism. Second, for the white Puritan settlers, America signified a place of spiritual renewal. America was to be created as an ideal New England, free from the corruption of the mother country. Third, the settlers were confronted by what they perceived to be a wholly alien environment, which exacerbated the need to define their identity in markedly exclusive terms (Zuckerman 1987). And their Puritan religion was especially significant here. As Richard Drinnon notes:

> By movement through space, this transplanted Puritanism had become the one true faith, and with no one – or no one recognizable – either above or below them, the emigrant middling men had become the only true men. . . . Hence, while the English Puritan version of the Protestant ethic was harshly intolerant, the New English variant was more so.
>
> (Drinnon 1980: 32)

Finally, the Americans became imbued with a sense that they were the Chosen People, whose ideological conquest of the world was but their Manifest Destiny (Horsman 1981).

This all culminated in an American sense of exceptionalism, endangerment, encirclement and hence paranoia and eternal vigilance against the Other (Campbell 1992: Ch. 5), which in turn promoted an identity based on 'regeneration through violence' (Slotkin 1973). This entailed not just a war with the Native Indian Other, but, above all, the subsequent construction and reconstruction of new enemies that could be repressed and defeated in order to reproduce American identity. In this way, with the completion of the Indian wars by the late nineteenth century and the 'winning of the Western frontier', so the Americans turned to the Final Frontier – the winning of the world. This entailed overseas expansion and the implementation of the American civilizing mission.

> By thus taking up the duty of 'regeneration and civilization', America could perform the noble work of teaching inferiors to appreciate the blessings they already enjoyed but were inclined to overlook. In turn, that would prepare them for the better days to follow under America's benevolent leadership.
>
> (Williams 1972: 60)

Directly reminiscent of the countless statements issued by Britain's imperial advocates, President Theodore Roosevelt laid down the racist formula of the White Man's Burden that would guide all subsequent US administrations: that it is America's 'duty toward the people living in barbarism to see that they are freed from their chains, and we can free them only by destroying barbarism itself' (cited in Williams 1972: 63). Indeed this idea has recurred time and again, finding its latest expression in George W. Bush's 'war on terror' particularly as it is applied in the Middle East (see Bowden 2002).

As with the British civilizing mission, so the American was no less founded on the same contradiction – between 'raising the barbarians up' (cultural conversion) and 'keeping them down' (containment). Again as William Appleman Williams (1972: 67) put it, the essence of the American global mission was firstly to wrench non-Western powers 'out of their neo-feudal . . . condition into the industrial era' (i.e. cultural conversion), but simultaneously 'to stop or stabilize such changes at a point favourable to American interests' (i.e. containment). Such a contradiction ensured that, like the British, so the American Mission would be based on a series of double standards.

Ultimately, the central prong of US foreign policy – like the British before it – has been the construction of external threats or scares, which constitute vital discursive vehicles that 'justify' the containment and cultural conversion of the Other in order to maintain 'superior' American identity (Campbell 1992). And, like those of the British before them, these strategies were based fundamentally on the 'market standard of civilization' (see also Bowden 2004c). Indeed the concomitant construction of the three worlds of capitalism that began with the British has remained an almost identical feature of the post-1945 world. Thus the modern (post-1945) 'First World' represents advanced civilization because it is scientific/rational, individualistic and liberal/democratic, while the savage 'Third World' is posited as such owing to its allegedly unscientific/irrational, collectivist and despotic properties – a view that finds its clearest expression in modernization theory (Rostow 1961). And once more, the collectivist/totalitarian 'Second World' (i.e. communism/post-communism) represents 'barbarism'. Accordingly, the *continuity* of the market standard after 1945 has constituted the vital discursive vehicle to justify America's racist imperial project of the cultural conversion and containment of the non-Western Other. To demonstrate this I draw on two main examples: the Third World debt crisis and US–Japan relations.

Imposing the market standard of civilization: constructing the Third World debt crisis

Materialist analyses assume that the 1982 Third World debt crisis was an *objective* fact: that debt levels as a proportion of exports or gross domestic product (GDP) had reached levels that could no longer be serviced. But what this misses is the discursive political process that constructs or defines a crisis in the first place. Surely, though, a 'crisis is a crisis is a crisis?' materialists might well reply. But consider the following example. Had unemployment levels risen to as much as 7 per cent of the total workforce in the 1950s, this would have been viewed as a major crisis of capitalism, and would have stimulated Keynesian governments to engage in 'crisis management'. But after 1980, Western neo-liberal governments not only saw such levels as *normal* but also viewed them as *necessary* in order to discipline labour. Accordingly, no political response was necessary. In other words, a crisis is constructed according to the identity or political ideology of the particular agent and can be manipulated to suit its particular political interests. How then and why was the 1982 debt crisis constructed?

At this time, the IMF – the US government's international disciplinary weapon of choice – had been eclipsed by the ending of the fixed exchange rate system in 1973 (see Michael Oliver's chapter in this volume). The US government sought to replace the 'lax' Eurocurrency markets with the more punitive IMF that, of course, attaches harsh conditionality clauses to its lending. Mexico's announcement of its debt crisis in August 1982 provided the opportunity for the US government to reintroduce the punitive IMF into the heart of the international financial system, which would then contain and impose cultural conversion in the Third World (see Jacqueline Best and Leonard Seabrooke's chapters in this volume). Within one year the IMF was intervening in forty-seven countries and imposing 'structural adjustment programs', which entailed the implementation of neo-liberal economic reforms. While the IMF claimed to be an apolitical instrument, which sought merely to impose neutral technocratic measures that would solve the crisis, nevertheless the result of the cultural conversion strategies was the exacerbation rather than the alleviation of the debt crisis (i.e. containment). As Gregory Fossedal put it:

> The currency devaluations drive up prices just as consumers are suffering reduced benefits and workers reduced wages. Resulting inflation creates Third World bracket gallop into high tax brackets that stifle entrepreneurship and growth. And the slowdown in economic activity deprives the government of revenues and exports, the provision of which the IMF sought in the first place. Any number of studies, including some by the IMF itself, have found that its programs tend to worsen, not improve, the national economies to which its mercantilist, budget-obsessed models are applied.
>
> Fossedal 1989: 207)

Proof of this lies in the fact that within three years alone Third World debt rocketed from $391 billion to $454 billion. If the US and IMF had been serious about solving the crisis they would have changed course at this point in the face of a deluge of testimonies made by many within the West and by the debtors themselves – that austerity was not working. But despite this the subsequent Baker plan imposed an even more severe neo-liberal program of cultural conversion. And while this enhanced the dissemination of Western civilizational practices (cultural conversion), its net effect again was further containment: by 1987 Third World debt had escalated to $528 billion.

Despite US rhetoric there *was* an alternative to IMF conditionality, cultural conversion and containment – most notably the Brandt Commission's *Common Crisis, North South* – which suggested a detailed alternative policy agenda as early as 1983 (Brandt Commission 1983: 50–100). But this was ignored because it did not mesh with objectives of the US civilizing mission. Clearly then the crisis had been politically constructed so that the US could punish the 'barbaric' Third World for its 'deviancy'.

Imposing the market standard of civilization: disciplining and punishing the Japanese Other

Why did the harmonious post-1945 US–Japan relationship take a turn for the worse during the 1980s? The traditional materialist account explains this in terms of an ever-rising US trade deficit that was caused by *unfair* Japanese trading practices. By the mid-1980s a fully fledged Yellow Scare acted as a spectre that terrified America. But the rising US trade deficit was a red herring because since the early 1990s – when the Yellow Scare died out – the trade deficits with Japan deepened. What made Japan seem so scary was that an Asian power with a different identity appeared to be challenging the supremacy of American liberal individualism. Japan had an economically proactive state and a relatively collectivist social structure, which stood in sharp contrast to the American way. Ezra Vogel captured the problem well as early as 1979:

> To expect Americans, who are accustomed to thinking of their nation as number one, to acknowledge that in many areas its supremacy has been lost to an Asian nation and to learn from that nation is to ask a good deal.

> Americans are peculiarly receptive to any explanation of Japan's economic performance which avoids acknowledging Japan's superior competitiveness. . . . It is disquieting to admit that the Japanese have beaten us in economic competition because of their superior planning, organization, and effort.
>
> (Vogel 1979: 225–6)

But rather than rectifying problems with the US economy, the Reagan government preferred to construct Japan as the latest Eastern threat to justify imposing cultural conversion and containment strategies in order to eradicate the Japanese threat and thereby reaffirm the 'superiority' of American values.

That this analysis betrayed a racist attitude is revealed by several points. The claim that the US trade deficits were caused by Japanese export surpluses is belied by the fact that 60 per cent of the US deficits were caused by the European Union. And no one was blaming the Europeans. Moreover, as Daniel Burstein noted of the prevailing Japan-bashing mood of 1987:

> Those bashing the hardest didn't stop long to explain why the United States was running a staggering trade deficit with nearly *all* its trading partners, not just the Japanese. If Japan's markets were as hermetically sealed as the bashers claimed, how could the Japanese import nearly $30b worth of American products annually – more than any other country besides Canada? Clearly, fundamental problems other than Japanese 'unfairness' lay at the heart of lost American competitiveness, but the unfairness issue provided a much more expedient political focus.
>
> (Burstein 1988: 85, 136)

Indeed Japan's low import ratio (7 per cent of GDP) was comparable to America's (10 per cent), as was Japan's low export ratio (9.5 per cent compared to America's 7 per cent). But listening to American rhetoric, one could be forgiven for thinking that Japan's exports were as massive as America's imports.

All in all, if there *was* a failing in the rise of Japan it was in its timing. For it came at a time when Americans perceived that their country was in decline and under threat. And like the New York Stock Exchange after a fall, the Americans were desperate to 'feel good again'. Constructing the Japanese threat as but the latest 'scare' could not have been more fortuitous. For it would enable the US government to deflect the weaknesses of the American economy on the one hand (i.e. scapegoat the Japanese), and simultaneously justify the imposition of cultural conversion and containment strategies on the other so as to punish the latest deviant Eastern Other. In such ways has American identity been maintained. How was this achieved?

Through the 1980s US governments beat the Japanese over the head with an extremely aggressive liberalization stick (i.e. cultural conversion), in order to open up their closed (i.e. protected) trading and financial systems on the one hand, and imposed a series of containment strategies on the other, all of which were designed to stall the Japanese rocket in mid-air. Ryutaro Komiya and Motoshige Itoh's words here are apt:

> Usually trade negotiations between two countries take the form of give-and-take, but in these negotiations, which have been going on almost continuously from 1976, the subject matter has been simply how much and how soon Japan would make concessions, with the United States offering little if anything in exchange.
>
> (Komiya and Itoh 1988: 202–3)

The first containment strategy took the form of a 'liberal double standard'. While the *leitmotif* of US government economic policy is that the market and not governments must determine the allocation of supply, in the 'besieged' industries the US turned protectionist against Japan. A staggering 30 per cent of Japanese imports were subject to what are euphemistically known as Voluntary Export Restraints (though these were coercively imposed). Most of the VERs were applied to cars. But this immediately led to 'economic blowback' as the Japanese relocated their companies within American borders and then imported Japanese car parts that, of course, led to further pressures on the US trade balance. The Americans then forced the Japanese to lower their tariff barriers. By 1984 Japanese tariffs on industrial goods were lower than American rates and there were fewer Japanese industrial quotas than in America (Komiya and Itoh 1988: 190–3). And yet the trade deficit continued to mount.

At this point the Americans targeted Japan's closed financial system as the scapegoat for their domestic production weaknesses. The background to this lay with the rapid rise of US public debt. The notoriously low US savings rate meant that the Reagan government had to look abroad for the necessary funds to pay for its rearmament program and the excesses of the wary US taxpayer. The government chose to lean heavily on Japan in order to extract the necessary funds. The stick used was the 1984 Yen–Dollar Agreement. First, this would force open the Japanese financial system so as to channel Japanese funds into US treasury bonds; and second, it would help strengthen the yen in order to provide relief for the US trade deficit.

But as with most of the punitive disciplinary measures, the result was for the Americans a mixed blessing. While they benefited from a mass Japanese buy-up of US treasury bonds, economic blowback ensued through a weaker yen and the massive exportation of Japanese capital abroad. Almost overnight Japanese banks stormed into the Top Ten global leader table that, in challenging US financial supremacy in the world, caused yet another body-blow to the wounded American psyche.

As the trade deficit escalated further, the Americans charged that Japan's 'unfair advantage' was conferred by its undervalued currency. In order to weaken the dollar and revalue the yen, the Americans pushed through the 1985 Plaza Accord in which the Japanese agreed (under coercive pressure) to revalue by selling dollars while the Americans sold dollars and bought yen. But while the dollar halved in value against the yen within three years, the deficit continued to mount and, worse still, the high yen led to the Japanese buy-up of American real estate, much to the chagrin of Americans. And when the Japanese bought the Rockefeller Center, this served only to exacerbate the Yellow-bashing mood (though no one in America seemed to mind when in 1988 the British bought up 400 American companies and spent almost three times more than the Japanese).

A similar over-reaction with racist overtones accompanied the Japanese purchase of Columbia Pictures. As Shintaro Ishihara noted, '*Newsweek* said of Sony's $3.4 billion purchase of Columbia Pictures that, "this time the Japanese hadn't just snapped up another building; they had bought a piece of America's soul"', to which he rhetorically replied, 'But who put it up for sale?' (Ishihara 1991: 89). Another example of this racist double standard was revealed in 1987 when the Japanese firm Fujitsu tried to acquire an 80 per cent stake in the American company Fairchild Semiconductor Corporation (which was a large supplier of computer chips for the US military). In the ensuing American uproar the Japanese diplomatically withdrew their offer. But the double standard lay in the fact that the Japanese were not trying to buy an 'American' company – Fujitsu was only trying to acquire the 80 per cent stake held by the French company, Schlumberger.

Interestingly, the language of the American analysis of the Japanese 'financial invasion' really gave the racist game away. Japanese intermediaries were thought of as invoking a 'termite strategy' by targeting 'vulnerable financial houses in the West' (Wright and Paul 1987: 98). The Japanese were not animals who had to be smoked out of their dens (as were the Native Indians before them and the Islamic terrorists after them), but were cunning 'insects' who 'gnawed' away at the foundations of the American financial and industrial structure. Exactly the same discursive weaponry had been deployed to marginalize so-called 'communist sympathisers' within America after 1945, who were described as 'moral termites from within' (Billy Graham), or a 'force of traitorous communists, constantly gnawing away like termites at the very foundation of society' (J. Edgar Hoover). And as Leonard Seabrooke notes: 'reminiscent of wartime propaganda, racist depictions of buck-toothed Japanese appeared in business publications and stereotypes of Japanese efficiency, diligence, and cunning were used to explain, poorly, Japan's financial status' (Seabrooke 2001: 140–1). The lesson was clear: the 'shifty slanty-eyed' Japanese could not be trusted and had to be contained – even though the 'financial invasion' was only made possible by American 'invitation'.

The Americans then set out to contain Japan's financial power by hobbling the competitiveness of its banks through the 1988 Basle Accord (Seabrooke 2001: 136–40). Japanese bank profitability immediately plummeted, and commercial and industrial loans dropped by some 25 per cent below their forecast level. By then, cultural conversion and containment had done their job. And so with the Japanese economy entering long-term recession in 1991, the ideological war had been won, thereby reaffirming the 'superiority' of American identity.

Thus it is clear that the Americans needed the 'Yellow Scare' in order to justify the punishment of Japan so as to reproduce 'superior' liberal individualism at home. That the emphasis on 'unfair' Japanese trading policy betrayed a racist construct is borne out by the fact that during the 1990s, at the time when the Japanese scare disappeared, the US deficits deepened. So while the Americans complained bitterly in the 1980s over the trade deficits, American complaints about the higher deficits in the 1990s were striking only for their absence. For, by then, the discursive function of the Yellow Scare had blipped off the US political radar screen.

Conclusion

Through the examples of the debt crisis and post-1980 US–Japan relations I have sought to show how the market standard of civilization as the discursive weapon of the American civilizing mission has operated. Other examples that could have been used are the Asian financial crisis of 1997, or the operations of US multinational enterprises or the imposition of free trade – especially under the World Trade Organization. But I hope to have provided sufficient evidence to reveal the *continuity* of the racist discourse of the market standard of civilization that has underpinned the British and American civilizing missions in the last two centuries. In the process I hope to have revealed the racist underpinnings of the modern global economy.

6 Civilizing the bad

Ethical problems with neo-liberal approaches to corruption

Mlada Bukovansky

The proposition that free markets exert a civilizing influence on human society has proven remarkably durable over the past three centuries. Despite critical rumblings about social justice and income inequality, economic modernization has remained a touchstone for those claiming to live in a 'civilized' society, and free-market capitalism is widely considered today to be the primary driver of modernization. Buttressed by the support and example of successful and dominant economic powers in the global economy, most prominently the United States, the message emanating from powerful national capitals and international economic institutions today is that open markets and the pursuit of economic self-interest by individuals and firms provide a solid foundation not only for a society's collective prosperity, but also for its political development. Pursuit of private interest also yields good public outcomes.

Despite such faith in the civilizing effects of markets, neo-liberal thinkers and policy analysts increasingly argue that markets need to be supplemented by 'good governance'; this insight has been accompanied by a focus on corruption as an impediment to the proper functioning of markets. Just as free-market ideology appears victorious against discredited alternatives ranging from communism to European socialism to state-led economic development, more and more policy experts and commentators are touting 'good governance' as a necessary ingredient to successful economic modernization. Greed may be good, but it is apparently not good enough. Market failure and the tendency of public goods to be undersupplied forces neo-liberals to attend to institutions. Corrupt government has generated a demand for 'good' institutions.

One might observe that neo-liberal theory continues to embrace the views articulated by thinkers such as Adam Smith and David Hume in the eighteenth century. For Hume, the pursuit of profit through market exchange drew people into peaceful relationships, allowed them to learn each other's manners and customs, and tempered those manners and customs with the habits necessary for conducting business. The behavior appropriate to market society was a welcome contrast to the aristocratic habits of military power struggle and status competition (Hume 1985 [1777]: 93–5). Hume further argued, against the traditional republican belief that commerce and luxury produced inferior, effeminate soldiers, that the luxury brought by commerce has a civilizing effect on public life without thereby endangering the love of liberty and willingness to defend one's country (Hume 1985 [1777]: 272–4; Pocock 1975). Satisfying private interest through commerce was also in the public interest, in Hume's view.

Despite the commonalities, however, Hume's theoretical orientation was very different from that of today's neo-liberals at least in one important respect: he had to argue against the prominent republican notion that commercial activity was corrosive because it distracted citizens from the pursuit of the public good. Hume's liberalism had a critical thrust that today's hegemonic neo-liberal theory lacks. Hume attempted to deploy the language of civic humanism to buttress his arguments about the civilizing virtues of a commercial society. Civic humanist (or republican) discourse, in the words of Istvan Hont and Michael Ignatieff, 'lamented the attenuation of martial virtue and the absorption in private self-interest of commercial peoples, exemplified in their delegation of martial functions to standing armies' (Hont and Ignatieff 1983: 7). Hume and his contemporary, Adam Smith, engaged in a critical dialogue with their republican interlocutors; this engagement led them to deploy substantive notions of public good drawn from the civic humanist tradition (Hont and Ignatieff 1983; Pocock 1975). They needed to respond to the challenges posed by republican insistence on the necessity of civic virtue, or public-mindedness, for the preservation of the liberty of a polity. In today's language, self-determination rather than accumulation of wealth was the republican preoccupation, and the latter was thought to endanger the capacity to sustain the former. Hume and Smith had to argue that this was not the case: accumulation of wealth could also enhance preservation of liberty.

By contrast, neo-liberal discourse today rarely articulates substantive ethical arguments about why corruption should be curbed, because that would be outside the scope of the scientific, rationalist methodology that informs most neo-liberal studies of corruption. Although the 'good' in good governance is presumably an ethical construct, neo-liberalism offers little guidance as to the content of this good, how it might be decided upon, and by whom. Consequently, the meaning of 'good governance' is quite thin in the neo-liberal approach, and is primarily centered around governments' acquiescence to integration into a global market economy. This entails, for developing countries at least, the imposition of severe limitations on governments' discretionary power, and the concomitant expansion of the regulatory power of international institutions, such as the International Monetary Fund (IMF) and the World Trade Organization (WTO), which are themselves committed to liberalization and integration into the global market economy (see Wade 2003). Such a value system is a far cry from the self-determination or preservation of liberty held dear by civic humanists.

In this chapter, I argue that although notions of corruption and its opposite, good (or civilized) governance, have irreducibly ethical connotations, neo-liberal discourse is ill-equipped to confront these ethical dimensions because it takes the ends of modernity as given. An alternative discourse on corruption might well correct some of the critical omissions of neo-liberal anti-corruption discourse.

The building blocks of such an alternative may be found in the civic humanist, or republican, tradition of political thought (Pettit 1997). Republican discourse offers richer and more normative notions of political agency, institutions, and public good than are available in neo-liberal discourse. It also offers more in the way of a self-determined notion of public good, and in a highly heterogeneous international system this may render its contributions particularly salient, though also problematic and somewhat unsettling.

Corruption is now bad

In the last decade, international organizations from the United Nations to the World Bank to the IMF have increasingly publicized their concerns about political corruption, commonly defined as the use of public office for private gain, or the illegitimate purchase by private actors of political consideration (see Peter Larmour's chapter in this book), primarily as a negative influence on economic development but also as the source of a host of other ills ranging from loss of democratic legitimacy to terrorism (for example Ashcroft 2003). The corruption issue has catapulted from the margins of academic and policy discourse to a position as one of the central problems facing transition economies and the developing world today. Moreover, international organizations and donor states, as well as students of economic and political development, are increasingly inclined to suggest that correcting the problem of corruption requires multilateral solutions and direct external pressure on sovereign governments (Mauro 2004).

This solidifying consensus raises a host of questions. Why has corruption moved from being a tacitly accepted, if unsavory, part of international transactions, to being considered a primary villain for underdevelopment and a host of other ills? Why does Samuel Huntington's assertion that corruption is an inevitable – and perhaps even a desirable – part of the process of economic and political modernization no longer bear the stamp of conventional wisdom (Huntington 1987)?

The international realm has traditionally been viewed as highly permissive with respect to bribery and other transactions that would be deemed corrupt in a domestic context. Only twenty years ago it was considered perfectly acceptable – and in many states tax deductible – to bribe 'foreigners' if not one's own nationals. Today, although such activities still routinely occur, they are no longer openly, publicly justifiable (Noonan 1984: 652–5). This aligns with a more general trend: the growth of a comprehensive governance agenda within international institutions and across a broader swath of non-governmental and trans-governmental networks, wherein the structure and implementation of domestic institutions and laws within sovereign states is increasingly subjected to external pressure to align with norms that have essentially become the new global standards of civilization (as presumed, for example, in Slaughter 1997). This holds true for the problem of corruption as well as for other governance projects such as democratization and advancement of human rights (Donnelly 1998; Bowden 2004a).

A perusal of major news sources will reveal plenty of corruption scandals in the advanced industrialized states, and within international organizations themselves, but, significantly, most international anti-corruption campaigns emanating from international organizations and aid donor governments are targeted at the developing world. Less developed countries are generally perceived as being far more corrupt than industrialized states, according to such indices as the Corruption Perceptions Index put out by Transparency International (www.transparency.org) (see Larmour chapter). In the past decade, charges that a country's development suffers because of corruption have become a widespread and routine way of addressing the 'development gap' between North and South. Despite sporadic attempts to restrain multinational corporations by prohibiting them from bribing foreign public officials, the bulk of multilateral anti-corruption rhetoric and policy is directed at the developing world, and at the transition economies of the former Soviet bloc.

The focus on 'transitioning' and developing countries invites the observation that current anti-corruption rhetoric represents an extension of wealthy country and corporate efforts to expand and solidify the institutional foundations for a global market economy. It also constitutes something of a departure from previous regimes geared toward this same end. The key point on which the anti-corruption discourse diverges from existing trade and monetary regimes is in its relatively explicit acknowledgment that a successful market economy requires *moral underpinnings*. But the normative character of anti-corruption discourse is in tension with the predominantly rationalist, technical, and instrumental justifications for open markets that have long dominated the academic and institutional discourse on international political economy. Blaming economic problems on corruption rather than, say, inappropriate tariff structures, unavoidably leads to the observation that individuals in authority are behaving badly, and that they need to behave better – with an eye toward the public good rather than their own personal or sectarian advantage – to ameliorate the problem. Evoking, however obliquely, the moral requirements for a liberalizing international economy also extends the neo-liberal institutionalist focus on transparency, separation of powers, and government accountability beyond the realm of institutional solutions technically conceived, and into the realm of ethical mores such as fairness and equality before the law (see Matthew Watson's chapter in this volume).

Despite its moral undertones, the bulk of contemporary anti-corruption discourse deploys the language and methodologies of economics and rational choice theory to render diagnostic assessments of the plight of the corrupt and less developed, and to develop 'cures' based on these forms of analysis (see Hopkin 2002). Advances in incorporating the study of institutions into analyses of economic growth and development, represented by the 'new institutional economics', have led to greater and more refined treatment of variables previously excluded from economic studies of development. Yet the analytical framework has not changed in one important respect: it is a framework where self-interested agents respond to a set of incentives in their environment, yielding either positive (wealth- and utility-enhancing) or negative (wealth- and utility-detracting) outcomes. Public policies aim to manipulate the incentive structures such self-interested actors face in order to achieve positive collective outcomes or at least minimize negative ones. Corruption control thus becomes a technical matter of effectively manipulating incentive structures.

While technical-instrumental approaches to the problem of corruption undoubtedly have merit, they fail to address a deeper set of conceptual issues, and they present an ethical problem. Advocating changes in incentive structures without addressing problems of political agency is likely to be an exercise in futility. It is well and good to ask that a country's tax collection system be reformed, but who is empowered to do the reforming? What forms of political authority are we advocating when we argue that incentive structures must be changed to limit corruption opportunities? Who are the authoritative agents, and what makes them legitimate? The liberal-rationalist approaches to corruption allow such questions to be evaded, because the ends of modernity, particularly economic growth and a governing structure that maximizes individual rights, are now taken as given and unproblematic (Euben 1989); neo-liberalism no longer needs to give a substantive account of political authority and public good.

Furthermore, the liberal-rationalist approach to corruption has not gone far enough in acknowledging the normative content of institutions; such content cannot be fully captured if we treat institutions simply as incentive structures that are part of the external environment faced by individual agents. To address the corruption issue, we need to deploy a notion of institutions that recognizes their capacity to be internalized, as normative, cultural structures, by social agents. This would give us a richer and more normative concept of political agency as motivation to act in accordance with internally held values rather than simply out of narrow self-interest. A richer concept of institutions, including the institutions and norms of modern market society, would also recognize their historical and sociological contingency.

We can also identify an ethical problem in the liberal-rationalist approach to corruption, because it implicitly advocates the external imposition of essentially modern, Western standards of civilization on societies that are not fully participating in defining those standards. As Robert Wade has put it, the neo-liberal agenda 'constitutes a shrinkage not only of development space, but also of "self-determination" space' (Wade 2003: 622). This problem needs to be faced not only for moral reasons but also for pragmatic ones as well; arguably the moral reasons partly constitute the pragmatic reasons. Externally imposed standards of civilization will lack legitimacy unless they are embraced and internalized by the culture on which they are imposed. Legitimacy of a law or standard is at least in part an ethical problem; a standard must be embraced as 'right' or 'fair' by a social actor to be considered legitimate. Standards that lack legitimacy (the ethical problem) are less likely than legitimate standards to be effectively enforced (the pragmatic problem).

Economic and institutional rationales in anti-corruption discourse

Although ethical terms and references to good governance are peppered throughout the key anti-corruption documents put out by institutions such as the United Nations (UN), the IMF, the World Bank, and the Organization for Economic Co-operation and Development (OECD) (Bukovansky 2005), in those institutions, as in contemporary academic discourse, the dominant rationale for the anti-corruption consensus has been economic, and to a lesser extent institutional (deploying a 'thin' conception of institutions as incentive structures), rather than normative. Many prominent theorists working in the rational choice tradition assert a complementarity between institutional effectiveness and economic performance (Davis and Trebilcock 1999; Keefer 2004; Rose-Ackerman 1978, 1999). Corrupt institutions are bad for the economy, in this view.

The consensus in recent economic studies is that corruption hurts economic growth because it siphons off resources and discourages foreign investment, and/ or because corrupt elites finance public projects in order to maximize their opportunities for monopoly rents rather than encourage sustainable growth (Shleifer and Vishny 1993; Rose-Ackerman 1999; Mauro 1995, 1997, 2004; Tanzi and Davoodi 1998; Ades and Di Tella 1997; Kaufmann 1997). Although many studies of corruption have focused on its effects on foreign direct investment (FDI), and although debate continues among economists as to the harmful or beneficial effects of FDI (see Kapstein 2002), economic growth remains the primary measure of development, and more open markets are widely seen as the best way to achieve such growth. In the neo-liberal anti-corruption discourse governing institutions are evaluated primarily on their ability to deliver and sustain economic prosperity conceived of as growth in gross domestic product (GDP), although to be fair income inequality often emerges as an important secondary concern (Husted 1999; Keefer 2004).

That said, the discourse supporting a world economy of relatively open markets has always included some discussion of institutional and even normative underpinnings (Best 2003b). After 1945 the consensus amongst American and West European elites was that international institutional arrangements were required to sustain a liberal trading order while allowing states to pursue social welfare policies – the 'embedded liberalism' compromise (Ruggie 1982). The international economic regimes underpinned by the IMF, World Bank, and General Agreement on Tariffs and Trade (GATT) emanated from, reflected, and were supported by the domestic structural conditions and values prevailing in the Western, industrialized states (see also Geoffrey A. Pigman's chapter in this volume).

The embedded liberalism compromise was not originally meant to be applied to the 'Third World' (Ruggie 1982), nor to the communist countries. After decolonization and the refocusing of IMF and World Bank lending on the developing world, the context in which these institutions operated changed radically, and with the recent wave of liberalization in the former Soviet bloc it has changed again. Thus, international institutional mechanisms for currency stabilization and structural adjustment lending no longer seem entirely adequate in a context of diverse levels of development and institutional heterogeneity amongst the states that are the main targets of IMF and World Bank lending. But although the means may have been adjusted somewhat to take account of the changed theater of operation, the broad ends of these institutions have remained fairly constant: liberalization and economic growth.

Because of the institutional heterogeneity faced by multilateral organizations initially created to deal with a more homogeneous group of states, the economic rationale for curbing corruption is now almost always buttressed by an institutional rationale (Rose-Ackerman 1999; Klitgaard 1988). In this sense, the anti-corruption consensus may be seen as an aspect of the broader governance – and civilizational – agenda that has emerged within the IMF and World Bank. But that agenda retains from its economic origins a technical-instrumental approach to institutions derived from the methodologies and techniques of economic analysis (see Jacqueline Best's chapter in this volume).

A wealth of literature has emerged in the past decade or so that applies the techniques of rational choice and quantitative methods to identify correlations and causal links between various 'governance' variables and outcomes such as economic growth or income inequality. This literature is critically, but sympathetically, reviewed by Philip Keefer, who notes that the most robust finding of the economic literature on governance is that secure property rights lead to more economic growth, while insecure property rights result in slower growth (Keefer 2004). Other studies isolate factors such as credibility of bureaucratic performance, voice, and accountability, though Keefer notes that these studies are more likely to face methodological problems (such as endogeneity and direction of causality), and thus present less robust findings than does the security of property rights hypothesis. Keefer concludes that much work needs to be done in disaggregating the concept of governance in order to refine tests of specific effects of discrete governance variables on economic growth.

It is worth noting here the inversion that has occurred since Hume's day. Rather than having to defend the argument that economic growth produces beneficial public outcomes (this is now a given), today's rational choice theorists writing on corruption are attempting to determine which public structures and policies are likely to promote economic growth. Where in the eighteenth century the economy was still in the service of the polity, the polity is now in the service of the economy.

In the policy domain, the economic approach to curbing corruption has more often than not led to recommendations geared toward cutting the size and scope of the public sector (Khan 2002). This is particularly true with respect to privatization and dismantling of state-owned enterprises. But some have argued that cutting the public sector can just as easily inhibit as encourage the development of democratic institutions of governance (Khan 2002; Hopkin 2002). International financial institutions and big aid donor states may want less corruption, but by advocating *smaller government* they are not doing much to contribute to – and may inadvertently be undercutting – the positive development of *good* government.

The idea that less government is better government can also be derived from an earlier strain of economic and political science literature that was more sanguine about corruption. Prior to the anti-corruption consensus, corruption was frequently seen as a way for multinational corporations to gain a foothold in developing country markets. Samuel Huntington's observations that corruption is a necessary part of modernization invite the conclusion that modernization and corruption might be complementary, rather than contradictory (Huntington 1987). Scholars who adopted this approach have argued (and a minority still do argue) that some forms of corruption may not necessarily be a bad thing; corrupt practices cut red tape and facilitate the smoother operation of markets, especially where governments are not subject to checks and balances, accountability, and transparency, and where they hold disproportionate power over state resources. Thus corruption could help rather than hurt development by allowing investors to elude inefficient laws and deny greedy officials the proceeds of legal but onerous tax revenues (substituting illegal but presumably smaller side-payments) (Lui 1996; Cheung 1996). Ironically, much of the pro-corruption literature actually dovetails nicely with the market-friendly notion that less government is better government, since corruption involves bypassing the inefficient public sector. Be that as it may, it is no longer in vogue to be pro-corruption.

Despite the plethora of economic studies of governance and institutions, in their methodological individualism and rationalism such studies do not leave much room for the possibility that politics could be an ethical endeavor grounded in commitment to a substantive public good. In an article first published in the 1960s, Joseph Nye defined corruption as follows: 'Corruption is behavior which deviates from the formal duties of a public role because of private-regarding (personal, close family, private clique) pecuniary or status gains; or violates rules against the exercise of certain types of private-regarding influence' (Nye 1967: 419). The liberal-rationalist discourse relies on a boundary between private interest and public good to define corruption. But the 'public good' has little substantive content, and thus lacks the positive normative appeal that would serve as a source of motivation. Since all rational actors are motivated by self-interest, how we determine whether or not a selfish act was corrupt depends ultimately on whether it broke a law. A corporate campaign contribution can be distinguished from a bribe only by reference to a law. The law is treated as an exogenous constraint on individual behavior.

But anti-corruption laws vary widely in different societies. Distinguishing between a gift and a bribe requires thick cultural knowledge of the particular society in question (Offer 1997). Further, many of the societies at which the new anti-corruption discourse is aimed do not have clear-cut rules delimiting the boundary between public good and private interest in specific transactions such as hiring family or using a government post to generate extra private income; judging such societies as 'corrupt' means deploying Western standards of civilization, which are not necessarily the standards of the societies to which they are being applied.

As Peter Euben has pointed out in a critique, Nye's discussion of the costs and benefits of corruption for 'development' carries with it an implicit normative judgment about the desirability of modernization. 'A good society is a modernizing one; a corrupt society is one that inhibits "development." But because the ends of modernity are regarded as inevitable, impersonal, and/or rational, they cannot themselves be the subject of rational dispute or "subjective" prescriptions' (Euben 1989: 244). The dominant values of modernity become reified. In the anti-corruption discourse, and in the governance discourse more generally, this often boils down to valorizing economic growth – measured in terms of GDP – as the end toward which public officials must strive. This not only inhibits critical political debate over the ends of the political community, but also leaves little room for agency as the conscious, willed reproduction of those values in daily life, and the moral self-restraint that this would imply.

These two problems – the reification of dominant (liberal) values and the neglect of moral and political agency – are at the heart of the elisions and omissions of the liberal-rationalist modes of anti-corruption discourse. Confronting these problems means *bringing politics back into the discourse* in such a way that it is not treated simply as a market-distorting or externality alleviating exogenous constraint, but rather as a process entailing the production of, and struggle over, collective identities and goals – the coercive and consensual process by which political communities are constructed and maintained (see also Barry Hindess's chapter in this volume). Only by confronting this process and its irreducibly political, normative, and contestable contours can we come to an understanding of corruption as something more than a transgression of arbitrary or exogenously imposed rules.

By linking the problem of corruption to the problem of underdevelopment, advanced industrial countries implicitly and unjustifiably claim the moral high ground for themselves, and ascribe to the 'developing world' the status of the moral reprobate while simultaneously making vague and possibly unworkable governance demands on developing countries. Further, by advocating pressure from outside as a primary mechanism for curbing corruption, we deny the capacity and agency of the actors in developing countries to determine for themselves the contours of political authority and the distinctions between public good and private interests, between gifts and bribes, between legitimate and illegitimate patronage. This may arguably be appropriate in some cases from a purely practical standpoint (as in so-called 'failed states'), though I believe further discussion is warranted even on this point. But as a matter of principle, and given that the economic framework of global capitalism is interwoven with a political framework of self-determination and formal sovereign equality, it may be worthwhile to develop anti-corruption discourse in such a way as to leave the question of the proper goal of political and even economic development open to discussion and critique, rather than treating it as a given. Otherwise, global standards of market civilization threaten to do away with self-determination, liberty, and real political agency.

Finally, pitching the anti-corruption discourse as a diagnosis for underdevelopment also absolves those living in liberal capitalist states from scrutinizing their own polities in terms of a discourse of corruption. But there is a long history in political thought of engaging in just such scrutiny (Arendt 1958; Habermas 1989; Shumer 1979), and, as the lobby for campaign finance reform in the US shows, for example, there is little reason to believe that critical scrutiny of the health of the modern liberal polity is no longer warranted.

Clarifying the moral and political dimensions of anti-corruption discourse

While there may be a number of institutional ways to check corrupt behavior. anti-corruption efforts ultimately require an image of 'good governance' that carries enough moral weight to motivate people, since ultimately public-minded behavior by individual human beings – usually the focus is on public officials, but clearly key private actors (as in the discourse on corporate governance) and community leaders of all sorts may be involved as well – is part and parcel of good governance. Although Susan Rose-Ackerman is an economist firmly grounded in the rational choice tradition, even she concludes her systematic discussion of the political economy of corruption by noting that, 'institutional incentives cannot be expected to substitute entirely for morality' (Rose-Ackerman 1978: 218). Nor, presumably, are consistently moral outcomes in the public sphere to be derived entirely from narrowly self-interested behavior.

Despite the fact that moral signifiers have seeped into international treaties (OECD 1997), the scholarly discourse has lagged behind in explicating the moral rationales underlying the anti-corruption consensus. This may be due to a preference for rational choice and quantitative methods in generating studies of corruption. To sustain the trappings of scientific methodology, most contemporary studies of corruption, whether articulated by way of formal economic models, rational choice theory, or new institutional economics, reify as institutional constraints or incentives the very values that should, in any successful anti-corruption effort, be internalized by powerful political actors and the politically aware publics that scrutinize their behavior. Institutions are not just constraints in the external environment faced by political actors; where they are most legitimate, their norms have been internalized by those who believe in their legitimacy and who allow their actions to be guided by such norms not out of fear of punishment but rather out of belief in their veracity. The subjective and intersubjective dimensions of values such as liberty, public-mindedness, fairness, transparency, accountability, and public trust are what render them potent and capable of motivating behavior. Furthermore, the ability of political actors to articulate and contest the meaning and interpretation of concepts such as the 'public good' suggests that political struggle is an irreducible element of defining corruption and its counterpart, a healthy polity that pursues the common good rather than being hijacked for more narrowly clientelistic or self-interested ends.

What if we ground anti-corruption discourse not only in the 'scientific' liberal discourse concerned with economic growth via the spread of capitalism, but also (or alternatively) in the republican discourse of political liberty and civic virtue (Pettit 1997)? Might this offer us a more substantive language by which to discuss self-determination, the meaning of public good, and to address questions of political agency? Without pushing the idea that Niccolo Machiavelli can save the developing world, there are nevertheless some good reasons to evoke republican concepts in the anti-corruption discourse; there are also limits to such evocations.

Republican – in contrast to neo-liberal – discourse suggests that the definition of corruption I gave at the outset of this chapter (use of public office for private gain) does not fully communicate the sense in which corruption can be thought of as a danger to the political community. Corruption is a term that, according to Quentin Skinner, 'the republican theorists habitually use to denote our natural tendency to ignore the claims of our community as soon as they seem to conflict with the pursuit of our own immediate advantage' (Skinner 1990: 304). The problem with this, from the point of view of republican theorists, is that such pursuit of 'immediate advantage' can lead a community to ruin. The ruin or corruption of a political community entails a loss of liberty, and a slide into dependency. In Machiavelli's *Discourses*, which states the republican position clearly and forcefully, a free state is one in which people legislate for themselves, with an eye toward the good of the community as a whole. By contrast, the corrupt state has lost its liberty and is in a state of dependency and bondage: either it is dependent upon a foreign power, or in bondage to a tyrant or a governing party that rules tyrannically only for its own advantage, or it may be subject to the brief anarchic rule of the mob (Machiavelli 1950: I xvi). None of these corrupt forms of rule is stable or secure.

In contrast to the often asocial individualism of liberal discourse (as represented by Thomas Hobbes's view of human nature), republican theorists deploy an Aristotelian notion of human nature as essentially social and political. Because human beings are social, they value the group to which they belong. But the group is often in danger, either from external threat or internal usurpations of power. Maintaining the group as a free, non-dependent (self-determining, in our parlance) political community demands the exercise of civic virtue. However it is defined, civic virtue entails behavior on the part of leaders and citizens that is geared toward maintaining a thriving and free political community. To do so, people must restrain their more narrowly selfish passions. Such sacrifice is worthwhile because it ensures that citizens will be able to live in liberty, and this includes security of their possessions and families (Pettit 1997; Skinner 1978: Chs 4–5).

Civic virtue is thus a moral concept entailing moral behavior, but such morality is also in the long-term self-interest of the citizen. According to Skinner:

> Belief in the idea of 'human flourishing' and its accompanying vision of social freedom arises at a far deeper level than that of mere ideological debate. It arises as an attempt to answer one of the central questions in moral philosophy, the question of whether it is rational to be moral. The

> suggested answer is that it is in fact rational, the reason being that we have an interest in morality, the reason for this in turn being the fact that we are moral agents committed by our very natures to certain normative ends.
>
> (Skinner 1990: 297–8)

Those normative ends derive from the value individuals place on the community. Rather than juxtaposing the requirements of moral behavior and the necessities of politics, as Machiavelli is commonly accused of doing, Skinner demonstrates that Machiavelli instead advocates a *different* sort of morality – different from the Christian virtues that dominated the moral discourse of his day – for those engaged in politics (Skinner 1978: 135). Such moral impetus ultimately springs from love of one's country, the *patria* of the Renaissance humanists (Skinner 1978).

Unlike earlier republican theorists, those of Machiavelli's time, and especially Machiavelli himself, were not optimistic about the capacity of human beings to sustain civic virtue based on love of country. As Machiavelli notes:

> men act rightly only upon compulsion; but from the moment that they have the option and liberty to commit wrong with impunity, then they never fail to carry confusion and disorder everywhere. It is this that has caused it to be said that poverty and hunger make men industrious, and that the law makes men good.
>
> (Machiavelli 1950: I iii)

Like Machiavelli, liberal rationalist discourse frequently places the burden of 'making men good' on institutional incentives. But unlike Machiavelli, current neo-liberal discourse has a very thin notion of institutions; it does not see them as organic entities capable of being either healthy or corrupt, according to the character and abilities of the human agents who govern them.

Republican evocations of the rule of law, the love of liberty, and the notion that arbitrary power must be restrained (most often through a 'mixed constitution' or, in more modern parlance, a system of checks and balances), all resonate with the contemporary discourse on governance of which the anti-corruption consensus is a part. But in so far as that discourse has remained dominated by a liberal, individualist rationalism, it fails to adequately articulate and fully explore the necessity of moral and political agency in the pursuit of collective good.

The articulation of a specifically political morality grounded in the love of country, of liberty, and of self-government, and the linking of such morality to the creation and maintenance of good institutions, are two contributions that republican political thought brings to the discourse on corruption and governance. For Machiavelli, as already noted, corruption was the core manifestation of the loss of liberty to dependency on either a foreign power or internal faction, as well as the symptom of institutions and laws that no longer worked to preserve the republic – either because they were once good but were no longer appropriate to the circumstances of a particular state, or because they were corrupt to begin with, or because citizens and leaders did not use the institutions effectively (Machiavelli 1950: I xvi–xviii).

Republican discourse leaves open this latter possibility of good institutions lacking any 'life' to them – that is, lacking good people to make them work. Again, however elaborate and detailed the debate may be on proper institutional and legal structure and form, republican discourse sustains an emphasis on human moral and political agency, where the terms 'moral' and 'political' may be construed as complementary rather than contradictory concepts. Here the difference between republicanism and the liberal discourse is stark, because the latter discourse for the most part adopts a Hobbesian view of man as naturally selfish (which the republicans do not deny) *and asocial* (which the republicans vehemently deny). It is worth noting that contemporary realism's tendency to tout both Hobbes and Machiavelli as founding fathers totally obscures this important distinction between them, and that Hobbes belongs much more to the liberal tradition than most contemporary international relations theorists allow.

Corruption in republican discourse can also connote a structural condition, a sickness of the polity that at worst can mean its destruction as a cohesive whole, or a 'loss of identity and definition' (Euben 1989: 222). Euben points out that one of the most exemplary historical cases of a polity that has become corrupt to the point of disintegration is Thucydides' account of the civil war in Corcyra; the term used in describing this disintegration is stasis:

> Under such conditions religion, family, and morality become instruments in their own destruction. Oaths are temporary strategies adopted only when one is outmaneuvered or outmanned by an opponent. . . . Morality and justice are rhetorical diversions which disguise secret hatreds and excuse private revenge. . . . Since everyone is a potential enemy, isolation is the only guarantee against surprise attack. In the beginning of civil war, men killed their enemies with the assistance of their party. But as the stasis intensified the number of potential enemies increased and the number of possible friends decreased until the only trustworthy friend was oneself and the only safe party was a party of one.
>
> (Euben 1989: 225)

It does not require a huge stretch of the imagination to apply this picture of a totally corrupted polity to some of the areas that have been and continue to be devastated by civil wars in our time. Corruption in republican discourse thus connotes loss of liberty, self-determination, and identity as a political entity; the corrupt state may break down, first into warring factions, and then warring individuals; it is not unlike the Hobbesian 'state of nature', or 'war of all against all'.

The republican discourse thus offers a richer and more resonant conception of corruption than does liberal-rationalist discourse. Richer, in its conception of institutions as organic entities whose norms are capable of being internalized, and that are capable of evoking emotional attachment and moral commitment, rather than merely exogenous incentive structures channeling the activity of narrowly self-interested actors. Corruption means that the institutions constituting the political community have decayed and no longer provide liberty and security. More resonant, in that it evokes the human capacity for moral agency in civic life. Corrupt people, and corrupt leaders, have neglected that dimension of action in favor of more narrowly selfish ends. But republicanism, no matter how cynical about the possibilities of getting human beings to do good for their community, still holds forth that possibility as a ground for moral action.

There are however limits to what republicanism can offer the anti-corruption discourse, and some accompanying dangers as well. The discourse is not conducive to the use of scientific and quantitative methods of analysis. It has little to offer in the way of systematically identifying variables that might be tweaked to make governance more effective. This is a limit, but not necessarily a weakness. Republican discourse can be thought of not so much as a science but as a language through which substantive political concerns may be critically debated. Rather than offering diagnoses, it offers fuel for debate and communicative action. Some of the other limits of republican discourse are more problematic. Grounding political morality in a love of country can be seen as antithetical to the development of a cosmopolitan morality that is dear to the normative liberalism of Immanuel Kant and his successors (cf. Bowden 2004a). Machiavelli's advice to leaders does not include an ethic of caring about what happens to those who live outside the polity, except in so far as they may pose a threat (in which case they need to be neutralized somehow). Despite his preference for a republican form of government, Machiavelli was not above advocating violence and princely rule to correct the problem of corruption in certain situations. And finally, republicanism is often deeply cynical about the possibility that good, non-corrupt governance can actually be realized.

This latter problem was to some extent addressed by the Federalists in the US, who sought to overcome the weaknesses of human nature by constructing institutions that would assure the survival of republican values without requiring the active deployment of republican virtues (Shklar 1990; Onuf and Onuf 1993). But that turning point in republican thought is what also fueled the liberal conception of institutions as exogenous constraints on selfish human behavior – a conception I have argued neglects the normative, motivational appeal of a more organic conception of institutions, one that recognizes their capacity to be internalized as motivators of moral and political (i.e. civic-minded) human action. Philip Pettit (1997) makes a strong argument for republican values centered on love of liberty, or the desire not to be dominated; such values make governing institutions 'good' in the sense that they inspire moral belief in the value of the political community. However one articulates the value of political community – and the danger that an exclusivist, virulent nationalism would be one such articulation – in the absence of such a normative motivation, moral behavior can only be induced by the exogenously constraining institutions. This in turn leads to the age-old question of who will construct such institutions where they do not exist already. And that is precisely the problem repeatedly faced in the anti-corruption discourse and the broader governance agenda in international political economy.

Rather than treating this problem as a technical one in need of institutional engineering by experts enshrined in multilateral institutions, we could instead consider it a political problem subject to reasoned public debate and discourse among those who have the greatest stake in it.

Conclusion

The emergence of corruption as a core issue in the global governance agenda raises important questions of political agency and moral action in politics, but up to this point these questions have been obscured by the technical-instrumental approach to institutions and the rationalist economic methods deployed in the prevailing liberal discourse constituting the anti-corruption consensus. Rather than assume that the ends of modernity can be bequeathed to the developing world and transition economies of the former communist countries via their unmediated integration into the global market economy, the anti-corruption discourse would benefit from an injection of alternative modes of deliberating about what corruption actually means, and what needs to be done to engage leaders and citizens in deliberation about the substance of the public good, and the pursuit of collective ends. That such pursuit involves some self-restraint and sacrifice cannot be plausibly denied. The motivation for such sacrifice must be normative and come from within individuals and societies. Normative motivations in pursuit of the public good are the result of moral commitments by human beings, commitments grounded in a devotion to one's political community.

At the outset of this chapter I noted that because Adam Smith and David Hume were engaged in dialogue with republican theorists who prioritized civic virtue above private interest, they developed complex and substantive notions of public good. The idea of public good has in the centuries since been hollowed out to the point where it is empty of content. Neo-liberal rationalism is a primary culprit in this evisceration. It might therefore be fruitful to bring a critical dialogue back into the mainstream discourse. A republican challenge to neo-liberal discursive hegemony is one way, though certainly not the only way, to inject a more critical strain into our thinking about corruption and good governance in world politics.

The practical conclusion of this line of argument, one which bears further study, is that externally imposed governance standards will have less legitimacy, and hence less capacity to motivate actors to follow them, than will standards that are deliberated and agreed upon by the political community in question. Self-determination needs to be brought back into the discourse of development and modernity in a meaningful way. From this perspective, the grassroots work promoted by Transparency International in setting up local chapters devoted to addressing the problem of corruption is more likely to be effective than is the imposition of conditionality attached to IMF or World Bank loans (see Larmour chapter). That is not to say that conditionality *per se* is bad or unnecessary, but that conditionality geared toward altering governance structures faces difficult practical challenges of agency and implementation, as well as the ethical pitfalls discussed in this chapter.

The republican legacy of the concept of corruption reminds us that public discourse about public good is a crucial aspect of politics, and that such discursive engagement is an important human resource. This holds true not only for 'developing' but also for 'developed' countries. According to republican definitions of corruption, not even the 'developed' world is in a good position to claim that its polities are healthy and vital rather than corrupt. It may be worth injecting the concerns and language of republicanism into the anti-corruption discourse so that the problem of good governance becomes once more amenable to communication, deliberation, and debate rather than technical prescription handed down by social scientists as though it were a cure to all that ails the 'developing world'. Although greed and selfishness may be constants, they are not all there is to politics; self-determination and the desire not to be dominated are surely more plausible as motivating public norms than are the constraints and conditionality of exogenously imposed standards of civilization and 'good governance'.

Part II

Contemporary cases

7 Civilizing techniques

Transparency International and the spread of anti-corruption

Peter Larmour

Transparency International (TI) is an international non-governmental organization (NGO) founded in 1993 to combat corruption in international business activities. This chapter looks at TI as an agent and critic of 'market civilization', paying particular attention to some of the techniques it has developed: the publication of an annual 'Corruption Perceptions Index'; the posting of a 'Source Book' on the web; the development of Business Principles for Countering Bribery; and the franchising of 'National Chapters'. Civilization may be a coercive process, and the chapter is particularly concerned with the kinds of power deployed in these techniques. It analyzes them as examples of 'policy transfer' and as the results of processes of mimicry and professionalization that lead to 'institutional isomorphism', and draws some conclusions about the spread of civilization.

In the absence of central authority, global standards may emerge indirectly, through processes such as emulation, conditionality or peer review. Adherence to standards may be required from those seeking membership of a club, like the European Union (EU) or the Commonwealth. Non-government actors may propose new standards or monitor their adoption. This chapter considers the example of the creation and promotion of global standards of civilization as they pertain to corruption and anti-corruption as outlined by TI. It will demonstrate how TI's standards are set, exported, and adopted, and how its techniques work, particularly the role of different kinds of power, and other social processes.

Transparency International

TI's founders considered several names for it, including 'International Business Monitor', before settling on 'Transparency International'. The initiative came from Peter Eigen, a World Bank official who had become disillusioned by the Bank's reluctance to confront corruption in projects it funded in Africa. Eigen became the first Chairman, and Jeremy Pope, who had been a senior official in the Commonwealth secretariat, became Managing Director. Other founding members included former ministers from developing countries, a retired businessman, a development economist, and an American 'global security expert' (www.michael-hershman.us). They looked for funding from the Ford Foundation, and lobbied at the World Economic Forum at Davos, Switzerland. Thus, they inserted themselves into the global architecture of 'market civilization'. Their strategy was to persuade rather than confront, and to create public, private, and NGO coalitions against corruption.

Their immediate concern was with international corruption, particularly the way Western firms bribed officials and politicians in developing countries, while international organizations kept silent about it. They had evidence in a book published by a supporter, a retired businessman named George Moody Stuart, which listed dollar amounts exporters typically paid to bribe ministers and senior officials (1997). He called this 'grand corruption' to distinguish it from the petty corruption of underpaid junior officials accepting bribes to do their jobs. TI was keen to deflate what it saw as Western claims to moral superiority in matters of corruption. It was also critical of the prevailing international relativism that had excused corruption in developing countries as 'the way things were done over there' (Transparency International 2005).

TI currently defines itself on its website as a 'global non government organization'. One of its founding fathers saw its early manifestations as more *sui generis*, personal, and opportunistic than an 'NGO'. It was a 'ginger group' (Transparency International 2005: 2) rather than the bureaucratic organization its Berlin Secretariat has since become. TI also now describes itself as both a 'movement' and a 'coalition' (Sampson in press, and for the literature on international movements see Eschle and Stammers 2004). From another perspective, watching its annual general meetings, TI also sometimes looks depressingly like the intergovernmental organizations some of its founders came from, with their national delegations, regional groupings, caucusing, appeals to points of order, and rifts between North and South. Its Secretariat is distinct from its National Chapters, many of which reproduce the insider-ish, non-confrontational style of its founders (De Sousa forthcoming).

While constitutionally TI's Berlin Secretariat is a German NGO, it is financed overwhelmingly by governments. Its 2004 audit report listed and grouped donors: 79 per cent of the total €5.7 million came from government agencies (the largest being the European Community (EC), followed by the Finnish Ministry of Foreign Affairs, then the German ministry for development co-operation, and then USAID). Only 5.5 per cent came from corporate donors, the largest being Sovereign Asset Management, Norsk Hydro, Shell, Anglo American, and Deutsche Bank. The rest came from various foundations and multilateral development organizations. TI's National Chapters find their own sources of funding, though TI occasionally provides seed money, and TI Germany provides a grant to the Secretariat.

TI was very successful in creating awareness of corruption within the international system in the 1990s. It has expanded its original definition of 'corruption' from 'the use of public office for private gain' to include 'the misuse of entrusted power for private benefit'. Its new definition aims to capture corruption within parts of the public sector that were privatized in the 1990s, and the private sector more generally. TI also takes a greater interest in political corruption, acknowledging differences between popular concerns and the worries of foreign investors. It is going through generational changes as its founding fathers step aside, as Eigen seems to be doing, or secede, like Pope and Fredrik Galtung have done. They have founded a new organization called TIRI (the governance-access-learning network) claiming it is part of a 'third phase' of anti-corruption activity, regaining some of the amateur enthusiasm of the first. Meanwhile, in 2003 TI adopted a more expansive mission to 'create change towards a world free of corruption'.

TI can be seen as both an instrument of market civilization and a setter of standards of market civilization, promoting principles of transparency and a level playing field between domestic and foreign companies. It can also be characterized as a critic, nagging governments to outlaw the bribery of foreign officials. Or it may be something in between, 'embodying its contradictions'. An ambivalent relationship with business and government is not unusual among contemporary NGOs and their activist officials or members. Their roles seem to be expanding as a side-effect of the rhetorical attack on states as 'rent seeking', 'predatory', or 'failing'. Certainties about 'left' and 'right', and the values of professions, are undermined by neo-liberal rhetoric about competition, choice, and clients. Tasks that governments used to perform are now being contracted out to the non-government sector. The personal political beliefs of its officials – in TI Berlin, for example, they seem to be mostly of the 'social market' kind – do not necessarily square with its doctrine, or with the ideologies of its financial supporters. TI's strategy of engagement and coalition-building predispose it to doctrinal fuzziness and compromise. In these ways it is rather like a political party.

Rather than trying to pin it down, this chapter asks how it works: what are some of the techniques it uses to promote the values it espouses, and what kinds of power are deployed in them? It is based on interviews with TI officials and documents available on its websites. I analyze some of TI's techniques in terms of 'institutional isomorphism' and 'policy transfer'. The first idea comes from the sociology of institutions, particularly the recognition that states were surprisingly similar in form, in spite of huge differences in their size and wealth. The second, logically a sub-set of the first, comes from political scientists, attentive to the way that the Organization for Economic Co-operation and Development (OECD) countries were increasingly borrowing ideas about economic and social policy from each other. But first I look at the 'civilization' side of market civilization, and its relationship to corruption.

Civilization and civilizing projects

The word 'civilization' does not appear on TI's website, and its officials would likely reject it as undiplomatic, and redolent of colonialism. Brett Bowden (2004a) found that the idea of a 'standard of civilization', distinguishing civilized from uncivilized states, fell into disuse and disrepute after the Second World War. However, he finds it, and ideas like it, to have revived in the triumph of the West after the end of the Cold War, and in Western projects to promote democracy or prevent state failure in what used to be called the third or developing world. Anti-corruption has become an integral part of many of these 'good governance' projects, and many of TI's National Chapters have benefited from them.

Civilization can refer to a particular entity ('European civilization'), to something more generic ('market civilization'), or to a process ('becoming civilized'). Ferdinand Braudel (1980) characterized civilizations as loosely bounded 'culture areas', engaged in continual exporting and borrowing of cultural goods, like the design of houses, recipes, and technologies. Nineteenth-century Japan, for example, deliberately borrowed institutional forms from the West (Westney 1987). Japanese business practices were copied by Western companies in the 1970s and 1980s. But civilizations also engaged in refusals, deliberate or implicit. They rejected ideas or reforms from abroad. Contemporary China, for example, is borrowing Western business practices, but rejecting Western democratic institutions. Japanese business practices have become less admired as the Japanese economy has stagnated in the 1990s. Renault now revives the ailing Nissan car company.

Braudel's approach would allow that behavior regarded as corrupt in one civilization might be acceptable in another. That kind of relativism dominated the international discourse about corruption until the 1990s. TI, however, is sternly opposed to it. Its 'Source Book' of best practice talks about the 'myth of culture' to reject 'cultural' defenses against charges of corruption (Pope 1996).

Braudel's account and the examples of China, Japan, and the West suggest a rough equality between particular civilizations, and the capacity to borrow and refuse. Often, though, the process is less symmetrical. 'Civilizing missions' are usually associated with European colonialism but Stephen Harrell writes about China's policies towards its minorities as 'civilizing projects' in which the civilizing center believes it is helping the peripheral people it dominates 'to attain or at least approach the superior cultural, religious, and moral qualities of the centre itself' (Harrell 1995: 4). Those superior moral qualities might include the absence of corruption. Civilizing projects were distinguished from outright conquest and subjugation by their ideology ('we are here to help'). They differed among themselves according to the degree of complicity among those being civilized. Conquest and attempts to civilize might also run together ('winning hearts and minds' in Vietnam). Civilizing projects might follow military success, for example de-Nazification after the Allied defeat of Germany in 1945. Anti-corruption might become part of a civilizing mission when it is attached to loan conditions, or enforced by police or military intervention.

Norbert Elias (2000) saw civilization as a more general process: the spread of social constraint enforcing self-restraint. He linked it to the increasing differentiation and interdependence of modern societies, where people had to take more account of others, and the monopolization of power by modern states that created 'pacified social spaces'. Warriors became courtiers. Just as violence was relegated to the barracks, other bodily functions like spitting were suppressed or screened off from public view. Civilized people were expected to show more self-control and kindness and less volatility and cruelty. There came more occasions to feel shame and embarrassment. Upper-class etiquette spread to the lower classes, and this process was recapitulated as 'the West' assimilated colonial elites and peoples. The process of civilization, as Elias had seen in Germany, was not irreversible. Nor was it planned, rather emerging as the unintended consequence of individual actions.

Elias's view helps us think about corruption and anti-corruption in more personal and physical terms. Corruption is often seen as something that happened before, but that we now feel ashamed about (see also Mlada Bukovansky's chapter in this volume). Practices that were once carried out openly – buying votes, promoting your nephew – are now carried out secretly, behind a screen of equality and impersonality, and would generate embarrassment if revealed. And as Elias described the civilizing process, the temptations and pressure of corruption are first felt most strongly within an elite, though elite values eventually permeate through the rest of the society as 'alien restraint' gives way to 'self-restraint'. The process is linked to the monopolization of force by the state. It is also reversible, as civilized societies might revert to corruption. This reversion might be particularly relevant in the circumstances of 'weak' or 'failing' states where many of TI's chapters in developing countries operate.

Institutional isomorphism

The emergence of 'global standards' is part of a more general process that sociologists Paul J. DiMaggio and Walter W. Powell (1983) call 'institutional isomorphism': the tendency of institutions to look the same, wherever they are (see also André Broome's and Leonard Seabrooke's chapters in this volume). The engines of this process, they say, are coercion, mimesis (copying of prestigious models), and professionalization. TI is involved in promoting isomorphism in several ways. Its Corruption Perceptions Index encourages countries to compare themselves with each other, and emulate those with a higher ranking. TI assembles and promulgates 'best practice', through its Source Book on the web. It works with another NGO to formulate a voluntary code of practice for businesses. It also replicates itself in eighty-five National Chapters, and is trying to enforce similar standards of accountability on them.

The Corruption Perceptions Index (CPI)

TI's CPI purports to rank countries according to perceptions of their corruption. It does not claim to assess the underlying rate. The perceptions are those of businessmen, journalists, academics, investment analysts, and risk assessors, which have already been surveyed by other organizations. So the CPI is a kind of poll of polls, if you will (Lambsdorff 2004). It is TI's signature product, but many of its officials and the National Chapters remain deeply uneasy about its methodology and impact. It started as an experiment, leaked to the German newsmagazine *Der Spiegel*, forcing TI's leadership to decide whether or not to disavow or embrace it (Lundberg 2002).

Ranking is a classic piece of indirect governance. By naming and shaming it is meant to encourage governments to improve their performance. They are not forced to do it. But if they do not, they will face embarrassment and loss of investment (the Malaysian government is said to have reacted at first with hostility to, and then engagement with, TI to see what it should do to improve its ranking).

The methodological arguments about the index, whether it imperfectly reflects reality, or elaborately constructs it, are part of a long-running debate in the social sciences between positivists and constructionists (my own instincts are for the latter). The main criticisms of its impact are that it reinforces prejudices, and fails to reflect improvements when they have taken place (Sik 2002; Galtung 2006). One TI official described it as a kind of 'bait and switch' – it attracted media attention that might then be pointed to more creditable activities.

The Source Book

The Source Book is a mixture of argument, exhortation, and statements of best practice (Pope 1996). Its length, continuing evolution, and multiple influences make it difficult to summarize. The central idea is of a 'National Integrity System' (NIS), described as 'an holistic approach to transparency and accountability and embracing a range of accountability "pillars", democratic, judicial, media and civil society' (Transparency International 2005). The categories of the Source Book have provided the framework for surveys of National Integrity Systems that are intended to capture national differences and opportunities for reform, about which the CPI is silent.

The idea of a 'system' counters the idea that anti-corruption is the responsibility of a single agency. It embodies the idea (from Montesquieu, James Madison, and the US Constitution) that potentially corrupt institutions might provide checks and balances against the excesses of each other, and remove the need for a presumably incorruptible sovereign to rule over them all. TI would draw civil society and the private sector into this structure of mutual supervision. The NIS is also systemic in TI's tactical sense of avoiding criticisms of individuals. It connects easily with the new institutional approach to corruption now influential in the World Bank. One of TI's founders commends Pope, its author, for being an institutionalist before that became fashionable among aid agencies.

Bryane Michael criticizes systemic approaches, including TI's, for committing the 'functionalist fallacy' (Michael 2004: 1070), which is the assumption that because a trait, or role, or organization exists, it serves some useful higher purpose. Certainly, institutions do not necessarily work either as they are supposed to, or together, for any particular purpose. The language of the Source Book shifts between description and exhortation, and subsequent studies of NISs expect to find a gap between the formal system, and what actually happens (Doig and McIvor 2003; Larmour and Barcham 2004). Explanations for that gap tend to step outside the institutionalist framework, for example into something more personal and evanescent called 'political will'.

The Source Book has been translated into many languages – versions in Albanian, Brazilian, Romanian, Serbian, Spanish, and French are on the web. TI is also concerned to adapt it to particular legal, cultural, and religious traditions. Yet there is often a tension between 'best practice' and 'best fit'. In one project to adapt the Source Book, local advisers are concerned that the translation should retain fidelity to Pope's original. Here the authority of authorship encourages standardization.

Business principles for combating bribery

TI's efforts to develop business principles are particularly interesting for arguments about 'market civilization'. Corruption is a fuzzy 'standard of civilization'. We do not know how much corruption there 'really is', and the CPI relies on a treadmill of reputations that always puts someone at the bottom.

The International Organization for Standardization has not yet produced an international standard for anti-corruption. However, it is working on proposals for a voluntary standard on 'social responsibility' that will 'promote and maintain greater transparency and fairness in organizations' and draw on sources including TI's 'Business Principles for Countering Bribery' (International Organization for Standardization 2005). The latter were devised by a committee including representatives of large international companies, some from transition and developing countries, chaired by TI and Social Accountability International, which is a US NGO dedicated to creating a standard to 'improv[ing] workplaces and combat sweatshops' (www.ceepa.org). The document they produced is intended to 'provide practical guidance for countering bribery, creating a level playing field and providing a long-term business advantage'. It sets out as the main principle, that 'the enterprise shall prohibit bribery in any form, whether direct or indirect', then provides advice about how a firm should implement this principle, for example in dealings with subsidiaries, agents, and clients.

Franchising National Chapters

TI's founders were initially reluctant to create or recognize national TI groups, but were persuaded by arguments that an anti-corruption movement would have to address day-to-day corruption concerns if it was to mobilize support for its founding preoccupation with international business transactions. Now TI has recognized over eighty-five National Chapters, but relationships between them and the Secretariat in Berlin often seem strained. A long-running issue has been the constitutional equality that National Chapters have with the members of the founders' *ad hoc* network of influential individuals. There has been annual tension as TI releases its CPI, and National Chapters have to take criticism from national governments that rate badly.

TI Berlin does not fund National Chapters, beyond occasional seeding grants. Only one of the National Chapters – TI Germany – funds TI's Secretariat in Berlin. In fact chapters might be competing for funds from donors who might prefer to fund activities in developing countries. Instead, TI Berlin has often had to adjudicate between local groups, or individuals vying to take on what has become an increasingly valuable brand name, 'Transparency International'. Its task has become one of brand management – ensuring that particular National Chapters, or people acting in its name, do not tarnish its reputation, and have some local accountability. It is now rolling out a program of re-accreditation. Already one troubled chapter, in Hungary, has decided to give up its franchise. Part of the strength of the brand comes from the CPI.

Coercion

DiMaggio and Powell's first engine of isomorphism was 'coercion'. Similarly, David P. Dolowitz and David Marsh (2000) scaled what they called 'policy transfer' along a dimension running from voluntary adoption at one end, through to imposition by military defeat on the other. In between were processes such as conditionality, whereby someone agrees to do something they would rather not in exchange for a loan or membership of an international organization. Harrell's idea of the civilizing project might fit somewhere in the middle of this scale: something less than voluntary, often involving complicity, but perhaps falling short of outright conquest.

For these authors, much then depends on what is meant by 'coercion' or 'power' more generally. TI, as an NGO, does not have direct access to power in Stephen Lukes's first sense of A getting B to do something they would not otherwise want to do (Lukes 1974). However, it may get its pet ideas attached to conditionality frameworks imposed by donors as conditions for loans or access to membership of valued clubs. Thus, for example, TI may find itself designing or monitoring anti-corruption strategies for countries wanting to borrow from the World Bank, or accede to the EU. Here it is piggybacking on the power of others.

However, Lukes (1974) went on to identify two other dimensions of power at which TI, and other NGOs, are adept. The second was the power to set agendas – to determine what issues were important, and what issues were not. TI has had startling success in getting 'corruption' onto the agendas of international organizations like the World Bank and the OECD. And the anti-corruption movement has also influenced national governments in their dealings with developing countries. Australia, for example, now looks at its neighbors through the lens of 'corruption', and the recent tsunami relief effort was precisely designed to avoid money going through a corrupt central government. The trouble with agenda setting is not so much what gets on it (attention to corruption being important) but what thereby gets squeezed off (corruption may not be the only important thing, and attention devoted to corruption has an opportunity cost).

Lukes's third dimension of power was ideology – the ability to affect hearts and minds – reflected in training and propaganda, but the more effective the less visibly it was exercised. Here again TI and its chapters devote effort to 'awareness raising' but the effort is sometimes paradoxical. Unlike say HIV/AIDS or global warming, 'corruption' is something most people are acutely aware of, though they may disagree about what counts as instances of it. 'Corruption' is a regular feature of newspaper comment, and a regular explanation available to victors in an election, or a successful coup d'état ('we got rid of our corrupt predecessors'). So much so that the 1990s anti-corruption movement in the formerly socialist countries of Eastern Europe have been accused of hyping the problem up (Krastev 2004). Martin Tisne and Daniel Smilov found anti-corruption rhetoric had been used to get support for reform, but lack of visible results was 'fuelling public distrust in government and the democratic political process, and creating a fertile ground for unconstructive populist critics of reform' (Tisne and Smilov 2004: 14).

Lukes's three dimensions do not exhaust understandings of power and the way an NGO like TI may deploy or enact it. Here I briefly consider three more. Stephen Gill's (1995) article on 'market civilization' draws on Antonio Gramsci's writings about 'hegemonic ideas', sustaining economic power, and the role of intellectuals in promoting those ideas. He writes of a global crisis of authority in which a transnational free enterprise system, centered on the Group of Seven (G7), struggles to manage and contain opposition to it. The system is a mixture of public, private, and other non-governmental actors. It is 'supremacist' rather than 'hegemonic', i.e. it is not necessarily winning. TI fits this picture: it is funded by business, NGOs, and governments (overwhelmingly the latter), and its strategy is to create coalitions between these three sectors.

Alain Desrosieres's (1998) history of statistics describes the controversies around statistical comparisons of unemployment, inflation growth, and poverty. The controversy over measuring corruption is only a more recent example. In this 'politics of large numbers' the objectification of data was linked to the growing power and reach of states (Desrosieres 1998). TI's CPI is part of a line of indices, from the World Bank and the United Nations Development Programme (UNDP), that are linked to the growing influence of international organizations.

Barry Hindess (2004a) also draws on Michel Foucault for his emphasis on the dispersed and de-centered character of power in a liberal regime that relies on inculcating responsibility and self-management. (It is rather like Elias's idea of civilization as 'the social constraint towards self-constraint' described above.) Hindess's paper on TI (Hindess 2004b) questions the direct, instrumental effectiveness of TI's non-confrontational anti-corruption strategies, but sees the attack on corruption performing an indirect, latent function of inculcating values that suit liberal regimes of self-management.

Mimesis

The second engine of institutional isomorphism is irrational mimicry. Faced with uncertainty, Di Maggio and Powell argued, organizations would copy the forms of prestigious others. A good example is the 'Westminster' constitution, which has been emulated around the world. Corruption involves high degrees of uncertainty that creates fertile ground for irrational copying. There are disagreements about what counts as corruption, and about what causes it. Corrupt acts often take place in secret. Governments uncertain about what to do about corruption often turn to the model of Hong Kong's Independent Commission Against Corruption (ICAC). Its three-pronged approach (prevention, prosecution, and education) has been mimicked in very different circumstances in Australia and Korea. TI has replicated itself, and the involvement of international organizations in anti-corruption activity has tended to produce national action plans that look remarkably like each other. However, Michael's analysis of the evolution of the anti-corruption industry suggests that, over time, a process of natural selection will lead to more international variety as locally appropriate plans and organizations survive, and inappropriate ones falter and become extinct (Michael 2004: 1080).

Professionalization

TI has an ambiguous relationship with the third source of isomorphism that DiMaggio and Powell identified with the professionalization of work. Overseas training, foreign consultancy, or expatriate workers are a powerful source of standardized models of 'best practice'. They might also produce a stream of 'solutions looking for problems': well-intended ideas, familiar to their proponents, but irrelevant to the local problems they are called upon to solve (Larmour 2005). Historically, the most promiscuous borrowers have been lawyers (Watson 1974). Much of TI's international success has been in the field of international legal conventions. Economists in the World Bank or Asian Development Bank, and accountants in international firms like KPMG, now also promote best practice. Some political scientists are involved in the transfer of electoral systems, and TI has also promoted electoral system reform in Papua New Guinea (Larmour 2003).

However, TI's Berlin Secretariat does not make a strong claim to professional expertise in fields traditionally associated with corruption – law, police, or justice. It does not hire ex-policemen or jurists, though these professions are better represented in some National Chapters. Nor, as a matter of policy, does it engage in consultancy work. Instead its professional skills lie in the promotion or dissemination of ideas in other ways: through lobbying, websites, and the media. Its early membership was a loose network of influential people who had ready access to world leaders and power-brokers. Expertise, when needed, was drawn in *ad hoc*. However TIRI – the 'governance-access-learning network' founded in 2003 as a breakaway from TI – proposes closer involvement in the training of specific professions, like judges, which would have the effect of homogenizing anti-corruption practices.

TI's expertise in networking is expressed in its doctrine of 'coalition building' and demonstrated in the global conferences it organizes, described by Steven Sampson (in press). It trades on the networks its founders brought with them – Eigen's relationship with the World Bank's network was initially confrontational, until James Wolfensohn took over as the Bank's President. Pope drew on his background in the Commonwealth, the quintessential network, with its copying of the prestigious Westminster model, and its dissemination of best practice through professional networks. TI's networks have now expanded and become more autonomous of their original individual sponsors. Networking is flexible, opportunistic, and light on administrative overheads. But it is also unaccountable, self-selecting, and open to the kind of nepotism and patron–client relationships that an anti-corruption NGO is meant to oppose. There is a weird institutional isomorphism between the corrupt networks – dependent on face-to-face contacts, trust, and a shared background – and the anti-corruption networks opposed to them.

Evaluation

TI has had some success in achieving institutional isomorphism, or policy transfer. It has certainly raised awareness of corruption among international agencies. Naming and shaming in the CPI has encouraged some governments, particularly Malaysia's, to address corruption issues. The Source Book is widely quoted, and used in training courses. Donor countries such as the UK and Australia have commissioned studies comparing developing countries against the template of a 'national integrity system' set out in TI's Source Book (Doig and McIvor 2003; Larmour and Barcham 2004). The next step might be for donors to encourage or insist that they conform more closely to that standard. TI's website does not yet claim any successes in the adoption of its business principles. Whether isomorphism or transfer will, in fact, lead to reductions in corruption is another, more complex, issue beyond the scope of this chapter.

Conclusions: TI and the spread of civilization

So what can a study of TI tell us about the spread of global standards of civilization, particularly market civilization? First we need to disentangle TI's techniques from the particular cause – 'anti-corruption' – that it has espoused. None of the techniques for achieving isomorphism is limited or specific to 'corruption' as such. For example, an NGO devoted to environmental protection might easily produce a ranking of countries according to expert perceptions of the degree to which they protect their environment; produce assessments of countries' 'National Protection Systems'; and devise business principles for protecting the environment. It could network and franchise national groups of 'Protection International'. It could be promoting anything; and indeed many of TI's officials and techniques could be promoting other good works, or have been doing so at other points in their careers (the new General Manager, for example, comes from Oxfam, and Galtung, who left to form TIRI, joined from another NGO). As we have seen, few of TI's Berlin Secretariat staff have any particular expertise in corruption, and its prevention, though such professionals play a greater role in some National Chapters. The professional skills evident at TI's Secretariat are in publicity, lobbying, running conferences and workshops, fund raising, information dissemination and websites, and the drafting of legislation. This is not to belittle these skills, but to point to their centrality to TI's purposes, and to their relevance to the promotion of other global standards.

Second, TI as an NGO can not force anyone or any country to do things they do not want to do, but its techniques are not completely innocent or absent of 'power' in several broader senses, particularly agenda setting, and the disciplinary power expressed in indices. That, as Foucault argued, might simply be part of life – all our relationships, he suggested, are saturated with power and resistance. But it does then raise questions of responsibility, accountability and internal democracy, expressed, for example, in the long-running debate about whether early individual contributors to the movement should continue to have voting equality with chapters claiming to stand for nation states. More broadly, processes of democratization need to take place within NGOs as much as governments or businesses.

Third, we do not yet know much about what Braudel called 'refusals'. TI's earliest opponent was the World Bank. Its legal department opposed financial support for TI on the grounds that it might be involving itself in defamation. TI's website describes how World Bank opposition came when TI proposed that companies sign 'integrity pacts' before being qualified to bid for projects: 'We were told it was anti-competitive bidding . . . and an attempt to introduce it in Nepal was blocked by an edict from Washington to the Finance Ministry in Kathmandu' (Transparency International 2005: 2). Relations between TI and the Bank became smoother after Wolfensohn took over the reins at the latter. However, Steve Sampson (in press) notices that no one speaks for corruption, in the way that the environmental movement must engage with pro-development lobbies. There are, he says, 'no pro-corruption forces'. Refusal is typically identified with politicians and the absence of 'political will' or reflected in 'problems of implementation'.

Fourth, the flow of anti-corruption ideas has not simply been from the center to the periphery, as the model of a civilizing project suggests. The model for the ICAC, often commended by TI, for example, comes from colonial Hong Kong in the 1970s. Integrity pacts are being developed most thoroughly in Latin America. Civilizing and applying standards of market civilization might mean moving ideas around the periphery as well as exporting prestigious models from the center. Or there might be a persistent double standard within 'civilization' – perhaps an anteroom where aspirants to civilization are told 'you need anti-corruption agencies that those of us in the heartland can get away without'. That is, we will tell you what standard of market civilization that you must measure up to but we might not necessarily conform to it ourselves.

Fifth, TI's history says something about the resurgent legitimacy of 'national' units of activity, in a purportedly globalized world. TI began in the thin air of international organizations and many of its founders were international civil servants, but they had to choose a national base (in Berlin) and to allow the creation of National Chapters. TI Berlin is largely funded by national governments. They also decided to play with nationalist fire, in the release of the CPI, which is supposed to harness volatile emotions of national pride and shame to reform. Now National Chapters claim the legitimacy of their national particularity, not any process of election (they were, after all, chosen by TI Berlin). The TI Secretariat diffidently describes itself on its website as the 'servant' of the National Chapters. Everyone, the founders, the new management, the breakaway TIRI, defers to the legitimacy of the National Chapters and the idea that the 'real work' of anti-corruption must and should take place at the national level.

8 Civilizing international monetary systems

Michael J. Oliver

One key demonstration that a state can conform to a global standard of market civilization is through its engagement with the international monetary system (IMS). How a state maintains and, in particular, defends its currency provides other states and private market actors with a clear indication of its capacity for socio-political self-management. An IMS can be understood as a 'set of arrangement, rules, practices and institutions under which payments are made and received for transactions carried out across national boundaries' (Solomon 1982: 5). This definition suggests order, structure, fairness, procedure, best practice, and other watchwords, which have become synonymous with demonstrating a capacity for 'civilized' self-management. The IMS has evolved to a considerable extent over the last 150 years and this chapter is a historical appraisal, rather than a contemporary account, of the distinguishing features of the different monetary systems. In essence, there have been three systems.

The first was the Gold Standard, which lasted from roughly the 1870s until the outbreak of the First World War. Reconstituted in a modified form during the 1920s, it had broken down by the mid-1930s. The Gold Standard embraced economic liberalism and accomplished its goals 'in an automatic fashion via the activity of self-regulating markets with a minimum of discretionary government involvement in the monetary sector' (Helleiner 2003: 214–15). Self-regulation in international monetary relations reflected 'civility' among tightly knit social networks within the dominant economic powers (see Seabrooke in this volume).

The second was the Bretton Woods regime, which most historians generally date as having existed between 1944 and the early 1970s. The Bretton Woods system is seen by many academics as the standard with which to judge all other monetary systems. It is revered largely because its system of fixed but adjustable exchange rates, administered by the International Monetary Fund (IMF), brought stability to the international monetary system after the interwar problems of confidence, liquidity, and adjustment. However, as Barry Eichengreen (1996: 7) points out, the Bretton Woods system is an aberration in the history of exchange rate regimes. It was a product of international negotiation, but, more commonly, monetary agreements have arisen 'out of the individual choices of countries constrained by the prior decisions of their neighbors and, more generally, by the inheritance of history'.

Finally, the period since 1973 has been the era of floating exchange rates. Floating rates did exist in the 1920s – before the inception of the gold exchange standard and after its demise in the 1930s – but they were a transitory affair and it is only in the last thirty years that floating rates have become widespread globally. It is true that there have been a variety of regional currency arrangements since 1973 (e.g. the European Monetary System), attempts made to fix the currency of small nations to larger states (e.g. the African Financial Community) and a recent attempt to introduce a single global currency and global central bank by 2024, but these are of second-order importance.

This chapter assesses how private and public agents have imposed civility in international monetary relations over the last 150 years. It explores why the 'market solutions' of the Gold Standard were replaced by a belief after 1944 that national governments should work with a supra-national institution (the IMF) to bring civility to the IMS. Under the Bretton Woods framework, co-operation between members was desirable in order to stabilize exchange rates, to regulate capital flows, and to guarantee that international obligations did not override domestic policy objectives. Due to a combination of factors, the tenets of Bretton Woods were challenged by the early 1970s but the introduction of floating exchange rates in 1973 did *not* herald a return to the ruinous nature and impasse of the interwar system. Moreover, financial markets began to impose their own discipline on states that failed in their capacity for economic self-management in the 1980s and 1990s. Not measuring up to the global standard of market civilization in monetary affairs imposes significant costs on such wayward states and provides incentive for them to conform. While the power and influence of financial markets have been criticized, this chapter concludes that history shows us that the only way to extend civility across nations and to stabilize the IMS is through market solutions, bolstered by effective supra-national institutions.

The Gold Standard and the interwar years

As Beth Simmons (2000: 575) has recently reminded us, the existence of the Gold Standard owed nothing to international legal agreements and its legal basis was enshrined in national laws. It is true that this 'decentralized system of regulatory harmonization' was not always a smooth and self-adjusting mechanism, but many of the strengths of the pre-1914 international monetary situation have not been replicated since (Bordo 1981). Indeed, the 1880–1914 period combined the remarkable trinity of international capital mobility, stable exchange rates, and fewer convertibility crises, at least among the core states (Britain, France, and Germany). This was achieved without recourse to supra-national institutions, bi-annual conferences between heads of state, or continuous government interference, and was the result of involved co-operation among banks on an unparalleled scale (Bordo 2003).

This co-operation worked out under what has become known as the 'rules of the game' (Keynes in Moggridge 1972: 259). The rules did not constitute a formal code of conduct written in tablets of stone; rather they were 'a set of crude signals and signposts' by which central banks were guided in formulating policy (League of Nations 1944: 67; McKinnon 1993: 3). The rules included maintaining convertibility at a fixed mint parity; absence of restrictions on the import and export of gold; gold backing for the currency; inter-bank co-operation in liquidity crises; and the contingent rule that, in the event of convertibility being suspended, it would be restored at the original mint parity as soon as possible (McKinnon 1993: 4). For practical purposes the chief operating maxim was that central banks should reinforce rather than counteract or sterilize the effects of reserve flows (gold and foreign exchange) on their money supplies, by which process the adjustment in payments imbalances would be speeded up through changes in prices and incomes in both gold-receiving and gold-losing states.

While these arrangements might not have provided heaven on earth, there were remarkably few financial crises among the core states between 1880–1914. Categorizing the distribution of crises according to 'industrial' or 'emerging' market, shows that three-quarters of all pre-1914 crises were confined to the Gold Standard periphery, while, during the interwar years, three-quarters of the observed crises were to be found among the Gold Standard core states.

As Eichengreen and Michael D. Bordo (2003: 71) have argued, banking crises pre-1914 did not undermine the confidence in the currency in the states that were at the core of the Gold Standard. Banks would suspend the convertibility of deposits into currency, currency would go to a premium and foreign capital flowed in to arbitrage the difference, provided the state remained on the Gold Standard. Civility under the Gold Standard required a commitment to constantly signaling financial rectitude (low fiscal deficits, stable money growth, and low inflation) to provide what Bordo and Hugh Rockoff (1996) have described as a 'good housekeeping seal of approval'. In turn, credibility and commitment were linked to international co-operation as central banks in England, France, Germany, Russia, and the US stood prepared to extend loans and ship gold to one another in times of distress (Eichengreen 1992: 31). The success of the system depended of course on a wide range of other factors that included the relative ease with which adjustments could be made, the steadfast commitment to 'regime-preserving cooperation' (Eichengreen 2004: 12), and the powerful influence of the Bank of England. The whole process was also facilitated by the fact that the costs involved could to some extent be shifted elsewhere, either on to the domestic economy or from core states to the periphery.

The pre-1914 Gold Standard was not restored after the First World War. In its place the Gold Exchange Standard operated, sandwiched in between two periods of 'managed fiduciary money' (Bordo 1981). Few had realized that the economic landscape would change so dramatically after 1914 and that the cornerstone of international economic policy, the Gold Exchange Standard, would be the prime culprit of the chaos. The Gold Exchange Standard was based on principles developed at the Genoa conference in 1922 (Eichengreen 1989: 263). Due to worries about the lack of gold reserves, states held their legally required reserves wholly or partly in the foreign exchange of a key currency (sterling and dollars) that were convertible. The private sector was discouraged from holding gold.

Why did the interwar system fail whereas the Gold Standard had worked prior to 1914? A major source of weakness of the post-war standard arose out of the stabilization process itself. Stabilization was a piecemeal and un-co-ordinated process extending over several years, carried out unilaterally by each state as and when it thought fit. Insufficient attention was paid to the shifts in relative costs and prices since 1914, and the somewhat haphazard choice of exchange rates, influenced in some cases by short-term capital movements and questions of prestige, meant that many states ended up with the wrong parities. The post-war standard started out from a point of serious disequilibrium. In essence, however, the post-war standard suffered because the three elements that were present pre-1914, namely adjustment, liquidity, and confidence, were not all present after 1914.

The adjustment problem arose from the moment that states adopted their new parities. These were regarded as sacrosanct, in much the same way as those under the pre-war system had been, so that they were reluctant to adjust them even when they were seen to be incorrect. The choice of wrong parity rates tended to magnify balance of payments problems and so the system was called upon to make adjustments on a scale far greater than previously and for which it was never designed, and at a time when, for various reasons, the adjustment mechanism operated less smoothly than previously (Redmond 1992: 358–9). Few states were prepared to sacrifice completely the stability of their domestic economies for the sake of external equilibrium. Those with overvalued exchange rates were reluctant or unable to make full adjustment to their domestic economies, while surplus states were unwilling to meet the former halfway. Within core states the rise of social movements with a very different conception of what market civilization should be providing them also provided a constraint on governments, as Winston Churchill's unhappy experience with trying to maintain 'strong sterling' in 1925 and the consequent General Strike of 1926 demonstrated.

Furthermore a confidence problem arose as there were sudden shifts among key currencies and between key currencies and gold. Gold Exchange Standard states built up their exchange reserve holdings through short-term claims on key currencies, notably sterling and the dollar. The accommodation of large holdings of foreign claims put a severe strain on the central money markets and increased market volatility. The potential for gold hoarding made matters worse as many states regarded the Gold Exchange Standard as a sort of halfway house on the way to the resumption of a full Gold Standard (Aldcroft and Oliver 1998: 35–6).

Perhaps the Gold Exchange Standard would have worked in more propitious circumstances, but during the interwar years international monetary relations were at best strained and, at worst, disastrous. To be sure, there was more evidence of co-operation among the major monetary centers than pre-war (Walter 1991: 134) and, for most of the 1920s, inter-bank co-operation, acting largely independently of governments, had predominated. However, it did not always work smoothly. The need for co-operation was especially important given sterling's weakened position, which required the support of New York and Paris in times of strain. The alternative was for one of the two centers to assume leadership in managing the system. In the event neither of these conditions was satisfied (Kindleberger 1973).

In the 1930s, national domestic policies determined by politicians intervened to weaken the power of central banks. Patricia Clavin has demonstrated how the priority of national economic policies effectively scuppered co-operative bank efforts at the World Economic Conference in the summer of 1933 and she singles out Britain who 'was not prepared to do any clubbing at the conference' (Clavin 1991: 513; 1992: 282, 310–11). Further efforts at co-operation three years later, when attempts were made to secure the alignment of some of the major currencies (the so-called Tripartite Agreement), had very limited success (Aldcroft and Oliver 1998: 82–4). In short, the central banks, constrained by national policies, political rivalries, mutual distrust, and conceptual differences about the role of the state in market civilization, hindered a return to a pre-war global standard.

The Bretton Woods years

The Second World War galvanized policy-makers in the US and the UK to consider how to strengthen the international economy in general and the IMS in particular for when the hostilities ceased. One of the most undesirable consequences of the Gold Standard was for some states to accumulate surpluses on their balance of payments and others a deficit. When a state had a balance of payments deficit it was required to reduce its domestic money base. John Maynard Keynes in particular wished to avoid the deflation associated with this adjustment mechanism that would produce a decline in national income and a rise in unemployment. In his original plan for an International Clearing Union (ICU), those states with a balance of payments surplus would provide credits to the deficit states through the clearing union. This was deemed unacceptable to the US (the state with the largest surplus). Instead, the US economist Harry Dexter White proposed the establishment of an International Stabilization Fund and an International Bank for Reconstruction and Development. The former would maintain stable exchange rates and provide finance for deficit states and thereby prevent members from having to deflate their economy and the international economy. The latter would provide credits for post-war reconstruction and long-term loans for development, and became known as the World Bank (see also Broome in this volume).

The discussions in the early 1940s were not confined to the US and the UK, and also involved the Soviet Union, the People's Republic of China, the free French, and a number of Commonwealth states. In1944 it was agreed that an International Monetary Fund (IMF) should be established. At the Bretton Woods conference, which determined the new formal global standard for market civilization, White presided over a commission on the setting up of the IMF while

Keynes took responsibility for the World Bank (US Department of State 1948). At the end of the conference, Keynes announced that

> We, the delegates of this Conference, Mr. President, have been trying to accomplish something very difficult to accomplish. . . . It has been our task to find a common measure, a common standard, a common rule acceptable to each and not irksome to any.
>
> (Keynes 1980: 103)

Keynes's statement of achievement, broadly speaking, contained three main features.

First, every member of the IMF had to establish a par value for its currency and to maintain it within a 1 percent margin on either side of the declared par value. Although currencies were treated equally in the articles, Article IV defined the linchpin of the system as either gold or the US dollar (the fixed price of gold was $35 per ounce). As the US was the only state that pegged its currency in terms of gold, all other states would fix their parities in terms of dollars and would intervene to monitor their exchange rates within 1 percent of parity with the dollar. In the event of a 'fundamental disequilibrium' with the balance of payments, the parity could be changed only if the fund member had consulted with other members (Article IV Section 5). The phrase fundamental disequilibrium was never defined and later proved to be a source of contention amongst some members. The escape clause differed from that of the Gold Standard because states were not expected at a later date to return their currencies to the original parity.

Second, under Article VIII members were expected to make their currencies convertible for current account transactions but were allowed a three-year transitional period to achieve this (Article XIV). Capital controls were allowed (Article VI Section 3) and members had to avoid discriminatory currency and multiple currency arrangements.

Third, the IMF could help finance members with short- or medium-term payments difficulties and issue sanctions against states with large surpluses. The rights of members to draw on the Fund, along with their contributions and voting powers, were based on members' quotas. The world share the member state had according to national income, international trade, and international reserves decided each quota. The quota would be paid by gold or US dollars (25 percent) and the member's own currency (75 percent). While members could draw on their quotas at will, stringent conditions were attached to further borrowing beyond the existing allotments. At the outset, the total fund was set at $8.8 billion and could be raised every five years by a majority vote.

The contrast with the interwar years, when there was a 'largely unsuccessful groping toward some form or organization regulation of monetary affairs' (Dam 1982: 50), was enormous. As Harold James (1996: 57) remarks, the Bretton Woods conference was the first to establish an institutional and legal framework, which guaranteed co-operation between states and required them to curtail their sovereignty for the sake of co-operation. It was not just in spirit alone that members were expected to observe the Articles of Agreement and it was required that they would also follow the letter of the law. Unfortunately, it took some time before Article VIII was satisfied, and, in the absence of convertibility, the essence of the Bretton Woods Agreement was put into cold storage.

By the early 1960s, a majority of IMF members had undertaken current account convertibility but there were still tight controls on the movement of capital. From its inception, there was a desire that the IMF would substitute private capital inflows and not complement them. The view expressed by the US Treasury Secretary Henry Morgenthau at the Bretton Woods conference, that the IMF and World Bank would 'drive . . . the usurious money lenders from the temple of international finance' (Gardner 1980: xix), was absorbed into official thinking amongst members for several decades. This new conception of, and desire for, monetary stability underpinned the view that market civilization should avoid its ruin. Accordingly, the role of the IMF in this era is that it was primarily concerned with surveillance of the exchange rate system and provision of temporary finance to manage current account deficits, a role it has now outgrown (see Best in this volume).

The growth in the Euromarket during the 1960s circumvented capital controls and, with the blessing of the US and British government, the market flourished (Seabrooke 2001: 61–6). As James (1996: 180) notes, banking in Eurodollars increased the international money supply and put it on collision course with the attempts made by national monetary authorities and the IMF to control the international money supply. Crucially, with greater resources now available to transfer money, it was only a matter of time before a new informal global standard of market civilization would impact currency markets and render fixed exchange rates meaningless.

Aside from the re-emergence of global finance, the other threat to the international monetary consensus was, ironically, the Bretton Woods system itself. During the 1950s, the system had evolved into a fixed exchange rate gold dollar standard and in the following decade the monetary authorities of member states became more unwilling to accept changes in parities. The IMF was cautious about giving states the option to alter exchange rates and, after 1964, its *Annual Report* did not mention the possibility of parity changes. As John Williamson (1977: 6) noted this meant that exchange rate changes were 'relegated to the status of confessions that the adjustment process had failed', despite the IMF having formal powers to make members adjust their rates (Gold 1988: 48). A move to floating exchange rates was recognized by core states as inevitable (Hamilton and Oliver 2006).

While floating rates threatened the surveillance processes inherent within the fixed exchange rate regime, they did offer several advantages including parity adjustment through a market mechanism, the cessation of exchange control, and greater flexibility in monetary policy. By the mid-1960s, there was a recognition that the IMS needed to be made more flexible although it was not until 1969 that the UK and the US undertook serious discussions on wider margins for currency fluctuations and crawling peg systems (Oliver *et al.* 2006). Harold James

(1995: 770) perceptively notes that, while the currency chaos of the early 1970s is seen as reflecting too much discretion in the system, it was in effect a cry to return to increased monetary management. Rather than *international* monetary management, however, with floating exchange rates states could take up the option of *domestic* monetary control. A new global standard therefore emerged on an assertion of domestic autonomy *with* market pressure.

Conflict and co-operation, 1973–89

The key issue for the IMF in the aftermath of the move to floating rates was to try to establish rules for a system that made rules difficult to implement. The IMF was now called upon to play the role of headmaster in a school of unruly pupils who refuse to sit still, become easily distracted and irritable with each other, and have considerable difficulty in behaving harmoniously. There was some success, however, and, between 1973 and 1976, discussions took place among members of the IMF to amend the Articles of Agreement. This prompted the Second Amendment, approved in 1978, which had at its core the acceptance that members should 'promote a stable system of exchange rates'. The wording was a result of the insistence by the US that floating exchange rates should now be *de jure* (James 1996: 271). Under the 'managed float' IMF members agreed to accept the principles that the exchange rate should not be manipulated in order to prevent a balance of payments adjustment or to gain an unfair advantage over other states.

The IMF did not always have to take the lead in the 1970s and 1980s, and, on occasions, several of the world's key states behaved like enlightened pupils and tried to sort out disputes between themselves. For example, intense diplomatic discussions outside the remit of the IMF evolved from the 'Library Group' meeting of March 1973 between the US, French, German, and British finance ministers and their deputies, which became the Group of Five (G5) ministers at Rambouillet in November 1975, and which from 1986 became the Group of Seven (G7). Compared to the 1960s, there were far fewer meetings of the Group of Ten (G10) in the 1970s. Aside from the establishment of the G5, this was also in part due to the divisions between the major industrial members on the questions of international monetary reform. The formation of the Committee of Twenty (C20) and then the Interim Committee also enabled key international monetary decisions to take place in a 'politically more acceptable forum' than the G10 (de Vries 1985a: 977).

The one major sticking point among members at the time of the move to widespread floating was the problem of capital flows. On the eve of floating, 'capital mobility had developed to the point where the Bundesbank could take in well over $1 billion in an hour when the market had come to expect that another parity change was impending' (Williamson 1977: 50). The C20's Committee of Deputies studied the problem of capital flows in depth but, although Western Europe and Japan strongly supported co-operative controls, the US was very reluctant to embrace co-operative initiatives and successfully destroyed all attempts at co-operation (Helleiner 1994: 108–9). Instead, the US was keen to move the international financial system onto a more liberal footing and managed to have Article IV-I amended to reflect that capital flows were now included in the framework of the 'essential purpose of the international monetary system' along with the exchange of goods and services among states (De Vries 1985b: 381–2).

As Eric Helleiner (1994: 111) has discussed, the attitude of the US reflected a new financial liberalism toward foreign economic policy that also extended into the domestic arena. In this approach, 'global finance' would replace the 'publicly managed' Bretton Woods order (i.e. private capital flows would replace government flows). With the relative size of the US economy, the role of the dollar as a vehicle currency, the prominence of US financial institutions, and the attractiveness of the US financial market, the US was able to 'change the range of choices open to others' (Strange 1988: 31; see also Seabrooke 2001).

Although the IMF had endorsed floating rates, it did not intend to allow national economic policies to go unchecked and sought new ways of surveillance. The new Article IV stated that the Fund 'shall exercise firm surveillance over the exchange rate policies of members, and shall adopt specific principles for the guidance of all members with respect to these policies'. It was decided at an Executive Board meeting in April 1977 that surveillance would be made 'within the framework of a comprehensive analysis of the general economic situation and economic policy strategy of the member' (James 1995: 773). As the fourth part of the IMF's official history shows, surveillance was hindered from the beginning because it lacked clearly defined objectives or standards. The essential difficulty was striking the right balance between procedures that were both even-handed and firm, and when 'wielding a club was not always compatible with being part of a club' (Boughton 2001: 42). The detailed account of the surveillance process discussed in James M. Boughton illustrates several other shortcomings, for instance the gaps in the timing of some of the consultations (the Executive Board did not hold a review of the Mexican economy from March 1980 until July 1982, a few weeks before the debt crisis hit) and the reluctance to 'name and shame' a member if the conduct of economic policy did not meet IMF approval and the member was not borrowing IMF funds. The two 'special' Article IV consultations on the Swedish devaluation in 1982 and the undervaluation of the Korean won in 1987 prompted complaints by other IMF members that general procedures were not being applied. The IMF's creation of a more 'one size fits all' policy framework, however, has received scorn from critics as too rigid (see Best in this volume).

James (1995: 774) notes that the provisions of Article IV with regard to exchange rate policy represented 'more of a pious code filled with a hope of liberalization than a serious attempt to change countries' policies by specific intervention by the IMF', but there was a wider problem with the entire process that became apparent in the 1980s. Without any special powers to enforce its policy advice, the only way the Fund could wield influence was through persuasion (Fund management and staff to state authorities), peer pressure (state to state in the forum of the Fund), and through publicity (Fund to the public) (Boughton and Lateef 1995). In theory, surveillance was applied to policies undertaken 'for balance of payments purposes' but exchange rates are dominated by domestic macroeconomic policy, which are outside the remit of the IMF's authority. In the early 1980s, the macroeconomic policies of the US caused a great deal of consternation for the IMF and the latter in particular really tested the limits of co-operation.

By the early 1980s, the United States had shifted decisively away from the aegis of co-operation. It was quickly made apparent to the rest of the world that America intended to form its domestic policy with little regard to the repercussions on the international community (see also John M. Hobson in this volume). In April 1981, the United States Treasury announced that it was no longer going to intervene in the foreign exchange market to stabilize the dollar, except on extraordinary occasions. As the US administration was following a mixture of loose fiscal policy and moderate monetary policy this raised real interest rates and attracted capital, placing upward pressure on the dollar that made the US less competitive. Another flashpoint was the size of the US budget deficit, which frequently provoked very heated discussions between the US Treasury Secretary and his foreign counterparts (Volcker and Gyohten 1992: 183). The US denied that there existed any link between the budget deficit, the strong dollar, and the growing trade deficit. In these sorts of circumstance, the limits of surveillance were sorely exposed.

There are three reasons to suggest that between 1985 and 1989 a transition occurred in the IMS that marked a transformation in market civilization that provided clear incentives for all states in the system to conform to a global standard. First, leaving the exchange rate to be determined purely by market forces no longer appeared an option among the developed states (in so far as it ever had), even for the pro-monetarist Thatcher government. At one point in January 1985, the pound was almost trading for a dollar and the monetary authorities decided that they would have to intervene to prop it up. The legacy of this episode was that some in the Thatcher government began to move away from monetary targets to an exchange rate target (Oliver 1997). If this most pro-free market of governments had indicated that the game was up, what hope for the rest?

Second, during Ronald Reagan's second term the US Treasury proved to be 'less doctrinaire' due to concerns about the impact of the high dollar on American business and industry (Lawson 1992: 475). Greater co-operation was required to solve international monetary problems and, accordingly, in 1985, the G5 Finance Ministers committed themselves to intervention in the foreign exchange markets when it was considered necessary. The most famous of these are the Plaza Accord of 1985 and Louvre Accord of 1987, both of which sought to revalue the dollar against the deutschmark and the yen.

Third, there were several new initiatives to address the resource issues of developing states. The slow recovery from the international debt crisis prompted officials in creditor states to develop new approaches (see also Seabrooke in this volume). These included more generous financing terms from commercial and regional banks along with the World Bank, as well as the IMF creation of a Structural Adjustment Facility (SAF) for developing states. SAF was built on the principle of the Trust Fund, established ten years earlier, but now lending would be given on concessional terms and provided for structural adjustment. Applicants had to submit three-year adjustment programs to address macroeconomic and structural problems, which prevented balance of payments adjustment and economic growth. SAF was joined a year later by the Enhanced Structural Adjustment Facility, to provide low-cost financing to the poorest developing states. The IMF's ambitious programs sought to provide borrowing member states with greater stability in the IMS.

The contemporary global standard in monetary affairs

The 1990s witnessed an intense debate about regional currency areas, the role of the IMF, and the growth of international financial markets, *inter alia*. These debates were largely propelled by the financial crises in Europe, Mexico, Brazil, Asia, and Russia (Oliver 2006). By the end of the decade, this had prompted several studies and numerous calls to reform the international financial architecture (e.g. Eichengreen 1999; Armijo 2002; International Financial Institution Advisory Commission 2000). In a thought-provoking analysis, André Cartapanis and Michel Herland (2002) have asked whether the lack of theoretical consensus over the dysfunction of financial markets in the 1990s, which led to a closer working compromise between the neo-Keynesians and neo-liberals, might be 'Keynes's revenge'. So far, it is not.

For one thing, the turmoil in the international financial markets during the 1990s, especially in the developing states, is a product of increased liberalization in capital accounts (Ahluwalia 1999). The costs of integrating into global financial markets and accessing international capital flows are greater volatility and instability, but this has not led to the closing down of emerging capital markets (see Seabrooke in this volume). Emerging markets have grown more cautious since the crises and the IMF has been afforded a far greater role in stabilizing and fostering capital flows (Bordo *et al.* 2004), but there has been no international agreement to restrict capital flows. The market provided a solution to one threat to systematic stability by reducing leverage in the international financial system after 1998. This was achieved by banks curtailing the amount of credit that they made available to hedge funds (Eichengreen and Park 2002). Concomitantly, floating exchange rates have also replaced fixed exchange rates in most of the developing states that suffered from financial crises which has been described as one of the most significant reforms of the international financial architecture by Eichengreen (2005). As a consequence of financial crises a plethora of new standards and institutions have been created within global capital markets (see Seabrooke in this volume).

Conclusions

Too often in current discussion on reforming the financial architecture, the lessons of history are ignored, avoided, or forgotten. This chapter has investigated the global standards of market civilization of the IMS through a historical framework and has not dwelt at length on contemporary issues. It should be stressed, however, that much of what is perceived as contemporary has deeper roots and so it is with the recent discussions on reform of the IMS.

The far-reaching changes to the IMS, enshrined in the Articles of Agreements at Bretton Woods in 1944, grew from the dissatisfaction with the interwar monetary system, which was a bastardized form of the Gold Standard. Although the Bretton Woods regime was an international agreement, brokered to benefit all of its members equally, the IMF was relatively ineffectual at penalizing those states that broke the rules. To be sure, members would incur the wrath of the IMF and were obliged to follow its directions if they sought resources from the Fund. Yet the system was flexible enough to allow states to go unpunished when they violated the rules of the system. As capital was liberalized in the 1960s, the IMF was only partially successful at regulating developments in the IMS effectively. The IMF was not redundant at the start of the floating era but was forced to rethink its role as markets came to play a more significant role in globalizing finance (see Jacqueline Best's chapter in this volume). By the 1990s, the IMF was reacting to crises *ex post* rather than preventing them in the first place. It is not surprising that, at the start of the twenty-first century, there is common ground between some *laissez-faire* liberalizers and anti-globalizers on the need to abolish the IMF and the World Bank (Armijo 2001: 382).

This chapter has not argued that market solutions are the elixir for civilizing the IMS but history has shown that it is chimerical to believe that neo-liberalism can be suppressed. As Maurice Obstfeld has pertinently noted:

> Postwar experience has been characterized by a growing acceptance of economic openness. Compared to the world of the late nineteenth century gold standard, however, we increasingly reside in broadly democratic societies in which voters hold their governments accountable for providing economic stability and social safety nets. These imperatives sometimes seem to clash with the reality of openness. Despite periodic crises, global financial integration holds significant benefits and probably is in any case, impossible to stop – short of a second great depression or third world war. The challenge for national and international policymakers is to maintain an economic and political milieu in which the trend of increasing economic integration can continue.
>
> (Obstfeld 1998: 28)

In the contemporary IMS there is a danger similar to the halfway house of the 1920s, that states must choose between allowing the market to civilize them or they can attempt to civilize the international system, as seen above, at their own peril. In monetary affairs the civilizing effects of the market are producing a global standard to which states must, and should, conform to ensure their own growth and prosperity.

9 Civilizing labor markets

The World Bank in Central Asia

André Broome

After the dissolution of the USSR in 1991 and the emergence of the former Soviet Republics as sovereign independent states, Central Asian governments publicly adopted the objective of moving towards a market economy with the assistance of international organizations. Among other recommendations for key economic changes, both the World Bank and the International Monetary Fund (IMF) emphasized the importance of reforming labor institutions in the former Soviet republics. Formal labor institutions play a crucial role in determining a country's economic performance and living standards, and can influence the level of public support for top-down structural changes to a country's economy. In Central Asia, the World Bank took a lead role in assisting states to construct new labor institutions, advising governments on what kind of formal labor institutions they should develop and what normative aims they should attempt to achieve through labor policy.

When taken at face value, the World Bank's objectives in Central Asia aimed to provide financial support and expert advice to governments as they made the shift from central planning to market capitalism. One can nonetheless draw comparisons between the World Bank's efforts to develop a particular form of economic life in Central Asia, and both European imperialist conceptions of undertaking a civilizing mission to enlighten 'uncivilized' peoples during the colonial era and Soviet 'developmental imperialism' in Central Asia following the Russian revolution (Pomeranz 2005). This chapter examines the World Bank's promotion of 'global standards of market civilization' in Central Asia, which defined the appropriate labor institutions and practices for states to adopt. The notion of global standards of market civilization raises questions about whether the Bank aims to universalize 'market civilization' as a set of ideal types with which to judge governments' policies and as a way of transforming the formal institutions and patterns of behavior in particular societies.

Like 'classical' theories of modernization and institutional convergence during the 1950s, the idea that governments should build institutions to regulate economic activities within their countries according to global standards determined by outsiders equates the definition of a 'modern' economy with a hypothetical template drawn from the particular experiences of Western economies. Against this view, scholars working in the emergent 'multiple modernities' approach argue that, while Western patterns of modernization may continue to be a global reference point for many non-Western societies, economic and social change in modernizing societies is a process that has been characterized by the 'continual constitution and reconstitution of a multiplicity of cultural programs'. The basic insight here is that modernization and Westernization are not synonymous, and that this plurality of changing cultural programs involves reconstructing a wide range of institutional and ideological patterns (Eisenstadt 2000). Through the promotion of global 'best practice' standards, however, the IMF and the World Bank classify institutions that do not correspond with the civilized market ideal as inferior forms of economic organization that governments need to reform (cf. Sachsenmaier 2002: 58). One can criticize such homogenizing standards on a variety of normative grounds, but this chapter aims to show how the World Bank's attempts to 'civilize' Central Asian labor systems actually proceeded in practice. I take this approach in order to supplement theoretical critiques of the World Bank's 'civilizing' role in supporting economic transformation. These frequently start and end with sophisticated deconstructions of the World Bank's normative agenda, ignoring how 'small-scale' everyday practices on the ground are able to influence macro-outcomes (Liu 2003), including whether or how the Bank's agenda is implemented in different domestic contexts.

To advance the shift to a market-oriented system during the 1990s, the World Bank encouraged post-Soviet states to adopt the same kinds of labor institutions based on an 'ideal' template (i.e. institutional isomorphism). This involved attempts to set common premises and standards for countries' formal institutions, which the Bank expected would help to change existing patterns of economic behavior and shape new patterns of action in accordance with market norms (on institutional isomorphism see DiMaggio and Powell 1983). To understand Central Asian responses to the World Bank's efforts to promote institutional isomorphism, I draw on an institutional approach that suggests that to successfully produce institutional change and the transfer of external policy ideas, governments must *translate* international ideas about formal institutions into domestic contexts (Kjær and Pedersen 2001). For comparisons across a large number of countries, considering the transfer of policy ideas as a process of generic diffusion (without significant modification of these ideas in each context) may be an appropriate approach to identify common patterns of change at the macro-level (Brooks 2005). I argue, however, that when investigating externally supported institutional change in a small number of cases, a context-specific translation approach is a more useful way of understanding the ambiguities and complexities of the World Bank's influence over this process.

Economic institutions take the form of both legally defined formal structures and accepted informal patterns of social behavior. This chapter focuses on the formal legal reforms the World Bank wanted the governments of Kyrgyzstan, Uzbekistan, and Kazakhstan to implement to their existing labor practices and institutions, but also discusses how people in these countries adapted existing practices to resist their governments' attempts to implement reforms. The aim here is not to put forward a different set of ideal labor policies that the World

Bank should have promoted in Central Asia. Rather, the aim is to examine how people responded to the institutional reforms the Bank did promote, both at an elite level and at the level of workers' and managers' everyday activities on the shop floor.

This chapter argues that when governments attempt to modify World Bank-supported institutional reforms through a process of translation, this constrains and distorts the Bank's attempts to create institutional isomorphism because it provides greater opportunities for people to contest formal legal changes through their everyday economic practices. I begin with a brief discussion of the economic and social context that Central Asian governments faced upon independence in 1991. I then examine the kinds of policies the World Bank wanted Central Asian states to adopt with regard to labor practices. Following this, I provide an overview of Central Asian responses to the World Bank's preferred labor reforms, and discuss their implications for the Bank's efforts to promote institutional isomorphism. I conclude by evaluating the World Bank's record on labor reforms in Central Asia against the concept of global standards of market civilization.

The post-Soviet context in Central Asia

The countries of Central Asia each faced a number of severe economic shocks in the early 1990s, including large declines in economic output, the emergence of high unemployment, and hyperinflation. A significant difference facing the Central Asian republics in comparison with the countries of East Central Europe was that no mass social movements existed that demanded independent statehood (Luong 2001: 105). Rather, a series of events resulted in the dissolution of the Soviet Union at the end of 1991 and the establishment of the Central Asian republics as independent states almost by default. Following independence, each of these governments began to apply for membership of international organizations such as the World Bank in order to access external financial support.

For its part, the World Bank had developed economic models and an organizational culture that were geared to dealing primarily with governments that had greater experience with market institutions. In addition, Kathleen Collins's research suggests that some characteristics of Central Asian societies constrained the efforts of international actors such as the World Bank to build new formal institutions. Collins argues that Central Asian clans (informal social organizations) have maintained collective identities in the region that are distinct from national, ethnic, and economic cleavages, based on actual or metaphorical kinship ties. Clans function as stable non-state support networks, which reproduce a range of reciprocal behavioral norms, including mutual assistance among clan members for social, political, or economic advancement. These established social groups were previously able to use Soviet institutions to advance their own goals, and since independence in 1991 they have limited the impact of legal institutional reforms by resisting formal changes outright, inhibiting the development of states' administrative capacities, and using state resources to support their own informal networks (Collins 2004).

On the one hand, because of the lack of experience with a market economy, it appears reasonable to expect that the World Bank would have a relatively higher degree of influence in shaping the transformation of the Central Asian countries. On the other hand, the path-dependent effects of economic and institutional legacies from the Soviet period, as well as the contestation of economic and political changes by strong informal social organizations in these countries, might suggest that to be effective the Bank's proposed reforms would have to be adapted to incorporate particular local conditions. In the event, after gaining membership of the World Bank during 1992, the new Central Asian states responded in varying ways to the Bank's policy reform proposals.

The World Bank and labor systems

Formal labor market institutions include agencies such as ministries of labor, departments of employment, and employment services, which share responsibility for the design and implementation of labor policies. These may include laws to regulate the activities of firms, employee–employer relationships, workplace conditions, and assistance to the unemployed. Labor policies can also include minimum-wage and employment protection legislation that regulates how and when managers can dismiss workers, as well as laws that govern the activities of labor unions (Cazes 2002: 3). Using a basic typology to classify forms of labor market regulation, policies that focus on the *supply* of labor (which may be 'active' or 'passive' policies) differ from those that focus on influencing the *demand* for labor. Labor supply policies target individuals who are already unemployed as a social group. Active labor supply policies aim to assist people to find new employment, whereas passive policies simply provide a basic level of financial assistance. In contrast, demand-focused labor policies encourage enterprises to retain or recruit workers (Verme 1998: 10–11). While scholars sometimes treat labor systems and social protection policy in advanced industrial economies as distinct areas of study, Central Asian states inherited institutional systems that tightly combined employment and social protection objectives.

What labor policies does the World Bank want governments to adopt?

The World Bank wants labor reform in 'transition' economies in order to rationalize the distribution of human resources through the creation of an efficient labor market. From the Bank's perspective, this will enable workers to adjust to the new circumstances economic change entails. The World Bank's main objective with regard to labor reform is that governments should allow markets to set wages, according to supply and demand. From the World Bank's perspective, the Soviet state maintained inefficient and overstaffed public enterprises. The World Bank wanted governments to adopt labor reforms that would stimulate the reallocation of labor from overstaffed, low-productivity enterprises to enterprises that are more cost-efficient. The Bank recognized that public sector job shedding would be a key feature of economic change in former communist countries, and estimated that the bulk of the resulting unemployment would be a temporary phenomenon while new labor market mechanisms took root. To achieve the shift to a market-based labor system after the Soviet system collapsed, the key areas of reform that the World Bank encouraged governments to adopt included:

1 Privatizing state enterprises and reforming the wage system to enable wages to reflect productivity, which would involve eliminating state guarantees of employment security and income security.
2 Removing direct and indirect restrictions on labor mobility, such as privatizing non-wage benefits and housing.
3 Redesigning the techniques and objectives of social protection, including eliminating universal subsidies and establishing targeted social assistance systems.

Establishing employment and wage flexibility

While the Soviet economy had a long-established norm of guaranteed lifelong full-time employment for most men and women of working age, the World Bank recommended that states immediately remove the guarantee of employment to rationalize and shed staff from public enterprises. The key goal the World Bank hoped to achieve by advising governments to abolish employment security was to devolve the responsibility for employment from the state to individual workers and employers, thus redefining and circumscribing the state's existing role (see also Barry Hindess's chapter in this volume). The Bank identified the core employment responsibilities that post-communist governments should assume as:

1 Shaping an economic environment conducive to private sector job creation.
2 Providing a minimum social safety net to assist people who were unable to find jobs and for those on very low incomes.
3 Accumulating information about labor market changes to inform future policy design.

To cope with the new problem of unemployment created by the elimination of employment security, the World Bank assisted governments to create employment services that would target the 'supply' of unemployed workers through both active and passive programs, including the provision of cash benefits, retraining programs, and assistance with job placement. World Bank programs in Central Asia aimed to develop the administrative capacity to register and pay the unemployed, to redeploy workers from public enterprises to the private sector, and to identify key problems in the labor market and to develop policy solutions. To aid the implementation of these formal changes, the World Bank assisted post-communist governments to build their institutional capacity to supervise labor developments. This included support to ministries of labor and employment services to develop computerized systems to collect, analyze, and disseminate labor market statistics, and assistance to create occupational classification systems that would enhance the ability of agencies to monitor changes as labor markets developed (Dar and Tzannatos 1999: 5, 27–8).

In the Soviet system, the state determined wage rates and maintained more egalitarian wage rates across the economy as a whole than in most capitalist labor markets. To help achieve the goal of reorienting responsibility for employment from the state to individuals, the Bank encouraged governments to reduce their responsibility for income security from setting pay rates to establishing a minimum floor for wages, allowing enterprises to determine each worker's pay rate above that level. The Bank considered that greater wage dispersion would heighten individual employees' incentives to work more productively, and would allow the owners and managers of enterprises to reward employees' different levels of skill and experience. From the Bank's perspective, therefore, increasing income inequality was both an inevitable and an advantageous component of the shift to a market system (World Bank 1995a: 104, 110).

Creating a mobile workforce

Many of the World Bank's proposed labor reforms for former communist governments aimed to redefine the functions of enterprises in order to establish greater labor mobility. Specifically, this involved reforms to break the existing link between social services and employment. Under the Soviet system non-wage social benefits were widely available, and managers often used non-monetary 'fringe' benefits as a way of rewarding particular employees (Namazie 2003a: 4). Workers' non-wage benefits covered a wide range of services, and could include access to housing, health services, child care, educational facilities, sanatorium visits, vacation homes, children's summer camps, sport and cultural facilities, and subsidized canteens. In Kazakhstan, for example, the Bank estimated that these 'in-kind' benefits comprised more than 40 per cent of total compensation to workers in 1992 (World Bank 1995b: 2, 5). While the World Bank noted that such benefits had helped to establish a large degree of income security for workers under the Soviet system, it viewed this 'social welfare' function of enterprises as imposing inefficient administrative and financial costs on firms. The Bank also argued that when non-wage benefits were available to all workers in an enterprise this prevented the establishment of a strong link between employees' rewards and individual work effort, and discouraged labor mobility because of the connection between job stability and access to benefits (World Bank 1994a: 1–2).

The World Bank therefore recommended that governments monetize social services, and establish uniform standards for service provision within each city. The Bank suggested that states could rationalize the provision of social services either through transferring the ownership, management, and provision of non-wage social benefits from enterprises to local governments and private companies, or through calculating the cash value of benefits and negotiating performance contracts with enterprises for the continued provision of services (World Bank

1994c: 18–20). In addition to changes to these constraints on labor mobility, the World Bank wanted governments to remove the *propiska* system of regional permanent residence permits from job eligibility criteria and to privatize housing.

Managing social risk

The third core area of labor reform the World Bank wanted Central Asian governments to adopt involved the creation of new methods to manage the social risks of unemployment and poverty. These embodied very different normative principles about legitimate government functions *vis-à-vis* firms, and aimed to demarcate state responsibilities for regulating labor practices from state responsibilities for providing social assistance. The World Bank wanted governments to remove implicit or explicit subsidies to enterprises and universal consumer goods subsidies, and to establish a clear distinction between *social insurance*, based on a link between individual contributions and benefits, and *social assistance* to the most vulnerable groups.

From the World Bank's perspective, while consumer subsidies may alleviate inequalities in the distribution of wealth they risk undermining the efficient functioning of markets because they distort price signals, can cause people to over-consume subsidized goods, and are a significant drain on government budgets. The World Bank therefore advised governments to shift from universal consumer goods subsidies to targeted systems of financial transfers to the poor. The Bank's main objectives were to make the system more cost-efficient through lessening the fiscal cost to the state and more effective by enhancing the delivery of assistance to the poor. Furthermore, the state previously underwrote workers' employment security by extending large subsidies to enterprises, either in the form of subsidized credit at negative real interest rates or through the subsidization of key inputs such as energy. The World Bank wanted governments to change these credit practices in order to enhance financial intermediation, to impose hard budget constraints on firms, and to impose greater financial transparency on firms' balance sheets and on government budgets. The Bank wanted markets to determine credit allocation rather than governments, based on standardized assessments of firm creditworthiness such as the ability to service debt. With regard to energy subsidies, the Bank recommended that governments liberalize price controls to allow energy prices to reflect production costs or their trade value (World Bank 1994d: ii–vii).

While the Soviet system did not distinguish between social insurance and social assistance benefits, the World Bank encouraged governments to establish a distinction between, on the one hand, unemployment benefits, pensions, and sickness benefits (social insurance) and, on the other hand, family allowances, maternity benefits, and consumer subsidies (social assistance). Like other reforms, the Bank wanted these changes to social protection methods in order to redefine the role of the state in the economy. For example, the Bank suggested that, while the state should provide targeted social assistance funded from general revenues, social insurance benefits should become self-financing and could involve private enterprises (World Bank 1994a: 57). The World Bank emphasized that governments should target social assistance at the poor. This required establishing new techniques for identifying poor households, and developing a hypothetical minimum subsistence level so that policy-makers could estimate an effective level of social assistance (World Bank 1994a: 54). To complement this approach to social assistance, the Bank advised governments to rationalize the 'insurance' component of their social protection systems in order to make social insurance benefits self-financing; that is, to link the benefits people can access over time (whether unemployment, sickness, or pension payments) to the previous payment of individual contributions (World Bank 1994b: 21). As with other Bank-supported changes, therefore, the underlying objectives of the Bank's recommended social insurance reforms included rationalizing and increasing the transparency of government expenditures, as well as devolving responsibility for economic choices from states to individuals (see also Matthew Watson's chapter in this volume).

Central Asian responses to the World Bank's reforms and the limits of institutional isomorphism

Despite similarities in the institutional legacies they inherited from the Soviet Union, Central Asian states adopted different economic policy trajectories during the 1990s to respond to their post-independence challenges (Pomfret and Anderson 2001). These responses appear to reflect in part policy-makers' strategic development of distinctive reform programs, as well as *ad hoc* responses to their different immediate social, economic, and political problems. Despite the World Bank's efforts to promote a high degree of institutional isomorphism for the regulation of labor practices in Central Asia as outlined above, in pursuit of their own interests and in response to their country's immediate priorities and circumstances Central Asian policy-makers engaged in a process of translation to produce institutional change. That is, policy-makers recombined Soviet-era institutional forms and practices in Central Asia (which in turn developed from a hybrid of both pre-Soviet and Soviet institutions) with elements of new institutional ideas and practices advocated by external international actors (Luong 2004). When policy-makers attempt to translate institutional change into domestic contexts, this process of modifying external ideas about institutional change involves domestic contestation that can alter the form of institutions and the practices that eventually develop. Although institutional translation occurred in each of these three countries as policy-makers responded to new economic challenges after independence, the degree of continuity with existing institutional forms and the fashion in which governments recombined them with new institutional ideas was different in each context. Kyrgyzstan came closest in the region to adopting a World Bank-'friendly' range of institutional changes, followed closely by Kazakhstan. Uzbekistan resisted much international advice, adopting some formal institutional changes while attempting to maintain an extensive role for the state in managing economic change.

Kazakhstan

At independence, Kazakhstan inherited favorable export opportunities due to a rich endowment of raw resources including oil, gas, and minerals. The Kazakh government moved quickly in some areas to establish an institutional environment for a market economy, while moving in a more *ad hoc* fashion towards creating the institutional parameters for a flexible labor market. In January 1992, for example, the government liberalized the bulk of prices from administrative controls (approximately 80 per cent of wholesale prices and 90 per cent of consumer prices); a measure that by World Bank estimates resulted in a 1,600 per cent rise in prices from December 1991 to December 1992. Hyperinflation in Kazakhstan and the other former Soviet republics affected labor practices because it increased the relative value of workers' non-monetary benefits, which offered some protection to people as their cash incomes rapidly declined and the effectiveness of minimum wage rates dissipated (World Bank 1993c: 14–15). In response to continuing economic contraction and hyperinflation in 1993 (when inflation averaged 1,400 per cent), the Kazakh government tightened remaining price regulations. Using an indirect system to influence prices through state procurement, anti-monopoly pricing, and directed credit practices, the government influenced an estimated 40 per cent of economic activity, aiming to protect public welfare during rapid economic change. Many managers notionally retained workers on payrolls to allow them continued access to non-wage benefits and to enable cash-strapped enterprises to avoid high redundancy payouts.

The government thus responded to the economic crisis with methods that were already familiar to policy-makers, shifting back to the pursuit of output and employment maintenance objectives at the expense of monetary stabilization and structural adjustment aims. This involved demand-based labor policies, including allocating credit through the central bank to alleviate firms' cash flow problems and providing implicit consumer subsidies to maintain household incomes (Verme 1998: 25). The World Bank argues that these practices were counterproductive because, by enabling significant wealth-transfers to groups that had privileged access to rationed goods and other administrative controls, they stimulated rent-seeking activities and contributed to the growth of an informal economy (World Bank 1994c: 2–8). Despite these substantial costs, this early contestation of the World Bank's preferred reforms by the government, workers, and managers arguably alleviated some of the extreme deprivation that people faced because of the lack of a functioning social safety net. Government employment figures suggest that aggregate employment declined by 13 per cent from 1990–6 compared with a 40 per cent decline in economic output during that period, although these figures do not include a potentially large number of unemployed workers who chose not to register with the Employment Service (Verme 1998: 18–23).

In the second half of the 1990s, the Kazakh government moved closer to the World Bank's preferred standards of labor regulation, supported by Bank reform programs. After 1993, the government began to remove methods that aimed at job creation, job security, and income maintenance through demand-based policies and the provision of non-wage benefits through enterprises (Verme 1998: 31–2). Moreover, the government's privatization of public enterprises greatly reduced public employment, which declined from 86.6 per cent in 1990 to 34.6 per cent in 1996 (Verme 2000: 699). Nevertheless, workers continued to contest the attempt to establish unemployment as an inevitable fact of economic life in Kazakhstan, using 'hidden' practices that included taking unpaid vacation or accepting very low wages for part-time work. These practices allowed many people to remain formally employed, which diminished their cash incomes but enabled continued access to some non-wage social services. Such methods also allowed workers who were unfamiliar with the personal embarrassment and decline in status associated with unemployment to avoid some of this social stigma, and to avoid relying on government unemployment benefits that were set at inadequate levels given rapid increases in the cost of living (World Bank 1995c).

In terms of social protection, Kazakhstan has been the regional leader in adopting the World Bank's preferred reforms in some areas. For example, the Pension Reform Act in 1998 established a new pension system that included both public and private components, and within two years contributions to private funds had increased to 45 per cent of total contributions (Alam and Banerji 2000: 11). Nevertheless, the high number of workers involved in the informal labor sector suggests that the scope of the government's formal institutions may exclude many people. Many people in Central Asia have sought income from 'informal' work in order to supplement low or non-existent wages. Informal work can include income-generating activities that are entirely separate from formal employment agreements and conditions, and additional income-generating activities that may take place within a formal employment setting (Namazie 2003b). Under Kazakhstan's new pension system, the government calculates benefits based on people's individual social insurance contributions through their place of formal employment. The system therefore excludes many workers who retired after 1998 but did not meet the eligibility criteria due to their reliance on informal labor activities (World Bank 2004: 14, 44). For some people, social transfers provided through family or clan networks may have alleviated this gap between the aims of the government's formal institutional changes and people's individual circumstances. For example, the World Bank estimated that private transfers in Kazakhstan in 1998 were more than double the amount of all government financial transfers excluding pensions (World Bank 1998: 26). International non-governmental organizations, religious organizations, and charities provided some of this support, but this indicates the significant role that clans in Kazakhstan have played in mediating the effects of the government's formal institutional reforms.

The Kyrgyz Republic

The Kyrgyz Republic faced severe economic constraints following independence, including few exportable raw resources and economic shocks caused by trade disruptions and the end of financial transfers from Moscow. The Kyrgyz government moved relatively quickly to change its institutional environment, with the aim of encouraging the development of a flexible labor market. In the early 1990s, however, the government encouraged enterprises to maintain existing relative pay differences among workers, who continued to participate directly in enterprise wage decisions. Kyrgyz policy-makers also continued to maintain the *propiska* system, which restricted the geographical area where individuals could work, and labor legislation adopted in 1991 retained formal guarantees of employment for some social groups, such as youth, single mothers and mothers with a large number of dependent children, workers close to the pension age, invalids, and others (World Bank 1993b: 98–101).

This approach to maintaining the demand for labor altered within a few years of independence, when the Kyrgyz government proceeded to introduce a greater range of the formal reforms promoted by the World Bank. This included both administrative reforms to change the functions, technical methods, and organizational cultures of state agencies responsible for labor regulation, and specific formal policy changes. Key labor policy shifts included allowing enterprises to set wage rates, some easing of legal restrictions on labor movement, privatizing housing, targeting social assistance benefits, separating social assistance support from social insurance, imposing hard credit constraints on enterprises to facilitate financial transparency and labor turnover, and introducing cost-recovery measures to workers' non-wage benefits and training programs (World Bank 1994b).

Like Kazakhstan, the privatization of enterprises rapidly reduced the government's direct role in managing employment, with public employment declining from 74 per cent in 1991 to 27.5 per cent in 1996. Combined with rising unemployment, underemployment, and the growth of a low-wage informal sector, the 'downsizing' of the state's role quickly increased the dispersion of wage rates (Vladimir and Heinrich 1999: 9). While the government adopted many of the World Bank's preferred labor reforms throughout the 1990s, however, a large implementation gap developed between the legal changes the World Bank achieved and actual labor practices. Although the government dismantled most of the protections of the Soviet system and replaced many of these with labor institutions and policies based on the Bank's preferred standards, for many people the new labor institutions were mostly paper constructions that provided limited substantive assistance. These formal changes perhaps impeded rather than aided the Bank's efforts to construct an efficient and effective labor market. According to the Kyrgyz Poverty Monitoring Survey, for example, 50 per cent of workers in the Kyrgyz Republic in 1998 did not have a written employment contract. While Kyrgyz labor legislation prohibits employment without a written contract, this figure suggests the pervasiveness of informal employment in the economy, and highlights the large number of people who do not have guaranteed access to paid vacation, sick leave, and other rights and protections specified in current labor legislation (Bernabè and Kolev 2003: 26–7).

From within the World Bank, the Operations Evaluation Department (OED), the Bank's formally independent unit for the assessment of its activities, has concluded that Bank staff in the 1990s sometimes designed reform programs and made recommendations for Kyrgyzstan based on existing economic reform templates from other countries. This included transplanting reform models from East Central Europe and Russia without taking into account the significance of Kyrgyzstan's particular circumstances, or the country's existing formal and informal institutions. The OED suggests that the Bank's use of a standard template for Kyrgyzstan contributed to the expectations of Bank staff that labor changes would develop in a similar fashion to countries in Eastern Europe. This led staff to assume that straightforward changes in formal policies would change people's economic behavior in the fashion desired by the Bank. Moreover, the OED notes the path-dependent effect of the Bank's initial assumptions and predictions, and points out that during the 1990s Bank staff were reluctant to acknowledge that the government often could not implement formal economic reforms on the shop floor. According to the OED, this implementation gap resulted in part from the Bank's lack of understanding about the country's extant economic and social processes. While the OED suggests that the World Bank itself could have done little to establish effective new institutions and to change people's behavioral patterns, this highlights the limits of the Bank's capacity to diffuse homogenous formal institutions. To get around this problem, the OED recommends that the World Bank's future approach should attempt to take greater account of the influence of clan politics in the Kyrgyz Republic, which has undermined the government's ability to implement top-down structural changes, and to build reforms where possible upon existing formal and informal institutions (World Bank Operations Evaluation Department 2001: 15–20).

Uzbekistan

Uzbekistan also faced similar challenges to its neighbors as policy-makers attempted to construct a stable national economy. Because Uzbekistan's economy depends largely on cotton exports, however, rising world cotton prices in the first half of the 1990s provided the new state with immediate export revenues that were totally lacking in Kyrgyzstan, while the time it took to develop Kazakhstan's oil sector put the Uzbek government in an initially more favorable position (Pomfret and Anderson 2001: 187–8). In comparison with the governments of Kyrgyzstan and Kazakhstan, the Uzbek government also made greater use of Soviet-influenced administrative measures, with the aim of maintaining economic and social stability. For example, in conjunction with the doubling of state-controlled prices in 1993, the government increased wage and benefit rates by 150 per cent in an effort to maintain their value (Pomfret 1995: 70). Although the World Bank estimated that real average wages declined by 47 per cent from 1991 to 1993, in contrast to both the Kyrgyz Republic and Kazakhstan the Uzbek government resisted the World Bank's recommendations to liberalize wage-setting, and restricted the increase of wage differentials in the early 1990s (World Bank 1993a: 103).

Uzbekistan nonetheless adopted some of the formal changes advocated by the World Bank. The Uzbek government moved quickly to privatize housing, transferring approximately 85 per cent of all state ownership titles to housing occupants at the end of 1993, changes the Bank expected would encourage labor mobility and labor shedding by public enterprises (World Bank 1994d: 3–4). Furthermore, the 1992 Law on Employment of the Population formally eliminated state guarantees of employment, and established an employment service and other agencies to deliver unemployment benefits and to finance retraining schemes. Despite these changes, registered unemployment only accounted for 0.5 per cent of the labor force at the end of 1993, because enterprises preferred to use underemployment practices such as placing employees on unpaid leave and shorter work shifts. The government also maintained most elements of the Soviet pension system during the 1990s (IMF 1998: 91), and developed demand-based labor policies and strict employment protection legislation against the Bank's advice. Although it is difficult to estimate aggregate public employment levels in Uzbekistan with confidence, from similar levels of public employment in 1990–1 to Kyrgyzstan and Kazakhstan, public employment has decreased more gradually in Uzbekistan during the first half of the 1990s. Estimates by the Bank, for example, suggest that the share of state employment declined by only 3.4 per cent in 1992 and a further 2 per cent in 1993. While informal labor activities also increased in Uzbekistan following independence, this did not appear to increase to the same extent as in Kyrgyzstan and Kazakhstan (World Bank 1994a: 20–3).

One of the Uzbek government's stated objectives throughout the 1990s was to avoid high registered unemployment, which policy-makers associated with the possibility of widespread social instability. To maintain employment levels, the state translated formal institutional changes that the government had previously adopted with the World Bank's advice to achieve labor policies that conflicted with the Bank's preferred standards. For example, in addition to providing benefit payments and helping people find employment vacancies, the functions of Uzbekistan's employment service included measures aimed at creating new jobs (through allocating low-interest loans to enterprises that took on new employees), financial support to promote the growth of small and medium enterprises, finance for public works programs, and placing unemployed workers on training schemes with state guarantees of a future job (World Bank 1994a: 26–33).

Because of the government's approach, Uzbekistan's relations with international organizations such as the IMF and the World Bank were difficult during the 1990s. While the government increasingly adopted World Bank-'friendly' reforms during 1994–6, relations with both the IMF and the Bank worsened at the end of 1996 following the introduction of a range of policy changes in response to a decline in export revenues as the trade price of cotton dropped (Pomfret and Anderson 2001: 189). These changes included new price controls on food, higher import tariffs, and the establishment of a complex system of multiple exchange rates (World Bank 1999: 4, 9). In addition to other aims, the government intended these policy shifts to promote export-oriented industries that could create new jobs, as well as to sustain household living standards. While emphasizing the economic costs of these arrangements, the World Bank acknowledged that the government's multiple currency practices and associated measures did contribute to supporting household welfare (World Bank 1999: 19,

21, 24). During the latter half of the 1990s, Uzbek policy-makers continued either to resist the Bank's preferred reforms outright or to adapt them to meet objectives that the Bank opposed. While the Uzbek experience in the decade following independence indicates that member states can sometimes continue to contest the World Bank's preferred institutional and policy changes over a sustained period, for Uzbekistan this approach was not without substantial economic, social, and political costs. These costs include exploitative labor conditions in the cotton industry in Uzbekistan, a decline and withdrawal of some foreign direct investment following the introduction of multiple currency practices in 1996, less financial support from international organizations compared with other former Soviet republics, and increasing public discontent with the government's approach to economic reform (Hopf 2002a). Nevertheless, the difficulty of distinguishing the effects of Uzbekistan's post-Soviet economic policies from the economic consequences of the country's initial circumstances at independence (see Taube and Zettelmeyer 1998) makes it hard to determine with confidence whether the costs of formally resisting the World Bank's reforms were greater or less than the likely costs of compliance.

Conclusion

The World Bank's role in the process of post-communist change in Central Asia has been to communicate 'global' ideas to national political elites about appropriate economic practices. The Bank's efforts to promote institutional isomorphism aimed to change people's everyday behavior, in accordance with global standards of market civilization about labor practices. This chapter suggests that although pressure from an international actor such as the World Bank can influence policy-makers to adopt the formal shells of new economic institutions, when governments attempt to translate change into domestic contexts people are able to use existing informal institutions and practices to resist formal changes (see also Peter Larmour's chapter in this volume). This is not to suggest that the ability of states to resist the World Bank's proposed reforms necessarily promotes the social good, *a priori*. Individual governments and social groups may regard global standards of market civilization as inappropriate because the attempt to impose changes in behavior from outside through institutional isomorphism neglects the differences of particular social contexts (see also Peter Larmour and Leonard Seabrooke's chapters in this volume). From this perspective, external attempts to promote institutional isomorphism may therefore have adverse effects on the development of indigenous institutions to manage social change. To look at the idea of standards of market civilization another way, however, some social groups may desire institutions that conform to external standards as a way of civilizing their own governments. Like the idea of modernization in general, global standards of market civilization concerning labor practices potentially offer the promise of great advantages to societies, in terms of increased living standards, greater social and geographical mobility, and rules that limit the power of economic and political elites over people's everyday lives (cf. Sachsenmaier 2002: 46–7).

During the first half of the 1990s, the World Bank expected that getting governments to establish its preferred formal institutional standards would automatically translate into behavioral change on the part of policy-makers, managers and employees in the workplace, and workers who were made redundant. Through removing some of the previous constraints imposed on established informal institutions by the Soviet system, however, the Bank's proposed formal changes may have functioned to bolster the informal social institutions that people used to contest the direction of economic change (Cooley 2000: 35). On the one hand, informal social institutions in Central Asia highlight some of the limits of the Bank's attempts to promote institutional isomorphism through formal institutional change. The World Bank designed institutions for Central Asia that were informed by ideas about human rationality as inherently individualistic, regardless of social and historical context, under the presumption that eliminating the formal institutions of the Soviet system would create an institutional space in which market structures could take root and change everyday economic practices (see also Matthew Watson's chapter in this volume). This ignored the importance of contemporary forms of social organization in Central Asia that are rooted in very different normative ideals and obligations, and embody a distinct form of political contestation that groups used to block or modify top-down changes (see also Collins 2004). On the other hand, the Uzbek experience points to the limits within which states can continue to contest global normative standards, limits that key international organizations and their dominant member states define. The government of Uzbekistan was certainly successful in using the Bank's formal institutional changes to *pursue* its own labor objectives, but this process generated public discontent and involved large political and economic costs, including a decline in international support for Uzbekistan's economic reforms.

This chapter has suggested that Central Asian governments during the 1990s sometimes used existing institutions and practices to translate the implementation of the World Bank's labor reforms, a process that enabled people to contest some of the core elements of top-down change through their everyday lives in the workplace. Workers and managers adapted practices that had developed under the Soviet system as a way of responding to their new circumstances. Whether the Bank's reforms would have created the conditions for increasing living standards and economic efficiency over time – if governments had been able to implement them – becomes a moot point for people on the ground when they face extreme economic hardship and uncertainty. By struggling to maintain access to non-wage benefits as their cash incomes declined, people were able to alleviate some of the negative effects of unprecedented economic crises and rapidly changing institutional environments, and were therefore able to contest the implementation of formal economic changes that failed to provide for their immediate needs.

10 Civilizing through transparency

The International Monetary Fund

Jacqueline Best

> Empire does not think differences in absolute terms; it poses racial differences never as a difference of nature but always as a difference of degree, never as necessary but always as accidental.
>
> (Hardt and Negri 2000: 194)

'Civilization' has become a powerful and even dangerous word in international politics. Samuel Huntington's *Clash of Civilizations* conjures up images of ancient and implacable cultural differences (Huntington 1996). George W. Bush's appeal to 'civilized nations' to join in the war on terror conveys a more singular notion of civilization while contrasting it with depictions of savagery and barbarism (Bush 2001, 2002). Such appeals to civilization evoke the rattle of distant sabers and the rumble of war. They depict a world divided.

Yet the language of civilization has also begun to appear in a rather different context and in a more hopeful tone. Recent statements by representatives of the International Monetary Fund (IMF) have invoked the idea of civilization in their discussion of the goals of financial reform. In the aftermath of a decade of financial crises, IMF-backed proposals for reform promise to both civilize the market and spread the civilizing powers of globalization more widely. Here the emphasis is not on entrenched differences but rather on the possibility of overcoming them – of bringing the benefits of a civilized world economy to all.

These recent interventions present us with two very different conceptions of civilization. In Huntington's conservative and pessimistic vision, civilizations are particular and exclusive. The IMF, on the other hand, invokes a more liberal and optimistic conception of civilization that is both inclusive and universal. Civilization is a word that contains profound tensions, gesturing to the past and the future, invoking universality and profound difference, inclusion and exclusion, war and peace, fulfillment and exploitation. The dark and light sides of the idea of civilization have always coexisted uneasily in our vocabulary and in our politics. Many uses of the concept, moreover, draw on both simultaneously. Bush's universalist appeal to a community of civilized nations, for example, depends for its clarity on its exclusion of those who would support the terrorists. Even the most universalist and optimistic conceptions of civilization must ultimately come to terms with the problem of the uncivilized.

Such ambiguities in the theory and practice of civilization have a long history. Over the past centuries both lofty ideals and naked interests have been wrapped in a language of civilization that has been at turns liberal and conservative, inclusive and exclusive, universalist and particularist. By the nineteenth century, the idea of civilization had been refined into a central tenet of international law: the standards of civilization. These standards sought to codify the criteria for membership in the 'family of nations' – the privileged circle of those who could enjoy the advantages of international law. They thus justified the inclusion of certain states, the exclusion of others, and the imposition of unequal treaties that guaranteed 'civilized' states certain privileges in their dealing with those deemed less civilized. The standards of civilization were born of both a liberal universalist faith in the civilizing force of free trade and a more exclusive and conservative belief in the essential inequality of different cultures and races. They expressed the ideals of an era and codified the interests of European states. These standards thus defined an idea of civilization that drew on both its dark and light aspects.

This chapter examines contemporary parallels with the concept of 'standards of civilization'. By returning to this earlier moment in the history of international politics, I seek to shed some light on the idea of civilization today. Specifically, I seek to understand what role this potent idea plays in recent IMF proposals for international financial reform. Together with the World Bank, the Fund has recently begun to introduce a wide range of universal standards in the areas of finance and macroeconomic management. These standards seek to define 'good' economic behavior in a broad range of different areas. The fact that they are being justified in the name of 'civilizing globalization' suggests, though, that they are more than that – that they may in fact constitute a new definition of standards of civilization.

What could the centuries-old discourse of 'standards of civilization' tell us about financial governance today? I will suggest that, in spite of important differences, significant parallels do exist between then and now, both in the ideas and the interests that have helped to shape the concept of civilization. A philosophical commitment to the civilizing role of a free-market economy plays a crucial role in both nineteenth-century and current conceptions of civilization. At the same time, both conceptions rely on a particular moral appeal to both civilizers and those who are to be civilized. Both discourses appear within the context of a globalizing world economy and help to foster the progress of globalization. Finally, both appeals to civilization bear the marks of power, working to the advantage of certain political interests and to the disadvantage of others.

This chapter begins by discussing the IMF's recent talk of 'civilizing globalization' in the context of proposals for reforming the international financial architecture, focusing in particular on the development of universal standards for good financial governance. I then explore the parallels and discontinuities between the past and the present. Ultimately, I will argue, recent proposals for international financial reform do in fact constitute an effort to impose a new set of standards of civilization. Moreover, the parallels between nineteenth-century and contemporary ideas of civilization should be of some concern. This study suggests that the dark and light conceptions of civilization are not as separate as they first seem in current debates. While we may have long ago formally rejected as racist the distinctions between savage and civilized that underpinned nineteenth-century standards of civilization, such implicit moral hierarchies continue to haunt current conceptions of economic civilization.

Civilizing globalization

While they were a creature of the nineteenth century, the standards of civilization did survive well into the twentieth century in various forms. After the First World War, the League of Nations set conditions on the recognition of certain states. Various treaties also ensured that states like Czechoslovakia, Poland, Austria, and Hungary protected minorities and guaranteed foreigners' freedom of transit and commerce (Hall 1924: 61–3). Thus, over time, more nations were included in the family of nations, if often with conditions attached. At the same time, extraterritorial provisions were gradually weakened in Siam, Turkey, and elsewhere. While China appealed to have its extraterritorial provisions lifted in the 1920s, the unequal treaty was only finally abrogated in 1942 after the bombing of Pearl Harbor (Hall 1924: 61; Gong 1984: 161). In fact, it was the experience of the Second World War that finally signaled the decline of the idea of standards of civilization. In the aftermath of the war, the growing global movement for decolonization condemned the standards as Eurocentric and imperialist. Meanwhile, Europeans were forced to come to terms with their own capacity for inhumanity. The Holocaust, the bombing of Dresden, Hiroshima and Nagasaki: all raised serious doubts about the West's claim to civilizational superiority. The language of standards of civilization thus slipped out of our political vocabulary.

Has the idea of standards of civilization been resurrected today? Jack Donnelly has suggested that its clearest modern equivalent is the movement for human rights. He suggests that the exclusive concept of civilization central to nineteenth-century standards has given way to a more inclusive and positive conception (Donnelly 1998). While the parallels that Donnelly points out are persuasive, they only tell part of the story. The nineteenth-century standards of civilization possessed a very important economic dimension, both in their conception and in their implementation. If we are to look for contemporary parallels, we should therefore pay some attention to economic ideas and policies to see whether the idea of standards of civilization has re-emerged.

In fact, we can find a parallel concept in contemporary debates about the reform of international economic governance. In the aftermath of the financial crises of the past decade, financial leaders, policy-makers, and scholars have all sought to develop a plan for reforming the international financial system. For their part, the IMF's representatives have developed a program that hinges on the introduction of new international standards with which all states should comply. The reappearance of the idea of universal standards has been discussed elsewhere (Eichengreen 1999; Kenen 2001; Gong 2002). What has not been noted, however, is the extent to which this return to standards has been framed explicitly in civilizational terms. In different ways, several of the major IMF figures have turned to the language of civilization to characterize and justify the proposed changes to the financial governance.

We can find the most comprehensive vision of standards of civilization in the speeches of Michel Camdessus. It was Camdessus who, towards the end of his tenure as Managing Director of the IMF, first championed the idea of universal standards. In a series of speeches and press conferences in 1998 and 1999, Camdessus presented these standards in the language of civilization, calling on the international community to help in the task of 'civilizing globalization' (Camdessus 1999c). What is the idea of civilization implicit in his vision for a reformed financial system? At one level, it is an international conception. Thus Camdessus calls on states 'to do at a world level what each of our countries has done during the last century: to establish order, discipline, and civilization, if I may say so, in the working of our domestic markets' (Camdessus 1998). The international economy must become a 'civilized environment' to enable the free and secure flow of goods and capital around the world. The single most important strategy for achieving this civilized global market, moreover, is the introduction of 'universally accepted rules and standards' (Camdessus 1999c).

What are these new standards that provide the hallmarks of a 'civilized' economy? In the words of the most recently retired Managing Director, Horst Köhler, they define 'sound economic and financial policies and corporate governance' (Köhler 2001). Together with the World Bank, the Fund has so far developed standards to cover twelve different areas of economic governance, ranging from accounting practices through banking regulation to guidelines for fiscal and monetary policy (IMF 2000, 2001). The development of these specific standards is embedded in a broader discussion of what have variously been called the 'basic principles' of good economic governance or 'good housekeeping practices', which include a much wider range of political economic norms (Larsen 2002; Goldstein 1999). These advocates for financial reform paint a very detailed picture of the kind of national economy that they would like to create: it will be tough on inflation, maintain a floating exchange rate, move aggressively on trade and financial liberalization, and, above all, limit the role of the state in the economy (Larsen 2002; Goldstein 1999; Eichengreen 1999). This, it appears, is the contemporary model of a civilized economy.

To these concrete standards, contributors to this discussion often add a more subjective dimension, pointing to the need to change the culture of finance. Thus both US Federal Reserve Board Chairman, Alan Greenspan, and Camdessus contrast the bad old days of 'crony capitalism' when governments retained close relationships with financial institutions and corporations, and the new era of universal, standardized rules and practices (Greenspan 1998; Camdessus 1999a). In spite of the fact that crony capitalism is alive and well in the Anglo-Saxon world, this term is consistently used to characterize a particular economic culture – the Asian model of capitalism that involves a much more central economic role for the state than is standard in either Britain or the

United States. (See Surowiecki 2002; Evans 1989; Singh 1999; Wade and Veneroso 1998. See also John M. Hobson's chapter in this volume.) This appeal to an international strategy for civilizing the global market thus appears to have a particularly Western inflection. Moreover, it becomes clear on closer examination that the Fund's attempts to civilize the *global economy* actually require civilizing certain *particular national economies*. In a comment on the progress made to date, Camdessus suggests, 'what we are seeing in many countries, is an improvement in governance, and the establishment of transparent, *arm's length* relationships among governments, corporations, and financial institutions, as are typical of *mature*, dare I say, *civilized* markets' (Camdessus 1999b, emphasis added). It is thus not only the international environment that must be civilized, but also, crucially, certain immature and uncivilized national economies who retain a too-close relationship between the state and the economy. What is the model they should use? This is clearly set out in the universal standards that, in Camdessus's words, 'build on and offer the potential to globalize the standards that exist within the most *advanced* nations' (Camdessus 1999c, emphasis added).

A return to standards of civilization?

These recent statements suggest uncanny echoes of a much earlier attempt to civilize the global economic and political order. Yet, such resonances do not in themselves adequately establish the parallels between then and now. If we are to understand the similarities and differences between these two appeals to the standards of civilization, we need to take a closer look at the context within which the contemporary discourse has emerged.

The intellectual context

The intellectual context within which nineteenth-century standards of civilization emerged combined several very different strands of thought. Chief among them was a liberal economic belief in civilizing effects of trade that drew inspiration from Montesquieu's suggestion that 'Commerce . . . polishes and softens (*adoucit*) barbarian ways as we can see every day' (cited in Hirschman 1978: 60). A second influential intellectual current was the conservative moral conviction that the existence of a hierarchy of civilizations created for the civilized states a moral responsibility to treat empire as 'a sacred trust' that was not to be abused (Pagden 2001). These liberal and conservative ideas combined with a new positivist certitude regarding the scientific laws of the world, be they economic, legal, or racial (Alexandrowicz 1973; Hall 1924; Lorimer 1883; Foucault 1970). This was a conception of civilization whose imaginative power was not diminished by its internal tensions – as inclusive and exclusive, historical and essentialist, light and dark conceptions of civilization all helped shape the standards of civilization.

In spite of the many years that separate us from the nineteenth century, we are nonetheless very much its intellectual heirs. It should not therefore come as a surprise that there are important parallels in the philosophical strands that inform the idea of civilization then and now. One of the most obvious of these is the central role of liberal political thought and *laissez-faire* economic theory and practice. While the nineteenth-century faith in the value of free-market economics took a serious beating during the Great Depression and the early post-war years, it has regained much of its former glory in economic and political circles in the past two decades (Best 2005, 2003a). Adam Smith and David Ricardo are once again the first names in a canon of economic theory that represents the discipline as a gradual refinement of the insight into the value of free-market society (see also Mlada Bukovansky's and Matthew Watson's chapters in this volume).

At the heart of contemporary new-classical economic theory is a conviction in the benefits of liberalizing economic relations – of significantly reducing national controls on international trade, finance, and investment (Best 2003a; Grabel 2000). In international finance, this conviction takes the form of a belief in the universal gains to be achieved by liberalizing finance, and thus eliminating controls over the movement of capital around the world (Eatwell 1997). While recent IMF proposals to reform financial governance have sought to mitigate some of the more destabilizing effects of this process, the liberalization of finance still remains the cornerstone of their vision of international economic governance and their efforts to implement it through the development of international standards. A belief in the social as well as economic value of a free-market society links past and present conceptions of the standards of civilization. Fund proposals not only seek to civilize the global economy but also to use the process of globalization as a tool for spreading civilization, echoing the Enlightenment commitment to the civilizing power of commerce.

I have used the terms 'conviction' and 'belief' to characterize the current dominant approach to *laissez-faire* economics. I have done so deliberately, in order to both highlight the strength of the attachment and to underline its moral dimension. I have pointed elsewhere to the increasingly explicit moral character of the debate on financial governance (Best 2003b). Here, I will simply emphasize the idea of civilization implicit in those moral arguments. Köhler was the most expansive in his articulation of the moral vision of the Fund, which he has outlined in numerous speeches (Köhler 2002, 2003c, 2003b, 2003a). In describing the ethical principles that he believes should shape global financial governance, Köhler emphasizes two central concepts: solidarity and self-responsibility. The duty of solidarity, he suggests, obliges affluent states to help those less fortunate by increasing development assistance and reducing trade barriers. The duty of self-responsibility, on the other hand, obliges poor states to take ownership of their own recovery and reform (see Barry Hindess's chapter in this volume).

These are clearly very different moral duties from those of *noblesse oblige* and obedience invoked by nineteenth-century moralists. The idea of self-responsibility emphasizes the capacity of underdeveloped nations to reform their own economies, whereas the nineteenth-century concept of a 'sacred trust' assumed that only advanced nations could initiate the process of civilization. Yet a whiff of paternalism still lingers around the Fund's idea of global ethics. For while poor nations bear responsibility for self-improvement, they are not necessarily trusted with the power to determine the nature of this reform. Theirs is the task of implementing the universal standards of a civilized economy. The responsibility for defining those standards still rests primarily with 'the most advanced nations' (Camdessus 1999c). I began this chapter with a quote from Hardt and Negri on the ways in which contemporary global politics 'poses racial differences never as a difference of nature but always as a difference of degree, never as necessary but always as accidental' (Hardt and Negri 2000: 194). The same logic is at work in new standards of civilization: a state's place on the ladder of civilization may be accidental rather than inevitable, but its economic values and practices are still judged and treated accordingly.

Just as *laissez-faire* liberalism and moral conviction form part of the intellectual context of both nineteenth-century and contemporary versions of the standards of civilization, so too does scientific positivism. The twentieth century witnessed the entrenchment of positivist epistemology in the social sciences. Nowhere was that trend more evident than in the field of economics. While positivist economics, with its assumption of the law-like regularity of the economy and of the rationality of the economic agent, provides the foundation for all Fund policies it has found a particular expression in the articulation of universal standards in the idea of transparency. In Camdessus's words, 'There is a strong consensus for making transparency the "golden rule" of the new international financial system' (Camdessus 1999c). In the past few years, the term transparency has become ubiquitous in international financial circles where it is defined as adequate information. The cause of the recent financial crises, particularly the Asian crisis, it is argued, was a lack of transparency. Crony capitalism, impenetrably complex economic practices, insufficient surveillance, and poor data combined to starve the markets of adequate information, a failing that was ultimately punished with financial crisis.

Transparency is a positivist concept *par excellence*. It assumes that knowledge can be rendered transparent – stripped of all interpretive ambiguity, cultural context, and uncertainty. The ideal of transparency reflects two related kinds of positivist conviction: it reveals a faith in the perfect representability of all economic and political truths; at the same time, it demonstrates a kind of market fundamentalism which assumes that the market itself will be capable of accurately processing all such information. Together, these two assumptions promise a world in which perfect information combines with an efficient market to produce optimal global economic conditions. The promise of transparency and the goal of universal standards are intimately connected. The possibility of transparent knowledge ensures that international standards can be unambiguously defined and measured. In turn, many of these standards seek to ensure greater political economic transparency – by imposing uniform standards of fiscal, monetary, banking, and accounting practice.

While the contemporary conception of universal standards thus shares with the nineteenth century a profoundly positivist worldview, it does not share that era's scientific justifications of racial inequality. The positivism of transparent economics assumes the equal rationality of all economic agents regardless of their origins. All are equally capable of functioning in a civilized economic environment; the problem of incivility lies with faulty institutions rather than with a failure of human nature. Yet, while the Fund thus rejects an essentialist conception of economic civilization, it nonetheless does buy into a kind of civilizational hierarchy. Fund representatives assume that there is only one form of economic civilization and one path for reaching it. Different forms of political economic organization are thus defined as earlier stages in a process of civilization rather than as different political choices (Eichengreen 1999; cf. Best 2003b).

The fact that this conception of economic civilization represents a kind of cultural hierarchy is concealed in part by the appeal to the universal value of transparency. Yet transparency is not an absolute concept. It is always partial and incomplete, relative and relational (Best 2005: Ch. 6). And it depends on specific contexts of communication and conventions of understanding. In this case a few major states have decided the conventions upon which to build a more transparent form of communication, and have based them on Western economic norms and practices. In spite of their historical and cultural specificity, these standards are represented as universally valid. Yet they impose an unequal burden on economies, requiring some to conform to the norms of others, sometimes at great cost in financial and political terms. Such costs, if they are acknowledged at all, are justified as necessary for the progress towards a universal goal – membership in that most charmed of circles, the 'club of countries with mature financial systems' (Eichengreen 1999: 50).

The intellectual context in which contemporary economic standards have evolved thus reveals some provocative parallels with the nineteenth century. Then and now we find a combination of free-market idealism, a certain moral conservatism, and a claim to authority based on scientific positivism. Linking them all is a conception of civilization that combines an appeal to universality and a hierarchy of differences.

The practical context

Perhaps the most striking parallel in the practical contexts within which the two standards of civilization emerged is the fact that both eras were in the thrall of globalization. In the nineteenth century, the British Empire relied on the standards of civilization to both impose and legitimize its interests, as formal imperialism was increasingly supplemented by an informal empire built on 'free-trade imperialism' (Wood 1983; Robinson and Gallagher 1981). The combined logic of civilization and empire was no more evident than in the Treaty of Nanking of 1842, signed after the Opium War, which the British fought in order to gain access to Chinese markets, and justified in the language of civilization. Writing shortly after the signing of the Treaty of Nanking, Lord Palmerston noted: 'There is no doubt that this event, which will form an epoch in the progress of the civilization of the human races, must be attended with the most important advantages to the commercial interests of England' (cited in

Greenberg 1969: 214–15). Of course, the form that economic globalization took then and now is different: the British Empire cast a long shadow over the nineteenth century's economic expansion. Yet the processes of informal empire that emerged in the nineteenth century do share certain concrete similarities with contemporary forces for globalization. Both have sought to legitimize globalization by linking globalization to the idea of civilization.

In practical terms, the introduction of universal standards has provided considerable support for the current process of economic globalization. The standards themselves help to both widen and deepen the integration of the global economy. Like their nineteenth-century precursors, these standards facilitate international trade and investment by making 'advanced' economic rules and practices the norm. The current appeal to universal standards can also be understood as a response to some of the difficulties that the process of economic globalization has encountered, both technical and political. The financial crisis of the 1990s posed serious technical challenges to the goal of economic globalization: large-scale financial instability is anathema to the global spread of investment and trade. The new international standards are intended to significantly reduce instability by clarifying existing rules, creating new ones, and imposing them consistently around the world.

At the same time, these universal standards – and the moral discourse within which they are presented – are designed to respond to the critics of globalization and financial liberalization (such as Germain 2000; Eatwell and Taylor 2000; Michie and Smith 1999; Scholte and Schnabel 2002; Stiglitz 2002). These new standards, it is argued, will alleviate the difficulties that developing and emerging economies have encountered in their efforts to liberalize finance – most notably the massive financial crises that they have faced. The problem, Fund representatives suggest, lies not with the process of liberalization itself, but rather with the weakness of the underlying domestic institutions and practices. By civilizing globalization through the introduction of new rules and standards, poorer countries will now also be able to enjoy the benefits of globalization (cf. Leonard Seabrooke's chapter in this volume).

Like their nineteenth-century counterparts, these standards work to support, to stabilize, and to justify the progress of a particular model of economic globalization. In doing so, they also work to advance certain interests over others. The interests aligned behind the current push for financial liberalization may not be as starkly evident as those who sought the expansion of the British Empire in the nineteenth century. Nonetheless, despite claims to the contrary, there is considerable evidence to suggest that some have benefited far more than others from the process of globalization. In his analysis of the impact of financial liberalization on developing economies, John Eatwell concludes that poorer countries have witnessed few of the beneficial capital inflows that were promised, while suffering from the deflationary bias and instability caused by financial liberalization (Eatwell 1997; Williamson and Mahar 1998). The former World Bank Chief Economist, Joseph Stiglitz, suggests that the current emphasis on liberalization not only disadvantages less developed economies but also actively serves the interests of the international financial community – rather than of the global economy as a whole (Stiglitz 2002: Ch. 8). Some would argue in response that the current move to reform international financial governance – including the development of international standards – is designed precisely to mitigate such inequalities by creating a 'level playing field' with clear rules and regulations.

Yet such arguments hinge on the assumption that these standards are politically neutral, thus begging the question of the role of power in this new pursuit of a civilized global economy. We have certainly come a long way from the gunboat diplomacy of the nineteenth century when unequal treaties were the normal means of imposing the standards of civilization. These new international economic standards have been designed and introduced by an international organization, not a collection of imperialist states. They are also voluntary codes: a country may gain certain advantages by following them but is not formally penalized for not doing so. The brutality of power exercised a century ago in the imposition of standards of civilization is not evident today. Yet, parallels do still exist. For when we take a closer look at the international politics of the nineteenth century, it becomes clear that power imbalances often took on subtler forms.

The informal imperialism of nineteenth-century Britain relied in part on the asymmetries of economic interdependence: a state's dependence on British loans or on access to their markets could just as easily provide leverage as the formalities of an unequal treaty (Robinson and Gallagher 1981: xix). Furthermore, even in the cases where treaties did play a crucial role, they were often only implicitly unequal (see also John M. Hobson's chapter in this volume). As Donnelly points out, Article I of the Treaty of Nanking granted equal rights to British citizens in China and Chinese citizens in Britain. 'China's profound lack of interest in obtaining such rights', he notes, 'was conveniently overlooked, and extraterritoriality was justified by appeals to "reciprocal" enjoyment of "universal" minimum standards of legal fairness' (Donnelly 1998: 7).

Similar claims today regarding the reciprocity of the international financial system and the fairness of the new standards should also be treated with a measure of caution. While the ideal of a level playing field is a noble one, in this instance it is rather misleading. The many different economies that make up the global order are certainly not equal. The vast discrepancies that divide the poorest from the richest have created structural inequalities in which deteriorating terms of trade, chronic poverty, and escalating debt increase the asymmetries of interdependence. Such countries often have little real freedom to choose or refuse to follow 'voluntary' codes. Such subtler forms of power are also reinforced by more blunt tools of coercion. Increasingly, the conditions for IMF funding include requirements to reform domestic institutions along the lines proposed by the international standards. There has also been some talk of late within the Fund and World Bank of making the adoption of standards mandatory, which would further blur the line between power and persuasion. For example, recent negotiations for standby agreements with Ecuador, Ghana, and Brazil have included references to demonstrating compliance with Reports on the Observance of Standards and Codes (ROSCs). Rodrigo de Rato, the new Managing Director of the IMF, has also suggested that the Fund consider linking a country's access to Fund resources to their adherence to standards and codes (Rato 2004: Schneider 2003). However level the playing field may appear, some states have set the rules of the game, while others are being required to adapt to them.

By examining the contemporary call for international financial standards in the light of what we know of the nineteenth-century appeal for standards of civilization, we are better able to understand both the intellectual and the practical logics at work today. Much has clearly changed between then and now. The moral character of the argument for standards has dropped its overt paternalism, while the idea of scientific racism has been rejected (cf. John M. Hobson's chapter in this volume). The role of power in the imposition of universal standards has also altered, relying more on subtle and systemic imbalances. Yet, the presence of these few differences makes the parallels all the more striking. Both attempts to define standards of civilization have been driven by a liberal political economic vision that equates free-market globalization with civilization. Both ideas of civilization have also contained an important illiberal dimension that assumes the superior capacity of certain Western nations to define, impose, and measure the standards of civilization.

Conclusion

In a recent press briefing, the current IMF Deputy Managing Director, Anne Krueger, reveals her conception of the link between globalization and civilization when she suggests that she is bewildered by some of the critics of globalization, given its clear and universal benefits:

> And I guess, on the one hand, those who really want to claim that they would like to stay with their ancient or their old culture and civilization and old standards of living and old standards of illness and illiteracy, et cetera, that's their choice. But that's not what most of the people in the world are choosing, and in that sense, what worries me mostly is that there are people who say they are anti-poverty, et cetera, who also say they're anti-globalization. (Krueger 2001)

While the word civilization only appears once in this passage, the concept actually figures twice, in different forms: once understood as particular, traditional cultures that resist the progressive force of globalization and once as a more universal force of progress that is synonymous with globalization. The Fund's vision of international economic governance promises the second more universal concept of civilization, but ultimately relies on the first as a foil – not unlike their nineteenth-century predecessors.

Krueger's remark is a response to a question about the clash of globalizations thesis. In fact, one could read the Fund's turn to the language of civilization as an attempt to respond to Huntington: their more optimistic and universalist appeal to the civilizing power of globalization ultimately seeks to trump Huntington's particularlistic civilizations. Yet, as Krueger's remarks reveal, the Fund also relies on a Huntingtonian conception of traditional civilizations as a way of explaining resistance to globalization. The fact that she can only understand dissent and debate by identifying them with 'backwards' civilizations and does not envision a central role for them in the construction of a new global civilization is cause for concern.

Civilization remains a dangerous concept. I initially invoked its danger in the introduction to this chapter in the context of Huntington's pessimistic conception of a clash of civilizations. Yet this danger is all the more pressing in the context of the IMF's more optimistic vision of a unifying global civilization because its optimism conceals its darker side. Those who seek to introduce these new economic standards reject the racist essentialism of the nineteenth century for a conception of economic civilization to which all can aspire. Yet they have introduced a different kind of fundamentalism through their insistence on a singular and absolute model of economic civilization. In their vision of a more civilized global economy, Fund representatives have also rejected the exclusiveness of the earlier approach to standards of civilization, promising instead the possibility of a universal civilization built on the progressive force of economic globalization. Yet contemporary economic standards remain gate-keeping mechanisms, separating the civilized from the uncivilized and placing them in a hierarchy of evolution. Inclusion, meanwhile, is deferred into the future for those who are too low on the ladder of progress and therefore have yet to qualify for membership. The Fund's universalist conception of civilization is still haunted by the problem of the uncivilized. We are witnessing a return to the idea of standards of civilization in the form of a call to civilize the global economy. Yet, if we have learned anything from the experiences of the nineteenth century, it is that such claims to civilize should be made very cautiously, if at all.

11 Civilizing global capital markets

Room to groove?

Leonard Seabrooke

The use of a 'standard of civilization', a preferred form of socio-political organization, in global capital markets presents both constraints and opportunities for creditors and borrowers. When imposed, civilizing standards may change how a borrower would prefer to conduct their affairs. Creditors, after all, do not have the time and money to check every little detail and want clear performance benchmarks in economic life. At the same time, borrowers may present themselves as conforming to a civilizing standard to access capital and give themselves a greater capacity to conduct their own affairs. As long as they stay within the parameters of legitimate financial practice, the 'groove', creditors may well allow borrowers room for change in self-determined ways.

During the last two periods of intense financial globalization in the late nineteenth/early twentieth centuries and the late twentieth/early twenty-first centuries, global standards of market civilization have firmly been in place. The character of these standards, however, has differed according to domestic political relations in the dominant financial powers of the day. Such relations, in turn, provided the context for investment from Western powers to 'emerging market economies' (EMEs), those states with a low- or middle-income economy and low-investible market capitalization relative to gross domestic product (GDP) (Mosley 2003b: 103–4). This chapter maps out the historical and conceptual terrain concerning civilizing ideas about the legitimacy of financial practices within global capital markets, and investigates the relations between Western 'civilizers' and EMEs during the last two periods of financial globlalization.

The chapter proceeds as follows: its first aim is to establish the historical context for the concept of civilization and its relationship to creditors and borrowers in both the public and private realms. Particularly relevant here is the importance of moral conduct in assessments of creditworthiness. The transition from community to individual assessments in creditworthiness over the last century, I argue, is analogous to the transition from assessments of clusters of like-states to independent sovereign states. The second task is to outline the domestic sources of civilizing ideas in the 'international rentier economy' of 1880 to 1915, particularly the importance of intense social connections for international investment that sustained an explicit standard of civilization. From there the third aim of the chapter is to discuss the domestic sources of civilizing ideas in what I call the 'international creditor economy' of 1970 to 2005, emphasizing the importance of financial 'disintermediation' to the increased surveillance of sovereign states and the role of credit-rating agencies (CRAs). Finally, I reflect on the rationalization of legitimate financial practices in global capital markets and what agency EMEs have in conforming to the contemporary standard of market civilization.

Civilizing ideas in capital markets: a historical sketch

For a state, firm, township, or individual to access capital it must successfully signal to a creditor that repayment can be made without much of a fuss. Equally so, the creditor must be satisfied with how the borrower's ability to repay has been calculated according to the rationalization of finance practices of the day. There are strong incentives for the borrower to demonstrate that it has met standards of organization and self-control to pass this test. The borrower must represent itself as rational and predictable, for the opposite will only increase the creditor's concern about repayment and lead to a refusal of access to capital or the imposition of a premium on the price of a loan to compensate for the increased risk. Above all, the borrower must present itself as civil in the sense of being capable of self-control, in being recognized as a legitimate authority among peers, and through a demonstrated commitment to laws of sustained, orderly conduct. In short, a borrower requires civilization to sustain capital inflows and avoid the incivility of default. This link between demonstrating a capacity for civilization and access to capital has always been the case and, for this reason, ideas of the state as civilizer of the market or the market as civilizer of the state are of interest to the historical development of global capital markets.

According to Max Weber, one defining aspect of the civilizations of Antiquity was the state's incapacity to convert hoards of precious metals into debt instruments to allow the flourishing of a capital market (Weber 1998: 45). Centralized monarchical systems in Antiquity preferred to tax their own populations rather than create credit from existing stores of value (precious metals, booty). They also placed caps on the capacity to make private profits to maintain an arm's length relationship with, and control over, private financiers. In contrast, Roman and Hellenic city states often taxed their domestic population to pay private financiers who effectively held them in debt bondage to extract higher profits (Weber 1998: 61–4, 211, 244).

In an attempt to tackle this problem, city states in the medieval period, such as Genoa and Florence, obliged their propertied class to invest in interest-free public debt. This did not, however, give states the upper hand. In the Genoese case power over taxing and governing the economy was ceded to creditors in the late fourteenth century upon default of repayment for funds lent for war-making. Creditors – in this case of the Bank of San Giorgio – were also able to use economic coercion to secure property rights more so than among political elites (Greif 2006: Ch. 8). Private credit relations engendered a civilizing process by mitigating conflict and providing more stable ground for the enforcement of contracts. Private markets, not the state, brought more civility to the growth of capital markets.

Prior to the building of legal and economic institutions that we identify as the modern state, most access to credit was city and township based, and private authority over them was commonplace. Credit relations were typically held within what Avner Greif refers to as a 'community responsibility system', within which the incentive to default on a loan was low as the costs to creditworthiness of the community were high (Greif 2006: Ch. 10). In Western Europe default on a loan to a foreign creditor would commonly mean that the community was obliged to repay the creditor and then seek its own means of extracting the lost funds from the borrower. Private actors were in the driving seat in assessing the creditworthiness of borrowers according to their capacity to behave in a civilized manner.

Community rather than individual obligations in assessments of creditworthiness also extended to the creation of fairs for the exchange of debt instruments (mainly bills of exchange), such as the famous Champagne fairs of the thirteenth century. At such fairs communities rather than individuals would be represented, with the threat of default resulting in the potential for a community to be discredited, banned, or physically punished (Greif 2006: Ch. 10). In Continental Europe this led to an enforcement situation that we would associate today with the behavior of organized criminal gangs, with creditors hiring 'hit men' in the form of mercenary armies to enforce debt repayment from another community. Such criminal-type behavior provided the foundation for the modern state (Tilly 1992).

In the English case the state rather than private actors sought to provide the standard of civilized conduct within financial markets. The English state asserted itself during the late thirteenth century by officially abolishing the capacity of debtors to extract rents from a community and encouraging the development of an individual-based contract system adjudicated by a central state administration. This change to a system we would identify as more modern, however, was hardly automatic and evolved over centuries. Moral conduct was still strongly associated with creditworthiness at a community level. Craig Muldrew's work (1998) demonstrates that within England between the sixteenth and eighteenth centuries there was intense pressure upon communities to conform to a standard of moral conduct. Such pressure led neighbors to pull each other into line for bad behavior, and to an explosion of literature on the moral decay associated with indebtedness, drunkenness, and other social sins, to curb impediments to creditworthiness.

Similar dynamics also occurred with foreign lending. Capital mobility within Europe increased greatly and the (now quarterly) international fairs provided means for creditors to not only settle bills of exchange but also to gather information on borrowers. This increased market integration permitted long-term loans to be made according to international rather than local interest rates, which also opened up space for outrage at usury within capital markets (Goldthwaite 1998: 497–9). The rise of Antwerp as the premier financial center with deep and liquid secondary capital markets for public debt also increased the intensity and volume of trading and raised questions about creditworthiness assessments being made by close personal networks (such as the House of Fuggers) where usury was rationalized as legitimate financial practice and not morally unacceptable (Germain 1997: 36–9). As Amsterdam took over as the world's principal financial center in the seventeenth and eighteenth centuries, usury was seen as an unfair practice (similar dynamics were present in Islamic societies and their prohibition of usury as 'riba'). Financial relations should not be, according to this new rationalization, based on gambling but on moral and rational standards. As with the development of double-entry bookkeeping, which was held by Weber and others as a key to modern capitalism, one could find self-improvement through order and civility in finance (Carruthers and Espeland 1991: 41; Weber 1976: 76). Within capital markets the new mix of morality and rationalization could provide the foundations for a 'universalisation and intensification of world credit practices' (Langley 2002: 45). This new frame for legitimate financial practice grounded civility in the moral self (see also Matthew Watson's chapter in this volume).

Control over capital markets, but not a monopoly over civility, was still in private hands and distanced from the state. One group in particular who lived off their private investments in public debts, 'rentiers', had gained in economic and political prominence (Germain 1997: 42–3). This situation was prominent not only in Amsterdam but also in London and was important in preventing the extension of credit, and the deepening of capital markets, beyond personal, if internationalized, networks within the finance capitals. For credit to be extended a new set of legitimating financial practices was required and needed to be supported by the state.

As signaled above, in the English case the state was the market civilizer. The creation of the Bank of England (BoE) in the late seventeenth century sought to 'connect savers and the English Treasury' and greatly expand the state's capacity for war-making without falling captive to private financial interests (Quinn 1997: 411–13, 427). This followed the desire to develop a financial system that would make credit creation 'less dependent on individual morality' (Muldrew 1998: 329). Such freedom permitted the formation of a deeper capital base and allowed the City of London to become the world's principal financial center. Other than providing a clearing house for bills of exchange (which also occurred in the European financial capitals like Amsterdam, Paris, and, to a lesser extent, Berlin), London was unique in its capacity for borrowers to access capital for long-term private and government debt in EMEs (Germain 1997: 52). And with increased English political and economic prowess came a new need for a standard of civilization in global capital markets that reflected domestic political wrangling over ideas about both the meaning of civilization and how the English state should regulate financial relations at home and abroad.

Civilizing ideas in the international rentier economy

One significant source of England's international financial power was the growth of provincial joint-stock banks during the nineteenth century that drew deposits not only from the upper classes but also the middle classes (Seabrooke 2006: Ch. 3). The deepening of capital markets was also largely dependent on industry during this period. During the late nineteenth century the Great Depression of 1873–96 sparked a significant change in the English financial system that was accompanied by a new government policy (by W.E. Gladstone) that sought to curb public expenditure and limit the power of rentiers who lived off government debt (Ingham 1984: 130, 234–5). Both factors led to a movement to concentrate capital in London by drawing it from provincial joint-stock banks. This trend increased during the 1880s and 1890s, leading to 'the breakdown of what had been for more than three decades, an efficient national market' and the establishment of an 'international rentier economy' (Davis and Gallman 2001: 890; Mann 1993: 292). This breakdown coincided with the development of intense personal networks among rentiers for creditworthiness assessment, the rise of imperialist 'finance capitalism', and an explicit standard of civilization concerning EMEs.

A key place to discuss which EMEs were creditworthy was gentlemen's clubs, whose membership ballooned during the 1880s and 1890s, the same period when rentier-type foreign investments into EMEs increased (Taddei 1999: 23). Consider, for example, the personal networks required for investment in the Argentine Canal Company, and the scandal that followed, which are detailed in Oscar Wilde's *An Ideal Husband*. While discussing personal creditworthiness related to the investment, Mrs Cheveley comments to Sir Robert Chiltern: 'My dear Sir Robert, you are a man of the world, and you have your price, I suppose. Everybody has nowadays. The drawback is that most people are so dreadfully expensive' (Wilde 1993: 33). Georg Simmel also noticed this trend towards increasingly personal and gentleman-based networks of creditworthiness within England (Simmel 1978: 479).

Within such networks the key civilizing idea at play was one of development and modernization in EMEs through a paternalist/colonist arm's length rentier-type investment. At its extreme, the attitude here was that while 'savages' or barbarians knew the immediacy of their economic desperation more than any 'civilized' person, they trapped themselves in their magics and irrationalities, and were unable to embrace capitalism and its 'rational orders' (Weber 1988: 449–50). The maintenance of an idea about who conformed to a standard of civilization and who did not – through a ranking of peoples and their capacity for socio-political self-organization – could therefore be justified (see also Brett Bowden's and John M. Hobson's chapters in this volume). The same applied for colonialism, whose 'watchword', as Norbert Elias famously commented, was 'civilization' (Elias 2000: 431).

The idea of an explicit standard of civilization provided a clear distinction on who qualified for protection under international law among a circle of civilized states, and who could be coerced, as seen in the proliferation of unequal treaties (see Jacqueline Best's, Brett Bowden's, and John M. Hobson's chapters in this volume). Moreover, the notion that arm's length investment was part of a 'civilizing mission' provided a moral justification for the use of coercion backed by public authorities should default occur. According to this logic, default provided a key indicator of a failing to provide socio-political self-organization, a failure to meet a standard of civilization that invited further intervention from European states on a moral quest to civilize.

While rentiers and others who frequented gentlemen's clubs preferred arm's length investments, they were certainly busy making deals. London-based investment ballooned during the period between 1890 and 1913, and by the eve of the First World War 44 per cent of global investment was made through the City of London (Fishlow 1985: 394), and one-third of British wealth was now being invested abroad (compared to 17 per cent in 1870; see O'Rourke and Williamson 1999: 208). Of this, the lion's share went to EMEs that, for the period, included states like Argentina, Australia, Denmark, Italy, Japan, Spain, and the United States (see Bordo *et al.* 1999: 51, n. 57). In fact during this period EMEs were receiving 63 per cent of global foreign direct investment, while in the last quarter of the twentieth century they received only 28 per cent (Baldwin and Martin 1999: 20). English portfolio investment went overwhelmingly into moderate-to-high-risk debt securities within EMEs and was heavily concentrated in government debt and heavy industries such as railways, mining, and metallurgy (Bordo *et al.* 1998: 17). In addition to investment in colonial territories and the US, which accounted for 44.8 per cent of investment in 1913–14, Asia and Africa received 25.9 per cent of investment and Latin America 20.1 per cent (Mosley 2003b: 255). A most popular and profitable investment – as Mr Wilde suggested – was in financing infrastructure projects in Argentina.

During this period of financial globalization, financial crises were infrequent but severe. Crises in Argentina in 1890 and the US in 1893 were worse than EMEs hit by the Asian financial crisis of the late 1990s (discussed below), with negative growth rates compared to the pre-crisis year of, respectively, 14 per cent and 24 per cent (Bordo *et al.* 1999: 53–4). Given that the stakes were high, rentiers and institutions in the City of London sought to protect their investment by two mechanisms increasing their power of surveillance over existing and potential borrowers. The first mechanism was through the formation of the Corporation for Foreign Bondholders (CFB) that was initially founded in 1868 but which received a big push from the English government when foreign investment boomed. From the 1870s, this creditor association negotiated with EME governments, such as Turkey, Peru, Mexico, and Argentina, with positive results in, according to the CFB's own reports, 'enlightened countries' (Mauro and Yafeh 2003: 9). Much of this success was from a growing surveillance capacity, whereby officers in borrowing countries would send back financial and political data to London to inform investors of the political and economic situation. Such surveillance gave EMEs strong encouragement to demonstrate their capacity for self-organization, particularly as recalcitrant borrowing states could be 'blacklisted' by the CFB from international borrowing (Kelly 1998: 31–6, 42). Clearly the CFB strategy had an effect. For example, Venezuela which had threatened default in 1902 was praised in 1908 as a model to their Latin American neighbors (Mauro and Yafeh 2003: 9, 12–13).

In cases of default with no capacity for immediate payment the CFB would arrange debt for equity swaps, acquire tax revenues, or seize physical assets for sale (note that the predominant forms of investment were in capital-intensive products). But how could a private association of creditors punish a government that failed to meet a standard of civilization by defaulting? The second mechanism used by rentiers and financial institutions to impose a civilizing standard was much more direct and involved their political links with the English state. The CFB had close ties to HM's Treasury and Foreign Office, as did rentiers. For example when the Venezuelan government proposed default to its creditors in 1902, the reaction from England, Germany, and Italy was to send naval forces. Venezuela paid up what was owing to these creditors within four years. Similarly, the US invaded the Dominican Republic in 1905 and seized customs revenue, and England threatened Peru in 1907 (Mosley 2003b: 270). This practice was not uncommon, nor was it particularly frowned upon. For example, the Hague Convention of 1906 accepted the use of force to guarantee investment in extreme cases where defaulters refused international arbitration (Mauro and Yafeh 2003: 23).

But like the change in ideas about usury a couple of centuries earlier, the imposition of military pressure within global capital markets became viewed as morally inappropriate and incongruous with the idea of civilization. In the early 1900s the Argentine jurist and foreign minister, Luis Drago, argued at international conferences that 'Britain's normal, if not absolutely invariable practice has been to take coercive military or naval measures, or to threaten them, in defence of her citizens, only when these were wronged by the seizure of their property or by personal injuries' (Lipson 1985: 54). The purpose of such a bold statement was to sway global public opinion against the use of the threat of force to secure repayment. At the 1906 Hague Conference, England dismissed such calls as piffle. England, so went the argument, had a right to intervene in 'countries of doubtful honour' (read: uncivilized) to protect the property of English citizens (Kelly 1998: 43). However, at the Hague Conference of 1907, in the same year Peru was threatened, England signed the 'Drago Doctrine' (named after the Argentine jurist) that publicly recognized that the use of physical coercion was neither morally appropriate nor a legitimate financial practice. So, why the sudden change of heart? In short, the use of publicly provided dreadnoughts for private profit had become politically unacceptable within the English polity. By 1906 the Liberal Party was in government and was pursuing an agenda that picked up on public sentiment against rentiers and their dependence on profits from international portfolio investment. The Chancellor of the Exchequer and future Prime Minister, David Lloyd George, publicly argued that rentiers were unwilling to pay fair taxation for the warships that protected their private interests. Lloyd George drew upon incidences such as those in Venezuela and Peru to put forward this case for increased taxation upon rentiers and the rich in the infamous 'People's Budget' of 1909–10 (Seabrooke 2006: Ch. 3).

During the period a range of political activists and scholars pursued a 'social liberal' agenda that saw the state as the ideal civilizer in capitalist market relationships, at home and abroad, and an idea of civilization as human betterment rather than material preponderance (see Bowden's chapter in this volume). John A. Hobson, for example, argued that imperialism was a 'mission of civilization' underpinned by a problem of economic underconsumption created by rentiers (Hobson 1902; Seabrooke 2004). As opposed to CFB's use of state coercion to created 'enlightened countries' receptive to capital investment, Hobson argued that a true meaning of civilization would compel the state to intervene into the domestic economy and redistribute wealth to create an 'enlightened community' by boosting the general standard of living and permitting more time for education and moral self-reflection (Hobson 1901: 254). The personal credit networks described above were deemed to be against the broader social interest. As 'credit is an essential element to liberty' it was the responsibility of the state, not personal networks, to assist the broader population in using credit to better their standard of living (Hobson 1909: 105–6). This domestic attitude should also apply internationally and, rather than imperialist financial practices that corroded 'the meaning of civilization', international institutions should be created to embody an idea of civilization as human betterment (Hobson 1936: 211). Within England, social reform movements called for the state to civilize finance for the betterment of all, while rentiers and the City of London clung to a conception of a standard of civilization that permitted imperialist finance capitalism. The result of such tensions could be seen in the English middle classes on the eve of the war, which Michael Mann refers to as 'superloyal schizoids': at once tied to the idea of social progress and imperialism (Mann 1993: 292, 583).

Ultimately the imperialist investments collapsed under the weight of the First World War and reflected their shaky domestic foundations. Capital flows to EMEs dried up in the 1920s to 1930s, and during the 1950s–1960s more than half of all capital going to EMEs was politically driven foreign aid rather than investment (Armijo 1999: 17). As we will see below, investment from Western powers into EMEs only picked up again in the 1970s and 1980s. Financial practices transformed to become less dependent on the kinds of personal credit networks described by Wilde and others, and more institutionalized and impersonal. The opportunity offered here was that the state could act domestically as guarantor to legitimate credit access for those previously banned, and that in global capital markets EMEs could present themselves as sovereign states who asserted their creditworthiness without fear of physical coercion. Akin to the transition from community to individual creditworthiness assessments described above, the new system offered greater *potential* for states to put themselves forward as single units rather than clustered together as barbarians under a civilizing mission. In this new 'international creditor economy' the idea of civilization would become intimately tied to institutional surveillance and less personalized markets. But the emphasis on EMEs demonstrating a capacity for socio-political self-government remained.

Civilizing ideas in the international creditor economy

For EMEs the modern story begins in the 1970s, following the collapse of the Bretton Woods system due to the US's incapacity to readjust the value of the dollar to gold within the fixed exchange rate system and its support for credit creation through private US financial institutions operating in the Euromarkets (Seabrooke 2001: 61–6; also Michael Oliver's chapter in this volume). During discussions concerned with how to put the world financial and monetary system back on track, the oil crisis of 1973, where oil prices quadrupled, led enormous amounts of capital to flow from Western powers to the Organization of Petroleum-Exporting Countries (OPEC). Most of this capital, some $30 billion in 1974 alone, was 'recycled' through the Euromarkets, then lent out to states whose balance of payments had been thrown into disarray (Frieden 1987: 88, 130). The oil crisis and the move to floating exchanges permitted a massive expansion in private capital through credit creation. While the amount of long-term private capital exports in global markets was 1:1 with public long-term capital exports from 1955–71, between 1972–6 the ratio changed to 2:1 (Germain 1997: 119).

As a consequence of the above changes a two-tier system of creditworthiness within global capital markets quickly developed. Western powers could borrow directly from global capital markets, particularly the Euromarkets, while EMEs relied on international bank loans (Cohen 1981: 50). Such lending was particularly attractive to Western states because domestic 'stagflation' was impeding their profits. The syndicated bank lending game, by contrast, was simple: a bank would go in with others to provide a loan to an EME, with the logic that being responsible for only one-tenth of a loan was sensible risk management. The lending of 'jumbo' loans of $500 million and 'mammoth' loans of $1 billion became commonplace, and, interestingly, 80 per cent of the borrowers were governments in EMEs. The International Monetary Fund (IMF) and the Bank for International Settlements (BIS) became increasingly concerned about this activity, since it was not clear whether the banking syndicates were sufficiently scrutinizing the borrower's capacity for socio-political self-organization; nor were they watching what other syndicates were doing. Furthermore, Western banks were halving the amount of capital they put aside in case of crisis in comparison to their assets (their 'capital adequacy ratio') (Seabrooke 2001: 95–8). They also assumed that international institutions would not permit a sovereign state to go bankrupt, increasing their 'moral hazard' and incentive to lend more to EMEs.

The banks engaged in syndicated bank lending to EMEs assumed that the borrowing government could sufficiently trade in international markets to gain the necessary export earnings to make repayments and avoid default. However, problems of 'surplus capacity' (a glut in trade) and an increase in US interest rates (most loans to EMEs were denominated in dollars) made this impossible. EMEs in Latin America soon began to default on their loans and a private creditor association, the London Club, and a public creditor association, the Paris Club, went into negotiations with the EMEs. As in the earlier period of financial globalization, default was interpreted as a failure in self-organization. However, unlike the CFB, these clubs' purpose was negotiation and not surveillance. The job of restructuring EMEs to meet a modern standard of market civilization fell upon international institutions.

Following the debt crisis, private lending to EMEs plummeted and foreign aid rather than investment was once again EME's largest source of capital (Armijo

1999: 17). During this low point a new two-tier system emerged in global capital markets during the 1980s and 1990s. Western powers became more enmeshed with global capital markets as they initiated a process, especially in the US, of financial 'disintermediation'. This process led to the replacement of traditional forms of lending from financial institutions, like bank loans, to the increased use of debt securities such as bonds and notes, as well as investment in stocks (Seabrooke 2005b). Surveillance of creditworthiness here was overwhelmingly conducted by private actors. EMEs increasingly engaged in this process but were now dependent on funds from international institutions and private bank lending when it was available. This was especially the case with EMEs who were financially insolvent rather than just strapped of cash. To make EMEs more creditworthy, international institutions promoted a rolling back of the state from economic management and encouraged a state's self-organization through 'neo-liberal' market mechanisms. The key policy changes included strict limits on government expenditure, the privatization of public assets and services, the introduction of a broad-based taxation system (such as Value Added Tax), a low debt burden relative to GDP, and an independent central bank that could keep inflation low. Clearly international institutions saw the market, rather than the state, as the chief civilizer. Furthermore, this new standard saw the 'neo-liberal' global market as the best means to bring democratization to EMEs and, in doing so, prevent political instability. While the previous period of financial globalization saw the use of an external military presence to civilize, the contemporary period saw the use of neo-liberal markets as a way of preventing internal military coups (Armijo 1999: 35; Haley 2001: 64–5). Through market discipline and democratization, so the logic went, an EME could become civilized.

The creation of this new two-tier system and the ideas that drove it reflected domestic politics within the principal financial power of the time, the US. When the debt crisis hit, the top nine US banks had lent 140 per cent of their capital to governments in Latin America (Reinicke 1995: 142). Such banks cried foul, arguing that the US and other Western governments had encouraged them to lend to EMEs 'as a matter of public interest', and that they should be bailed out by the US taxpayer (Cohen 1986: 40). A range of community groups, activists, and politicians contested the legitimacy of this claim and argued that rather than a bail-out, any US banks with bad debts to EME governments should have a premium placed on their borrowings within the US domestic financial system. Such a severe reaction was soon legislated through the International Lending Supervisory Act of 1983 and sounded the death knell to international syndicated bank lending. This domestic political reaction was also timed during a 'rentier shift' in which excessive entrepreneurship and permissive regulation fostered domestic bank and thrift crises, furthering domestic concern about creditworthiness assessment. The subsequent reforms to the US financial system in the late 1980s and early 1990s reflected the need to tighten creditworthiness criteria and encouraged the rationalization of its assessment through 'objective' financial and social data. Within the US, activists and community groups campaigned for minority groups to have increased access to personal credit, particularly for housing. As a consequence of political wrangling, legislation was passed, such as the 1989 bolstering of the Home Mortgage Disclosure Act of 1975, that required financial institutions to take data from all potential clients about their gender, ethnicity, and age to prevent banks from 'redlining' communities they considered as not able to manage their own affairs, those not considered fully civilized. In addition, the new financial practice of securitization – where the flow of capital from a dependable asset, such as a home mortgage, was 'pooled' with others and then sold as new debt to a third party – was also becoming prominent and of great personal benefit to 'ordinary Joes' (Seabrooke 2006: Ch. 5). The domestic encouragement of disintermediation and securitization led to deeper domestic capital markets and furthered use of debt securities in global capital markets. It also gave rise to the explosive growth of institutional portfolio investment that followed the rationalization of creditworthiness through objective financial data.

The growth of institutional portfolio investment and the mechanisms through which it sought to assess the creditworthiness of EMEs provided a new standard of civilization in global capital markets. In contrast to the intense personal networks within gentlemen's clubs and the City of London more generally, institutional investors relied, primarily, on depersonalized information from international public and private institutions. Rather than an explicit discourse about how global capital markets could provide the uncivilized with civilization (as long as there was a dreadnought in their harbor to remind them to pay their dues), the modern standard of civilization relies on impersonal market signaling. As portfolio investment in types of debt securities like bonds (basically 'IOUs' with interest) and equities (shares in an enterprise) are the responsibility of the recipient government or private enterprise, EMEs were actively required to demonstrate to market actors that they have the capacity for economic and sociopolitical self-organization.

EMEs in the contemporary period include most states in Latin America, East and Central Europe, and East and Southeast Asia (poorer states in Africa, Eastern Europe, the Caribbean, and South Asia are now referred to as 'Frontier Economies'; for a list see Mosley 2003b: 104). During the 1980s many EMEs embroiled in the debt crisis were encouraged to convert non-performing syndicated bank loans into bonds, such as the Brady Plan's creation of 'Brady Bonds' from 1989 onwards (more than half of all EME government debt bonds were of this type in the mid-1990s). While for much of the 1990s Eastern European and Southeast Asian EMEs relied on international bank loans (from European and Japanese banks, *not* US banks), EMEs' issuing of bonds grew considerably in the late 1990s, from $13.9 billion in total in 1991 to $127.9 billion in 1997 (Mosley 2003b: 108). Indeed, by the early twenty-first century, EMEs were using the issue of debt securities as their key means of financing. Between 2000 and 2004, EMEs issued an average of $92.5 billion in bonds and $28.2 billion in equities per year. The lion's share of new debt issued (including loans) was by Asian EMEs with $83.5 billion and Latin American EMEs with $50.6 billion (IMF 2005: 11). For EMEs this market could provide greater flexibility and potentially more investment, while the creditors and portfolio investors had a relatively easy means of pulling out one's capital in times of trouble.

The key concern for investors in EMEs is the capacity to repay and, when there is a perceived lack of financial information to assess creditworthiness, who governs the state (Mosley 2003b: 124–7). The financial crises of the 1990s would confirm this view. For example, between 1990 and 1993, one-fifth of all net capital inflows to EMEs went to Mexico, and particularly US private investment into government debt securities denominated in US dollars called *tesobonos* (Strange 1998: 96–7). An increase in US interest rates led to speculation on the Mexican government's capacity to pay on all outstanding *tesobonos*, which then fuelled fear and capital flight, leaving Mexico with $55 billion in outstanding debts. Mexico then went cap in hand to the IMF, who were unable to lend the sufficient funds alone due to a US veto (the US owns the largest share of the vote – 17.4 per cent – on all 'special decisions' within the IMF that require 85 per cent of members to be in favor). Similarly the Asian financial crisis of 1997–8 was worsened by unrealistic expectations about the value of international investments in real estate and stock markets that could not be sufficiently verified to calm investors' nerves (Seabrooke 2001: 165–7, 180–7). Again the IMF was embroiled in a struggle with the US in trying to lend; a struggle that is fundamentally steeped in US domestic politics, particularly the view among the US public that under no circumstances should US taxpayer monies be used for bail-outs from financial crises (Broz 2005).

Perhaps as a consequence of being short on funds, the IMF has redefined its purpose from providing funds for balance of payments problems to, instead, making surveillance of economies the 'very core of the institution' (Pauly 1997: 41), and presenting itself as a 'technocratic shepherd of the wayward [with a] . . . "neo-civilizing mission"' (Hall 2003: 95). As a consequence, EMEs who borrow from the IMF have increasingly learned to 'talk the talk' in adopting the 'civilized' institutional structures without actually changing political and economic practices on the ground: a scenario that has led the IMF to talk increasingly about its frustrations with the lack of 'political will' and reform program 'ownership' within borrowing states (Seabrooke 2005a). It is also in this context that the IMF has called for EMEs to increase their reportage of their observance of standards and codes to demonstrate their 'transparency' to unmask barriers to 'political will' (see Best's chapter in this volume).

One lesser-known but vitally important actor that operates a standard of civilization in contemporary global capital markets are CRAs who seek to provide 'developed country "government-at-a-distance" over developing countries' (Sinclair 2005: 147). CRAs such as Moody's and Standard & Poor's (S&P) rate the creditworthiness of EMEs for both sovereign and corporate debt securities according to set objective criteria (overwhelmingly financial data) that further the rationalization of financial practices within global capital markets and follow a neo-liberal view of the market as civilizer. Their power is considerable. For example, during the Asian financial crisis CRAs quickly and severely downgraded Thai government and corporate debt, creating fear among investors that other EMEs in the region were likely to have repayment problems, which then furthered financial contagion. Such behavior is complicated by the fact that CRAs have a track record of only downgrading EMEs' debt securities once the crisis has begun, prior to which they were enthusiastic supporters of more investment and lending into EMEs (Rojas-Suarez 2001: 6). In addition, there is evidence to suggest that CRAs retain cultural and societal preferences, a ranking of peoples to put it crudely, within global capital markets. Asian EMEs, for example, are thought to be favored over Latin American EMEs as more reliable (Sinclair 2005: 137).

In considering CRAs, however, we should note that rationalization of financial practices provides both constraints and opportunities for EMEs. For starters, there is significant path dependence in CRA ratings (from 'AAA' or 'Aaa' for best quality through to 'C' or 'D' for lowest grade). Layna Mosley found that 97 per cent of states rated with an S&P 'AAA' receive the same rating the following year, with such continuity only diminishing to 75 per cent for states rated as 'B' (Mosley 2003b: 141). Such path dependence suggests that CRAs are not looking as closely as market actors would hope. Also, research suggests that in the most recent financial crises, such as in Asia in 1998, Russia in 1998, Turkey in 2000–1, Argentina in 2001, and Brazil in 1998–9 and 2002, EMEs were able to lessen the negative impact of CRAs by signaling financial data, such as consumer price index information, directly to institutional investors (Andritzky *et al.* 2005: 15–16). EMEs have actively engaged CRAs. During the 1990s there was a sevenfold increase in the number of EMEs who wanted their debt securities rated by CRAs (IMF 1999: 202).

As Timothy J. Sinclair's work establishes, CRAs propagate an '"operating system," or mental schemata' for how EMEs should self-organize their economy and, implicitly, their polity based on a neo-liberal model that favors the US (Sinclair 2005: 177). These civilizing ideas are powerful and provide a framework for action, but they also open up potential space for EMEs to have agency. For example, there are good grounds for thinking that CRAs, and financial market traders in general, are not watching every movement within EMEs. Javier Santiso's (1999, 2003) extensive interviews with market participants in emerging-markets trading demonstrate that the rationalization of financial practices within contemporary global capital markets is increasingly self-referential and based on a short-term trading memory. He found that a debt securities' turnover timing (ninety days, yearly, five years) is the only time of assessment for most traders, leading to trading based on key indicators according to global standards of the day and with little memory of what has occurred in the past. As one of Santiso's interviewees stated, 'The market is a giant autism' (Santiso 1999: 318). Similarly, Ezra W. Zuckerman's research (1999, 2004) on stock market activity within the US finds that as long as actors provide market signals that conform to expected standards and perceptions of legitimate financial practice, the market will not scrutinize them intensely as outliers.

While it is indubitable that the predominating structures within global capital markets are stacked against EMEs, the contemporary system places the emphasis on EMEs signaling their creditworthiness to the market rather than being lumped under an explicit civilizing mission. And while this may be no less invasive to EMEs than the previous period of financial globalization, EMEs arguably have greater agency to attract investment without the use of force and with the capacity to signal information to market actors in their hands. The same, however, cannot be said for the 'Frontier' economies, most of which are African, that are heavily dependent on international institutions like the IMF and the World Bank. These Frontier economies must follow the IMF and World Bank's standard of civilization, through the Highly Indebted Poor Countries (HIPC) and Poverty Reduction and Growth Facility (PRGF) initiatives, to effectively demonstrate their creditworthiness prior to having access to, or interest from, global capital markets.

Conclusion

This chapter has traced the development of civilizing ideas and financial practices between the state and the market, and between Western powers and EMEs, in global capital markets. We have seen a shift between the idea of the state as the civilizer of markets and the counter-notion that the market should civilize. One vitally important process to understand in the creation of standards of civilization in global capital markets is the process of rationalization of legitimate financial practices. As discussed above, morality is intimately tied to assessments of civility and creditworthiness. In the medieval period we noted that the creation of 'rational' and orderly financial practices was tied to the moral self, and that this micro-level behavior was then translated into macro-level changes with the rejection of usury as morally repugnant. Morality and civilization are, however, ambiguous bedfellows. In the international rentier economy, a moralizing discourse about the West's civilizing mission permitted investment in EMEs based on a notion of civilizational superiority that should be backed by military force.

The contemporary standard of civilization in global capital markets has eschewed explicit moral language and concentrates instead on 'objective' financial data assessed by institutions (MacKenzie 2003; cf. Best chapter in this volume). As the rationalization of financial practices is not natural but constructed by the ideas of actors engaged in capital markets, it can be contested. Indeed, moral pressure placed upon EMEs by institutions can also run both ways. For example, to garner international legitimacy, since 1999 the creators of contemporary global standard of market have sought input from EMEs (mainly through the Group of Twenty (G20)) in discussing the 'Global Financial Architecture' and financial stability (Germain 2001: 422).

The rationalization of civilized standards in contemporary global capital markets provides clear incentive for EMEs to conform to standards if they wish to attract investors. This is particularly the case as institutional investors make up 90 per cent of their investment (Haley 2001: 33–42), and the top 20 EMEs – assessed by capital inflows – attract 83 per cent of all investment to EMEs (the top five in 1997 were China, Brazil, Argentina, South Korea, and Mexico, see

Mosley 2003b: 107). One may therefore expect a great deal of 'institutional isomorphism' among EMEs who wish to signal to actors in financial markets that they are a safe but lucrative bet (DiMaggio and Powell 1983; see also Andre Broomé's, Gemma Kyle's, and Peter Larmour's chapters in this volume), and many political economy scholars have noted the extent of policy diffusion and convergence in how EMEs govern their economies (Simmons and Elkins 2004; Chwieroth 2005). EMEs, however, do not simply adopt 'policy diffusion' or international norms on financial practices lock, stock, and barrel. Rather, propagated ideas and principles go through a process of bricolage where local content is added to make changes more domestically acceptable (Campbell 2004: 65; see also André Broome's chapter in this volume). We should not automatically assume that conformity with neo-liberal institutions places EMEs on path-dependent development from which they have no capacity to deviate (Crouch and Farrell 2004).

Contemporary global capital markets are rationalized around the gathering and analysis of financial data to the extent that as long as borrowers demonstrate their conformity with civilized institutions and legitimate financial practices they may have 'wiggle room'. This is not to dismiss the great structural constraints that private financial actors and international institutions place upon EMEs to impose a standard of civilization to produce a certain type of socio-political self-organization. Many will agree, myself included, that a standard of civilization should not be imposed where it is not wanted. At the same time, we should not discount the fact that, with sovereign protection and the responsibility for market signaling in their court, EMEs' access to global capital markets provides a hitherto unavailable capacity for a state's self-flourishing with policies it can inform and shape to accord with social norms and domestic political institutions (Guillén 2001; Brooks 2005). Surely this is superior to having a foreign warship in the harbor or, worse still, being ignored. In conclusion, and to take a twist on Mosley's (2000) view of developed states having 'room to move' in global capital markets, as long as EMEs can 'talk the talk' to signal that they are operating within the parameters of civilized standards and legitimate financial practice, they very well may have more 'room to groove'.

12 Civilizing tax havens

The OECD and the harmful tax practices initiative

Gemma Kyle

Taxation is intimately tied to state sovereignty. It is a key power exerted by states over the economic activities taking place within their jurisdiction and is their primary source of income. The definition and enactment of effective and efficient laws designed to protect states' rights to tax are therefore a central concern of all states. In particular, state legislators are concerned to define and maintain secure boundaries around what is and is not taxable. The collection and distribution of tax is also considered an expression of a civilized state whose citizens contribute to the wealth and well-being of society in general (Hobson 1919; Schumpeter 1942). Both the efficacy and economic efficiency of tax laws are compromised when national or international boundaries are breached. Secure boundaries on a national level obtain when taxable income is not easily redefined as non-taxable. Secure international boundaries obtain when taxable income is not easily shifted outside state boundaries and beyond the reach of domestic tax authorities to overseas tax havens and offshore financial centers (OFC).

Revenue leakage across state boundaries to overseas tax havens has grown as a concern with increasing globalization of trade, and the advances in communications technology and capital liberalization policies that have fostered it, together with innovation in financial instruments that have enabled more sophisticated taxation planning. In particular, the increasingly rapid growth and development of each of these two factors, globalization and financial planning, is at odds with the slow pace of legislative change aimed at combating these powerful threats to the ability of states to raise revenue both effectively and efficiently through taxation (Simmons 2001). Not only is legislative change within states slow relative to the changes that underpin globalization and more sophisticated tax planning, co-operation on a multilateral level is non-existent other than bilateral double taxation agreements (DTA). This, more than anything else, is the lynchpin around which the security of tax revenues at the state level revolves. There are at present no universally agreed-to rules, language, or application of tax law that allow for full compatibility between jurisdictions. In addition, there are no universally agreed-to international tax principles. Yet without such rules and principles to define and provide effective multilateral co-operation between states, globalization and more sophisticated financial management will continue to widen the breaches in state boundaries through which taxation revenue is leaked into outside tax havens.

This chapter deals with attempts by the Organization for Economic Co-operation and Development (OECD) to establish international tax standards through the harmful tax practices initiative (HTPI) that protect states' tax bases from erosion. This necessarily entails the privileging of OECD member states' fiscal sovereignty above the legal sovereignty of tax havens and promotes a predominantly Western model of international taxation that protects the extraterritorial extension of developed states' domestic taxing rights. The chapter proceeds in section two with an analysis of tax havens' resistance to the OECD initiative. I suggest that the OECD's strategy to combat harmful tax competition has a profound practical impact on small-island tax havens and raises deeper conflicts over the norms surrounding sovereignty and private-property rights. This ongoing conflict frustrates OECD attempts to establish global standards in international tax competition with which to civilize tax havens.

Civilizing international tax competition

Tax havens and offshore financial centers have been critical in creating opportunities and incentives for tax avoidance and evasion. In 1998 Oxfam estimated that developing countries lose more than US$50 billion each year to tax evasion, and the US alone loses US$70 billion annually through offshore tax evasion (Kimmis 2000). The IMF estimates that deposits in OFCs exceed US$5 trillion (Tanzi 2000). As a consequence of the threat to fiscal sovereignty and revenue leakage posed by globalization and low tax jurisdictions, international tax co-operation at the multilateral level has taken on increasing importance.

In response to these concerns the OECD launched the Harmful Tax Competition Initiative in 1996 whose goal was to, in effect, civilize international tax competition in general and tax havens in particular through the establishment of international tax standards. At this time anti-money laundering and good governance policies were becoming key concerns of the international financial institutions. Tax havens and OFCs in particular were coming under increasing scrutiny and pressure to end their bank secrecy regimes and introduce international financial regulatory standards to combat the economic instability and international financial crime associated with globalization (Hampton 2002). The September 11, 2001 terrorist attacks on the US and subsequent US-led war on terror, with its focus on the exchange of information to combat terrorist financing, further raised the profile and importance of the HTPI.

Appealing to the principles of fairness, transparency, and disclosure, the HTPI draws a distinction between good and bad tax competition, and establishes a central role for the OECD in the international tax architecture to ensure that the integrity of domestic tax regimes is upheld and that global welfare is maximized. These principles are embodied in the initiative's civilizing ideal for international tax competition of the level playing field. The establishment of a level playing field, the HTPI states, 'is essential to the continued expansion of global economic growth' (OECD 1998: 12). While the HTPI does not make explicit reference to the term 'civilization', it is implicit in its language and intent, and its appeals to 'fairness', 'global welfare', 'good governance', and 'legal compliance' (OECD 1998).

The HTPI released its first report in 1998 entitled *Harmful Tax Competition: An Emerging Global Issue* (OECD 1998), which set out the criteria for identifying harmful preferential tax regimes and tax havens. These are:

1 no or low effective tax rates;
2 'ring-fencing' of regimes (no substantial activity test for tax havens. Ring-fencing is the practice of isolating a beneficial tax regime from the domestic economy, such that only non-residents have access to the regime);
3 lack of transparency;
4 lack of effective exchange of information (OECD 1998).

Such harmful tax practices, the report goes on to argue, 'diminish global welfare and undermine taxpayer confidence in the integrity of tax systems' (OECD 1998: 8). In addition such practices have the potential to distort patterns of trade and investment, erode national tax bases, alter the structure of taxation and shift the burden from income to consumption (OECD 1998: 14–18).

Of greater concern, however, is that such tax practices have the potential to drive the effective rate of tax levied on income from international financial activities significantly below rates in other countries. This represents a threat to the current tax practices of OECD member countries who do not wish to face the politically unpalatable option of raising revenue in alternative ways (the report explicitly refers to consumption taxes as one concern) or reducing fiscal outlays. By framing the debate surrounding international tax competition in terms of global welfare the initiative seeks to delegitimize tax havens by designating their economic practices as normatively bad (Hall 2003). This, in turn, legitimizes the strategic action of economic sanctions that isolate tax havens from the global economy if they do not agree to change their fiscal regimes.

The OECD's mission to civilize international tax competition did not receive full membership support. Luxembourg and Switzerland abstained in council on the approval of the 1998 report and the adoption of the Recommendation to commit to combating their harmful tax practices (OECD 1998). In their dissenting statements both Switzerland and Luxembourg argued that they did not believe that bank secrecy was necessarily a source of harmful tax competition, that the report appeared partial and unbalanced, and that the exchange of information should be provided only in accordance with general legal principles and respective national legislation (OECD 1998: 75). Switzerland also stated that it considered the protection of the confidentiality of personal data to be 'legitimate and necessary' (Switzerland *Statement of Abstention* in OECD 1998: 77).

In the subsequent 2000 report entitled 'Towards global tax co-operation: progress in identifying and eliminating harmful tax practices', the HTPI identified thirty-five jurisdictions that met the tax haven criteria and forty-seven potentially harmful preferential tax regimes in OECD countries (OECD 2000).

More importantly, the 2000 report established procedures through which tax havens that did not commit to combating their harmful tax practices would be officially and publicly listed as un-co-operative and subject to co-ordinated defensive measures. The first list of un-co-operative tax havens was released in May 2002 with seven jurisdictions listed. By 2005 only five tax havens remained on the list – Andorra, Liechtenstein, Liberia, Monaco, and the Marshall Islands. Luxembourg and Switzerland are not qualified as tax havens by the OECD and thus are not listed despite their refusal to end their bank secrecy regimes. Of the preferential regimes identified in the 2000 report most have been abolished, amended, or found not to be harmful after the harmful tax criteria were reduced in 2001 to just transparency and exchange of information (OECD 2004b).

The civilizing strategy

There are three key elements to the HTPI through which the OECD seeks to civilize international tax competition in general and tax havens in particular. There is the key civilizing idea that certain forms of tax competition are harmful. The key civilizing policy through which such harmful tax practices are combated is the exchange of information, which in turn facilitates the institutionalization of the civilizing ideal of the level playing field for cross-border tax activities. As the OECD has no formal powers of enforcement it relies upon a more discursive strategy to engender consensus and compliance with these key elements of the harmful tax initiative (Steffeck 2003; Campbell 2004; Finnemore and Sikkink 1998). This strategy includes the collaboration with other prominent international institutions, organizations, and initiatives, diffusion of international tax principles through existing tax treaty networks, the blacklisting of non-co-operative jurisdictions and reliance upon its own structural power within the international financial architecture. In particular the OECD maintains close institutional linkages with the United Nations (UN), the International Monetary Fund (IMF), and the World Bank. In addition its member countries include the most powerful economies in the world, which are also members of the G7 (Group of Seven), G20 (Group of Twenty) and European Union (EU).

Through its strategic collaboration with the Financial Action Task Force on Money Laundering (FATF) and the Financial Stability Forum (FSF), the OECD has related its own work on harmful tax to the broader good-governance agenda and drawn a powerful discursive link between harmful tax and international financial crime, corruption, and terrorist financing. The identification of countries as tax havens and engaging in harmful and potentially criminal activity is reinforced through the discursive practice of 'blacklisting' un-co-operative jurisdictions, which in turn encourages increased scrutiny from public and private authorities whether the economic activities are legitimate or not. These discursive practices have been successful to date in reducing financial flows to listed jurisdictions and encouraging identified tax havens to commit to the OECD initiative (Sharman 2004; Hampton 2002; Persaud 2001).

As an indication of its success to date, the OECD points to the thirty-three tax havens that are now participating partners in the HTPI and the design of a model Taxation Information Exchange Agreement (TIEA) that sets out the international tax standards to which the OECD appeals. The HTPI has also received statements of support from the G20, UN, World Bank, IMF, and APEC (Asia-Pacific Economic Co-operation). For all intents and purposes multilateral co-operation between national tax jurisdictions should be increasing, there should be a proliferation of negotiated TIEAs, and the diffusion of the OECD's international tax standards within domestic legislatures.

On the contrary, identified tax havens have refused to sign a multilateral TIEA and only a handful of bilateral TIEAs (between the US and Caribbean tax havens) have been negotiated. Key OFCs are yet to commit to the initiative, including Switzerland, Luxembourg, Singapore, Hong Kong, and Macau. Significant political resistance to the initiative has been raised by private actors and the US, who in turn has threatened to withdraw its funding for the OECD if the initiative is perceived to be 'anti-competitive'. The legitimacy of the OECD to pursue tax co-operation on a global scale has been brought into question and there exists no economic consensus on whether internationally mobile capital should be taxed in the first place. The future of the HTPI and its proposed international tax standards now appears to be in doubt.

Contestation and resistance

Attempts to civilize international tax competition have proved to be more difficult than first anticipated and, by 2004, the HTPI had narrowed its focus almost exclusively onto the activities of small-island tax havens, neglecting the more sophisticated harmful tax practices of developed economies such as the US and Singapore.

In no way should we be sanguine about the financial abuses that tax havens and bank secrecy facilitate. Drug cartels, traffickers, organized crime, and terrorist groups all use bank secrecy to conceal their activities. Corrupt government officials exploit bank secrecy laws to evade economic sanctions and siphon off desperately needed development finance (Wechsler 2001; Kimmis 2000). However, rather than civilize the tax havens in order to allow for better self-management, the OECD initiative undermines the economic sustainability of small-island states by isolating them from the global economy. This arises because it is the tax havens that are seen as corrupting the market and undermining the ability of civilized states to enforce their tax laws and achieve their political, economic, and social welfare priorities.

As a consequence of the threat to their sovereignty and economic sustainability, tax havens have strongly resisted attempts by the OECD to impose the international tax standards promoted by the HTPI. The tax havens have concentrated their resistance to the HTPI on contesting the discursive claims and strategies surrounding the key elements of the initiative. As stated previously, there are three key elements to the OECD's HTPI through which it seeks to institutionalize international tax standards and civilize tax havens. These are:

- the *key civilizing idea* that certain forms of tax competition are 'harmful';
- the *key civilizing policy* of information exchange through which such harmful tax practices are addressed and the level playing field realized; and
- the *key civilizing ideal* of the 'level playing field', with its associated appeals to equality, reciprocity, and mutual respect.

A focus on the discursive strategies through which policy ideas are translated into practice brings to the fore the contingent nature of norms and enables the study of the contestation that lies behind the construction of new international civilizing standards and their associated institutional arrangements (see also André Broome's and Leonard Seabrooke's chapters in this volume). I take the term discursive strategy to mean the way that the material world is given meaning through the construction of sign systems that enable people to identify and differentiate things (Millikin 1999; Wiener 2004). There are two other important aspects of the strategic design of discursive structures for this present study. First, discursive structures are productive, that is they help to produce the world that they seek to explain. This enables an understanding of how the OECD is attempting to do more than just establish international tax principles that regulate and constrain actors but also seeks to constitute the very actors whose conduct they seek to regulate (Katzenstein 1996: 22). The productive capacity of discursive structures reminds us that the study of policy ideas by itself is not sufficient, but must also include the study of policy implementation which constructs the social space and practices that reinforce the identity of the object requiring regulation (Foucault 1977; Millikin 1999; Wiener 2004; see also Jacqueline Best's chapter in this volume).

Second, discursive structures reflect (and often reinforce and legitimate) prevailing relations of power. This enables an understanding of how the increasing supervisory and regulatory roles of international organizations, such as the OECD, do not necessarily constitute a consensus on global economic governance but rather reflects the structural power of dominant economies to impose their will.

Contesting the idea: harmful tax competition and tax havens

The HTPI was developed in response to OECD member country concerns regarding the erosion of their tax bases as a consequence of what was perceived to be harmful tax competition. It is their fiscal sovereignty that they are concerned to protect from tax havens who maintain fiscal regimes that undermine their ability to enforce their own tax laws.

Being branded a tax haven is now considered to carry serious reputational risks, especially if accompanied with blacklisting and the threat of countermeasures (Sharman 2004). Once listed as un-co-operative, these states attract increased scrutiny from government authorities and public and private ratings agencies, discouraging foreign investment and leading to the closure of banks and accounts (Sharman 2004; Zagaris 2001c; Persaud 2001). This renders the discursive practice of blacklisting as tantamount to economic sanctions, undermining the ability of small-island tax havens to participate in the global economy despite the fact that they engage in many genuine economic activities and offer a variety of legitimate financial services (ATO 2004; Zagaris 2001b; Persaud 2001).

The tax havens appeal to their sovereign rights as independent states and the principle of non-intervention to defend themselves against the HTPI. They argue that the OECD has no mandate to act beyond its group, and no legitimacy, as a matter of public international law, to use 'propaganda' and threaten sanctions to violate the absolute sovereignty of states over their fiscal affairs (Zagaris 2001a: 524; Webb 2004). In what Alan C. Hudson refers to as the 'unbundling' of sovereignty, tax havens exert the legal right to establish an OFC with its minimal regulations and bank secrecy, and relinquish their fiscal right to impose direct tax on the economic activities carried out within their jurisdiction (Hudson 2000). The unbundling of sovereignty in response to the globalization of economic markets represents a reinterpretation of states' rights and capacity to operate in the international political economy, and is considered to be an alternative solution to the contradictory spatial logics of states and markets (Hudson 2000; Palan 1998). Consequently, the tax havens challenge OECD claims that the HTPI would reassert state sovereignty over capital flows. Alternatively the tax havens argue that it is the fiscal sovereignty of OECD member countries and their associated claims to the right to tax the worldwide income of their residents that is placed above the legal sovereignty of tax havens and their right to non-interference in the design of policies to attract foreign investment.

In contesting the key idea of harmful tax competition the tax havens also accuse the OECD of engaging in double standards by not subjecting its own tax havens of Switzerland and Luxembourg to the same discipline applied to small-island tax havens, despite their refusal to co-operate with the initiative (Webb 2004: 807). They also point to the discrepancy between the treatment of low tax and bank secrecy as harmful, yet the more sophisticated non-resident tax regimes employed by OECD countries are characterized as 'potentially harmful preferential tax regimes', despite the fact that they were designed to attract the same financial investments (OECD 1998; Webb 2004). The targeted application of the concept of harmful, the threat of financial protectionism, and the unwillingness of the OECD to override the fiscal sovereignty of its own tax havens has led the small-island tax havens to accuse the OECD of pursuing harmful tax competition for the benefit of their own economies (Webb 2004; Sharman 2004). This, for small-island tax havens, renders the HTPI a vehicle for tax harmonization and not tax competition.

Contesting the operating mechanism: exchange of information

The OECD proposes to combat harmful tax competition through the institutionalization of high standards of transparency and exchange of information

(OECD 1998). These standards are set out in the OECD model Taxation Information Exchange Agreement. OECD commentary on Article 5 of the model TIEA, *Exchange of Information*, states that:

> information must be exchanged for both civil and criminal tax matters; [and that] information in connection with criminal tax matters must be exchanged irrespective of whether or not the conduct being investigated would also constitute a crime under the laws of the requested Party.
>
> (OECD 2002)

Ordinarily, information is only exchanged between states on the basis of dual criminality. That is, the prosecution of a criminal act for which the tax information is required must be considered a crime in both the home and host country. It is precisely this principle that has frustrated attempts by tax authorities to gain information from Switzerland on crimes such as tax fraud, because under Swiss law tax fraud is a civil, not criminal, offence. Dual criminality is the cornerstone of the international contractual legal system as it protects national legal sovereignty and is embodied in all treaties between states, including double tax agreements. The principle of dual criminality is one of the critical reasons why anti-money laundering, anti-bribery, and anti-terrorist financing conventions require the criminalization of such acts, otherwise offenders can evade prosecution by hiding in those states where it is not a crime. Article 26 of the OECD model DTA has recently been updated to reflect the new exchange of information standards contained within the model TIEA. It did not, however, incorporate the requirement that the principle of dual criminality be ignored. The model TIEA also excludes the principle of non-discrimination, which is included in the OECD model DTA. This means that income attribution regimes that discriminate against investment in tax havens by automatically attributing income derived from tax havens back to the home jurisdiction for tax purposes can continue.

There is an inherent residency tax principle bias within the key mechanism of information exchange being promoted by the OECD. This is what Karen Brown refers to as the 'hegemony of the principle of capital export neutrality', which assumes that global economic welfare is maximized when the worldwide economic activity of individuals and companies are taxed in their home jurisdiction alone (Brown 1999: 313). This residency bias also exists in the OECD model DTA and is one of the key reasons why the UN developed their own model DTA that is more applicable to the tax practices of less developed countries. This in turn highlights a critical difference between the policies promoted by the FATF and FSF and the key policy of information exchange being pursued by the OECD. While the others seek to facilitate the international flow of capital through the standardization of banking and financial regulatory practices, the HTPI promotes and protects the extraterritorial extension of domestic tax laws, so as to ensure the global enforcement of predominantly Western domestic taxing powers.

The exchange of information takes away a tax haven's competitive advantage as it allows the home country to tax the economic activity of their residents in the host jurisdiction. If tax havens do not commit to the exchange of information then they will be blacklisted and potentially subject to countermeasures, which in turn discourage foreign investment. This leaves tax havens in a no-win situation. Tax havens have, however, so far resisted signing TIEAs with OECD member countries on the grounds that the imposition of obligations that do not represent agreed international standards and that are not universally applied is illegal, and not consistent with the norms of multilateralism and non-discrimination enshrined in international public law (Easson 2004; Sanders 2002; Zagaris 2001a). In addition sanctions are to be applied against non-signatory states 'without any right of appeal to a tribunal on findings of fact or interpretation' (Zagaris 2001c: 996). This renders the OECD unaccountable for its actions towards tax havens. Concerted action by tax havens against such discriminatory practices led to the OECD conceding in the 2001 HTPI Report that 'coordinated defensive measures would not apply to uncooperative tax havens any earlier than they would to similarly situated OECD member countries' (OECD 2001: 10).

There remains a question, however, as to the legality of the proposed defensive measures under World Trade Organization (WTO) rules as the HTPI is not officially recognised by the WTO as a legitimate basis on which to discriminate against another country (Gross 2003). This in turn is indicative of the potential for clashes between civilizing ideals as more global standards are added to the rubric of good governance.

Despite most tax havens having now agreed to commit to the OECD's higher standards of information exchange, mainly so as to avoid being blacklisted, they have made their commitments conditional upon the achievement of the level playing field. As Antigua and Barbuda Prime Minister Lester Bird remarked at the October 2003 Caribbean Financial Action Task Force (CFATF) council meeting, 'the offshore financial centers in the Caribbean would effectively be dead if they were made to exchange information while European centers were allowed to maintain bank secrecy' (Bird in Easson 2004: 1065). More recently, after the refusal of Switzerland to exchange information under the EU savings directive, Antigua and Barbuda suspended its commitment to the OECD and urged other Caribbean countries to do likewise (Hampton 2002).

Contesting the civilizing ideal: the level playing field

The key civilizing ideal of the harmful tax initiative is the establishment of a level playing field for cross-border tax activities in the areas of transparency and exchange of information (OECD 2004a). The concept of the level playing field as employed by the OECD embodies the norms associated with the international system of states, including equality, reciprocity, and mutual respect (OECD 2004a). The effect of employing the imagery of the level playing field and associated normative connotations is to mask the structural and economic inequalities that exist between states, and the privileging of a predominantly Western model of international taxation.

Tax havens argue that the playing field being promoted by the harmful tax initiative is far from level. On the contrary, the more common refrain is that the initiative is neo-colonialist in its intent, with rich countries of the OECD seeking to recapture foreign investment and destroy their economic livelihoods (Sanders 2002; Sharman 2004; Persaud 2001; Hampton 2002). To support their stance the tax havens point to the limited membership of the OECD and the lack of consultation prior to the drafting of the harmful tax criteria and international tax standards designed to combat them. They also point to the lack of reciprocity in the HTPI, with tax havens currently bearing the full burden of adjustment without appropriate compensation for the loss of economic activity, without the promise of OECD membership and without access to the lucrative DTA network, which encourages investment between countries through the assignment of jurisdictional taxing rights. The tax havens have sought to enforce some reciprocity through the TIEA negotiation process. In particular they have argued that they will not sign a TIEA without the negotiation of a DTA, a non-discrimination clause and development assistance.

Tax havens emerged as a consequence of the desire of financial institutions and banks to escape strict regulatory controls at home and the desire of small-island states to find an alternative path to development (Hudson 2000; Palan 1998; Persaud 2001). Indeed, the development of an OFC was encouraged by colonial powers as an alternative approach to economic development for small-island economies that had no natural productive base (Persaud 2001; Hampton 2002). In what Hampton refers to as 'mismanaged dependency', tax havens are now dependent upon the sustained presence of OFCs for their survival (Hampton 2002). The ability of tax havens to shift away from their current tax practices would be greatly enhanced if financial and technical assistance were to be provided (Sharman 2005). This would also strengthen the moral justification for defensive measures (Hampton 2002). Yet, the OECD offers little guidance in the way of practical relief or adjustment assistance and OECD member countries appear reticent to provide such assistance to encourage tax havens to shift away from their offshore activities (OECD 2000; Persaud 2001; Sharman 2005). This again highlights the inadequacy of the OECD approach of pursuing the problem of tax evasion in isolation, without due regard for the historical development of such practices or tax haven dependency on them.

Not only do many small-island tax havens stand to lose economically from the initiative, there is also a greater potential for instability if economies falter, resulting in unemployment and poverty, fomenting civil and political unrest. And, indeed, global welfare is not served by establishing initiatives that do not accommodate the development priorities of their target countries and thus undo the work performed by other agencies and aid programs (Sharman 2005). Consequently, small-island tax havens maintain very real concerns about their political and economic sustainability in the absence of an offshore market.

US structural interests and private capital

The US and private capital have also been supportive of tax havens' resistance to the HTPI, although not for entirely benevolent reasons. In the debate over what tax practices should be considered harmful, whose sovereign rights should prevail, and what is the appropriate mechanism and institutional design for achieving tax co-operation internationally, there is one country whose contribution to the debate is perhaps more important than most others. The OECD initiative is unlikely to succeed without the support of the US, because of the size and prominence of its financial market internationally (Wechsler 2001; Simmons 2001; Webb 2004). Under Bill Clinton's administration, the US endorsed the recommendations of the 1998 OECD Report (Wechsler 2001). The Bush administration has subsequently retreated from this position with Treasury Secretary Paul H. O'Neill stating that 'the [OECD] project is too broad and it is not in line with this administration's tax and economic priorities' (O'Neill 2001).

The Bush administration's stance towards the initiative has been influenced by the intense petitioning from a wide range of think tanks, tax analysts, and lobbyists who oppose the OECD's agenda. Arguing for 'ancient rights to financial privacy' (Isaacson 2004), over thirty of these organizations were successful in petitioning the US Senate Appropriations Committee to put forward a funding bill that would 'prohibit the OECD from receiving US taxpayer funds if it has tried to identify, report on, or penalize any country that encourages foreign investment through tax incentives' (Rahn 2004: 1). However, not all opposition has been from the right of the political spectrum. An influential letter signed by twenty-six members of the congressional Black Caucus (all of them Democrats) was also submitted to Congress, 'expressing concerns as to the effects the OECD initiative might have on small nations in the Caribbean' (Easson 2004: 1059–60).

Reflecting on the concerns of both private capital and the tax havens, O'Neill stated that 'the United States does not support efforts to dictate to any country what its own tax rates or tax systems should be and will not participate in any initiative to harmonize world tax systems' (O'Neill 2001). Concerned about the US's wavering support, the OECD negotiated a compromise that saw the refocusing of the initiative onto transparency and exchange of information only. This meant that the 'no substantial activities' criteria would no longer be applied to determine whether a jurisdiction is considered to be un-co-operative and 'ring fencing' would no longer be considered a harmful tax practice. Thus, offshore regimes such as the New York International Banking Facility (IBF) would not be targeted by the OECD initiative. For the OECD the US *volte-face* saw the scope of the project considerably reduced, exposing it to further claims of partiality (Easson 2004; Webb 2004).

Non-state actors have been influential not just in the US but also in their support of tax havens' claims to sovereignty and campaign of resistance. Private actors play an important role in the debate surrounding international standards as they are often at the coal-face between policy and practice, and provide insight as well as influence. As Layna Mosley has demonstrated in her study of the development of global standards in international finance, markets play an increasingly important role as partner to national governments, making the future effectiveness of international standards more likely (Mosley 2003a). Private capital reacted harshly to what they perceived to be attempts by the OECD 'tax cartel' to harmonize taxes. They accused the OECD of blurring the boundaries between legal tax avoidance and the criminal act of tax evasion and promoting financial protectionism against tax havens so as to protect their own high tax practices and tax base from competition (*Economist* 1998; Mitchell 2001). In response private capital sought to frame the OECD proposals as inconsistent with the shared norms of liberal economic ideology and an infringement of individual and market freedoms that would damage the global economy (Webb 2004). Indeed, one commentator likened the OECD's initiative to 'as much an action against globalisation as are the street protests against the World Trade Organisation meetings' (Vlcek 2004: 227). Alternatively, private capital emphasized the importance of tax competition and tax planning to realizing the benefits of economic liberalization, promoting efficiency, and warding against the profligacy of national governments (Gaffney 1998/9; Easson 2004).

The US stance towards the harmful tax initiative is not driven by special interests groups alone. The US tends to not support the development of international standards that would constrain its capacity to influence the international economic agenda. Such state capacity is derived in part by its ongoing ability to attract international financial capital (Seabrooke 2001). The OECD project directly threatens US interests in this regard because it proposes to enable non-resident tax authorities to trace investments residing in the US, undermining its tax competitive status and thus attractiveness to foreign investment. As William Vlcek explains,

> by far the largest tax haven, at present the US neither taxes the savings and investments of non-resident foreign individuals or firms, nor reports their accounts to their state of residence. As a result, some $9 trillion is believed to be invested in the US by such agents, and some fear this wealth would leave the US economy if it were to become subject to taxation at the rate of their state of residence.
>
> (Vlcek 2004: 240)

Consequently, despite the increasing importance the Bush administration places on the exchange of information in the wake of September 11, in practice it is more the *provision* of information, as opposed to the *exchange* of information, that the US seeks.

There are also good economic reasons why the US would resist the OECD's proposed international tax standards. The US currently faces very large twin deficits, an uncertain US dollar, massive tax cuts, and a war in Iraq (McLure

2005; Vlcek 2004). The potential capital flight that could be triggered from the collection of information on interest payments to foreigners, as Charles E. McLure aptly points out, 'would lead to higher interest rates, make it more costly to finance the deficit and put further pressure on the dollar' (McLure 2005: 96). Of course in the absence of US exchange of information, the playing field for international tax co-operation will be far from level.

Conclusion

The development of international standards is not simply about accepting or rejecting new institutional arrangements. It's about the construction of new identities, new relations between structures and agents, and the reinterpretation of prevailing practices and norms; it is a dynamic and highly contested process.

The OECD harmful tax initiative was designed in response to the rapid growth in international finance and the threat to fiscal sovereignty posed by tax havens and the associated rise in access to and incidence of tax evasion. In developing their international tax standards the OECD ignored the inherent residency bias in their tax model. It also neglected the historical development of the symbiotic relationship between tax havens and international finance, such that tax havens are now dependent upon their OFCs for survival (this includes, it may be argued, the US). What this means is that, although the OECD has generated consensus on the recognition of the problem of tax evasion, and by extension the very real dangers of bank secrecy in facilitating international financial crime, they have so far been unsuccessful in generating consensus on the appropriate policy practices to civilize international tax competition.

Alternatively the HTPI has relied upon the use of discursive strategies and coercion to create an environment in which tax havens could neither reject the initiative outright nor fully commit to changing their practices. The OECD points to the commitment of thirty-three tax havens to the initiative as a mark of success. The OECD has not, however, been successful in convincing other major tax havens, such as Switzerland, Singapore. and Luxembourg, to commit to the initiative. The unwillingness of the OECD to override the fiscal sovereignty of OECD member countries and enforce the higher standards of information exchange demanded of tax havens exposes the OECD to accusations of double standards and undermines its capacity to institutionalize international tax standards with which to civilize the tax havens. Indeed, it is the ability of tax havens to withhold or withdraw their commitment to higher standards of information exchange in the absence of a level playing field that is one of the key weaknesses of the initiative.

The international financial community and the US have also been circumspect in their support of the OECD initiative. Despite a few loud but minority voices both within the Bush administration and taxpayer lobby groups, very few people question the importance of information exchange in the wake of the September 11 terrorist attacks on the US. And, indeed, tax authorities have long relied upon the exchange of information provisions within their bilateral DTAs for the enforcement of jurisdictional taxing rights. Yet the OECD maintains that the principle of dual criminality, which has protected states and individuals alike from incursions on their legal sovereignty, should not hold in the field of international tax competition. This has exposed the OECD to accusations of both violating legal sovereignty and tax harmonization as high tax jurisdictions can prevail over low tax jurisdictions.

Finally, and most importantly, the economic consequences for small-island tax havens, private capital, and US structural interests have brought to the fore conflict and contestation over the norms surrounding sovereignty and private property, fomenting strong resistance to change. This renders the institutionalization of international tax standards under the current OECD harmful tax initiative highly unlikely.

Norms and social practices are mutually constitutive and change as underlying conditions change (Kratochwil and Ruggie 1986; Ruggie 1993). Consequently, in the process of re/constructing identity, authority, policy practices, and regulatory spaces in response to globalization, not only are normative structures re/interpreted and re/constructed, but also present and future conditions for strategic action are also reconstituted (Hall 2003). What this means, as Ruggie succinctly states, is that 'processes of globalisation entail a shift not in the play of power politics but of the stage on which the play is performed' (Ruggie 1993: 139–40). The failure of the OECD to institutionalize international tax co-operation under the harmful tax initiative highlights the inability of territorially bounded regulatory powers to resolve conflicting claims to jurisdictional taxing rights. However, in the process of contesting the constitutive norms of the international system of states in the context of international tax co-operation, it raises the potential for conceptualizing state co-operation in profoundly new ways.

13 Civilizing drugs

Intellectual property rights in global pharmaceutical markets

Jillian Clare Cohen

One of the conundrums of public policy is the question of how a government can ensure that health objectives are achieved at the same time that it promotes economic growth. Fostering economic growth and seeking to ensure health of a population does not always mean trade-offs for governments. However, in the case of pharmaceuticals and patent protection, as this chapter will discuss, governments are often in the uncomfortable position of having to determine what matters more – health or economic growth? In a world that has distorted drug access, the World Health Organization (WHO) reports that about one-third of the global population lacks regular access to medicines (WHO 2004). This is a morally compelling reason to identify potential obstacles to drug access so that they can be dismantled. This goal may however be in discordance with trade objectives. The potential impact of trade on health outcomes is a research area that has gained considerable interest from both policy-makers and researchers. A wealth of literature has addressed the conflict between trade and health objectives (Jacobzone 2000), particularly in the aftermath of the creation of the World Trade Organization (WTO) in 1995. At stake are two notions of standards of civilization clash. The first is the idea of standards of civilization permitting human betterment and human flourishing. The second is that, in economic life, a standard of civilization will ensure the protection of property rights and enforce contracts.

This chapter proposes that public policy, such as trade agreements, which can indirectly influence health outcomes, must be scrutinized for its health implications as rigorously as those policies that are explicitly directed to health outcomes. The WTO and the Doha Accord do provide a global standard of market civilization, with the idea that the reform of international and domestic markets – pharmaceutical markets in this instance – toward a global standard will improve the capacity of developing states to organize themselves politically and economically, and lead to improvements in health. But this intention may be undercut by economic interests that forcefully promote their agenda in international organizations.

The Doha Accord of August 2003, at a cursory level, seemed to usher in a concern for protecting and promoting health over and above trade. The Accord marks a 'civilizing' or legal softening of trade agreements in terms of their real or potential impact on health. But embedding special provisions into trade agreements in order to protect health (or more narrowly access to medicines) is not a novel outcome and is reflected in the General Agreement on Tariffs and Trade (GATT) Treaty decades earlier. The question remains then why the Doha Accord was necessary if the primacy of health goals were historically accepted? This question suggests that, despite explicit mechanisms to safeguard health concerns when trade obligations potentially can overturn them, governments have chosen, or have been compelled, to place greater primacy on economic matters than health concerns.

Health has a moral importance. because of its status as an end of political and societal activity. According to Aristotle, society's obligation to maintain and improve health rests on the ethical principle of 'human flourishing' – the ability to live a flourishing, and thus healthy, life. Flourishing and health are inherent to the human condition. Indeed, certain aspects of health sustain all other aspects of human flourishing because, without being alive, no other human functionings are possible, including agency, the ability to lead a life one has reason to value. It can be argued, therefore, that public policy should focus on the ability to function, and that health policy should aim to maintain and improve this ability by meeting health needs. This view values health intrinsically and more directly than solely 'instrumental' social goods, such as income or health care. It gives special moral importance to health capability: an individual's opportunity to achieve good health and thus to be free from escapable morbidity and preventable mortality (Prah Ruger 2004).

Government action to support the intrinsic value of health for individuals and populations should not be undercut by second-guessing these motivations in light of trade relations. For instance, a government that decides to use health safeguards within a trade agreement to protect its population may be accused of using the safeguard to protect local interests. Whether a government is motivated by concern for health, economic interest, or some combination of the two should be irrelevant as any action directed towards improving the health outcomes of its population should be exempt under trade rules as an indication of health's primacy over trade.

There is no simple answer to the question of how to align trade and health objectives seamlessly. Perhaps, because of this, the subject is a rich area for research. This chapter intends to make a contribution to the debate by demonstrating that there is a continual need for legal mechanisms to protect health concerns, specifically with regard to the issue of patent protection for pharmaceuticals. The modification of trade-related patent laws as they govern pharmaceutical products and processes has become a subject of much research and policy discussion since the enactment of the 1995 Trade Related Aspects of Intellectual Property Rights (TRIPS) Agreement. The need for special provisions for the disengagement of international standards imposed on pharmaceuticals – which hence have a potential to impact on access to drugs – demonstrates the need for health to trump trade and not vice versa.

In this chapter I try to answer the question of why special provisions to protect health are necessary in trade agreements. The chapter is organized in the following manner. First, I discuss the GATT Treaty and its Article XX, which was developed with the intent of protecting health. Second, I examine the TRIPS Agreement and its implications for pharmaceutical access, as well as possible policy levers that can ideally mitigate the harshest impact of the TRIPS Agreement. Third, I then turn to a brief review of how the WTO is managing issues that demonstrate how trade and health objectives can be at odds with each other. Finally, I conclude by proposing a more humanistic patent regime for pharmaceuticals. Here, I call for reform of the WTO so that health outcomes are explicitly integrated into its institutional mandate. The need for greater moral clarity, such as concern for a global health problem, like the lack of access to medicines, must inform trade decisions that spill over or cut across in to the health sector. As Sabina Alkire and Lincoln Chen point out, 'an appeal to moral values will motivate people to support a set of actions' (Alkire and Chen 2004: 1074). Strengthening this view, access to essential medicines has become a central topic at the international policy-making level. It is also increasingly viewed as a fundamental human right (Cullet 2003), with international human rights law placing attendant obligations on states to ensure access.

The GATT and its provisions to protect health of populations

The GATT Treaty that has governed international trade since 1947 was conceived as an interim agreement designed to protect the tariff concessions resulting from the 1947 Geneva meeting and to help ensure a more robust global economy that would encourage peace and prosperity. The GATT never came into force officially but was applied provisionally to reduce trade barriers on a reciprocal basis and to eliminate discriminatory treatment. The GATT thus can be conceived as an institution designed to create global standards of market civilization and, importantly, as a realm of possibility for the inclusion of civilizing standards in both senses of the term, through the Havana charter that incorporates a wider global governance role than the GATT provided in the end.

International obligations can mean the imposition of standards and designs that may be inappropriate and/or vastly different from local ones. In this case, often there is a push–pull dynamic between global and local standards that may lead to very different results depending on the incentive structure and institutions that must be navigated. Dani Rodrik argues that multilateral institutions need to encourage a greater convergence of policies and standards, with 'deep integration' only among those countries that are willing to do so in order to reduce tensions from the differences in national standards (Rodrik 1997: 82). Here Rodrik's 'trilemma' of globalization suggests that states must forfeit autonomy and submit themselves to a global standard of market civilization to reap eventual benefits. This argument, akin to Thomas Friedman's 'golden straitjacket' of globalization (Friedman 1999), puts forward the notion that it is in developing states' interest to transform their socio-political self-organization in accordance with global dictates for their own good. At the same time, however, they also must allow for selective disengagement from multilateral standards for countries that need breathing room to satisfy domestic requirements that are in conflict with liberalizing trade (Rodrik 1997).

The importance of permitting a government to selectively disengage from international obligations, particularly in terms of health concerns, was apparent early on in the GATT Treaty. Article XX allows for a number of exceptions to the GATT obligations in order to protect 'human, animal or plant life or health' (GATT 1947). The language of this Article is arguably broad enough to allow for its application. The intent of this inclusion was that any exceptions concerning health, which a government would seek to apply, could not prevent the import of certain goods unless it was considered a reasonable precaution to take. The Committee responsible for drafting this safeguard made it plain that they were against the use of the provision as a measure of protection in disguise. However, the likelihood was that governments would have different interpretations of Article XX according to their national interests and this, in turn, would generate debate.

For instance, in May 1989, following a suspension by the US of Chilean fruit imports on the basis of suspected food contamination, the government of Chile underscored the need for a crisis management body that allowed for consultations among contracting parties for the exchange of information and joint decision-making. This was to ensure that measures adopted under the health exception were in keeping with the seriousness of the threat. According to the delegate from Chile, 'hundreds of millions of dollars of fruit and vegetables [were] destroyed or re-exported, confiscated or prohibited from entry because two grapes had been found to contain toxic chemicals' (GATT 1989a: 24). While many delegates recognized the legitimacy of Chile's concern and supported Chile's proposal, delegates from Canada, the US, and Japan defended the right of governments to act expeditiously when human health was endangered, without being required to consult extensively on the trade impact of their actions. Shortly after this, in October 1989, the Council agreed to the Chairman's proposal that in the event of a trade-damaging act, 'a measure taken by an importing contracting party should not be any more severe and should not remain in force any longer, than necessary to protect the human, animal or plant life or health involved, as provided in Article XX(b)' (GATT 1989b: 6–7). This recommendation ensured contracting parties' right to take action to give priority to health over trade concerns while protecting commercial interests as much as possible.

In short, the tension between trade and health objectives is a longstanding conflict that has not been resolved by an inclusion such as the GATT Article XX(b) that acknowledges members' rights to take measures to restrict imports or exports when necessary to protect human health. These measures are permissible if, and only if, they are not deemed as protectionism in disguise and do not impose any more trade restrictions than necessary. The health exception of the GATT Treaty was an imperfect inclusion that did not always guarantee a government's right to give primacy to national health policy objectives over commercial interests. However, at a minimum, it did recognize the need for mechanisms to allow governments the right to protect the health of their populations. As will be discussed below, the complex intersection of trade and health objectives did not subside with the creation of the World Trade Organization. In fact, its TRIPS Agreement propelled this issue squarely into the international health policy debate.

The TRIPS Agreement: tripping over the disconnect between trade and health objectives

The Uruguay Round of trade talks took place from 1986–94 and addressed a wide range of issues, including intellectual property rights on pharmaceuticals, and eventually led to the passage of the TRIPS Agreement. This Agreement covers a range of intellectual property issues such as patents, trademarks. industrial designs, and copyright. In other words, the TRIPS Agreement created global standards for intellectual property law with real power. However, market standards for pharmaceuticals create dilemmas given that they are both a market commodity and a necessary health commodity that can prevent and cure.

The TRIPS Agreement, furthermore, requires each member state to maintain sufficient procedures and remedies within its domestic law to ensure the protection of intellectual property for both domestic and foreign rights-holders. The minimum legal obligations concerning pharmaceuticals include, first, that pharmaceutical products and micro-organisms are patentable for up to twenty years from the date the inventor files for patent application, and, second, that discrimination against patent rights for imported products is not permitted. Third, exclusive marketing rights are granted until patent expiry, and, fourth, there is a transitional period of one year, which can be extended to up to ten years, for developing countries without pharmaceutical product patents (Redwood 1995). The WTO Treaty states that 'membership in the WTO entails accepting all the results of the Round, without exception' so members must comply with the TRIPS requirements as part of membership conditionality.

The Agreement does however include some provisions that allow developing and least developed countries some 'breathing space' in terms of its applicability. It allows developing countries a general transition period of up to five years to amend their patent legislation so that it is in accordance with WTO standards. This means that all countries are obliged to adhere to one global standard, or what we are calling here a global standard of market civilization. A longer time-frame, up to ten years, was allowed for developing countries that have not provided product patent protection for pharmaceuticals, that is, countries that have 'process' patents in place but no protection for the final product. Least developed countries were originally given up to eleven years, but this was later extended to the year 2016 when it became obvious that the initial timeline was unrealistic in terms of its feasibility for implementation.

Advocates of TRIPS argued that pharmaceutical patents were required to provide incentives for large multinational pharmaceutical firms to invest resources in the research and development (R&D) of new drug therapies. But the difficulty with this line of reasoning stems from the fact that R&D expenditure does not even remotely address the needs of developing countries. Médecins

Sans Frontières (MSF) estimates that 90 per cent of the world's health R&D expenditure is devoted to conditions that affect only 10 per cent of the world's population; with priority conditional upon ability to pay (MSF 2003). This prioritization of diseases affecting the developed world is reflected in the fact that of 1.393 new drugs approved between 1975 and 1999, only thirteen were specifically indicated as targeting tropical diseases (Trouiller *et al.* 2002). Tropical diseases are known to largely affect poor populations and account for 12 per cent of the global disease burden (MSF 2001).

Detractors of the TRIPS Agreement point out that the Treaty could exacerbate the already existing inequity in pharmaceutical drug gaps because it effectively limits the production of drugs in the global market. Prior to TRIPS, the pharmaceutical patent regime of developing states was, for the most part, considerably below the minimum criteria of TRIPS. Many developing states, such as India and Brazil, had adopted an explicit policy to disregard intellectual property protection for pharmaceuticals in an attempt to be self-sufficient in the production of basic medicines and to develop a competitive local industry. Domestic producers, both private and public, could then supply their populations with basic medicines at prices often considerably lower than those of the research-based pharmaceutical industry and learn by doing so through 'reverse engineering'. As such, critics of the agreement argued that its implementation would result in higher prices for drugs, widen the access gap to essential medicines between developed and developing countries, further exacerbate existing imbalances in the R&D of drug therapies between developed and developing states, and threaten the viability of local industry by having a negative effect on local manufacturing capacity. Finally, longer patent regimes would prevent generic competition that, in turn, helps make pharmaceuticals more affordable. Generic competition will significantly reduce drug prices if the correct market structures are in place. Pharmaceutical product prices fall sharply when generic entry to the market occurs following the expiration of patents (Scherer 2000).

The TRIPS Agreement is a product of extensive negotiations and thus includes provisions within the text that demonstrate where concessions were made, particularly for developing and least developed countries that were concerned about its application on drug access. The Agreement contains provisions that may be used by governments to ensure that health objectives are not compromised. However, although there is language in the text of the Agreement which suggests that governments may place health needs over and above trade needs, the reality for many developing and least developed countries is that they do not make use of the provisions due to administrative, political, and knowledge barriers. As such, I have highlighted some of the provisions that are potentially beneficial to governments that want to ensure that health objectives are not mitigated by the application of trade obligations.

One example of a potential policy 'release' from the TRIPS Agreement is Article 27.2, which allows a government to deny patent protection for specific inventions. This restriction on the patentability of inventions in order to protect 'human, animal or plant life or health' allows governments the freedom to give priority to human life or health in order to protect '*Ordre Public*'. However, there is no universally accepted definition of what this term means so potentially it gives a government ample scope for its use (or conversely, no scope). Of equal importance, Article 31 provides governments with the authority to issue a compulsory license for a pharmaceutical license without the permission of the patent owner in situations of national emergency, particularly for public non-commercial use and to remedy anti-competitive behavior. TRIPS gives states significant leeway in determining what constitutes a national emergency, allowing countries the freedom to pursue public health goals. WTO members' freedom to do so is explicitly articulated in Article 8. which authorizes members to 'adopt measures necessary to protect public health and nutrition, and to promote the public interest in sectors of vital importance to their socio-economic and technological development', provided that such measures are consistent with the TRIPS Agreement.

Furthermore, Article 6 does not prohibit the parallel import of drug products and permits countries with relatively high drug prices to import a patented product from a country where it is priced lower. While these provisions in the Agreement indicate that states can adopt measures necessary to ensure access to medicines for all, in practice, many governments have not applied these safeguard provisions (Cullet 2003). The reasons for this are many and include the lack of capacity to make use of provisions (such as in the case of compulsory licensing, which until the recent Doha Accord required a country to have manufacturing capability) as well as political pressure to respect intellectual patent law for pharmaceuticals thus not making use of potential health safeguards.

The significant potential of the TRIPS Agreement to impact drug access has prompted the World Health Organization to become involved in trade issues ('t Hoen 2002: 35–6). The fact that an international organization focused on health has engaged in trade issues demonstrates that the intersection of trade and health has very real potential to adversely impact health outcomes unless appropriate policies are in place. In 1996, a Resolution on the Revised Drug Strategy requested the WHO to 'report on the impact of the work of the World Trade Organization with respect to national drug policies and essential medicines and make recommendations for collaboration between WTO and WHO, as appropriate' (WHO 1996: para 2(10)). Two years later the Executive Board of the WHO issued a recommendation that the Fifty-first World Health Assembly adopt a resolution to 'ensure that public health rather than commercial interests have primacy in pharmaceutical and health policies and to review their options under the TRIPS Agreement to safeguard access to essential drugs' (EC 1998). It is debatable whether the WHO is the most appropriate institution to address issues dealing with international standards for pharmaceuticals. Irrespective of this, what is significant and meaningful is that, along with very active non-governmental organizations (NGOs), such as MSF, Consumer Project on Technology on Health, and Health Action International, the WHO is monitoring the impact of trade agreements on health, notably in the area of pharmaceuticals, and is advocating for the primacy of health over trade.

The policy watershed: the Doha Accord

Public health activists and a number of developing-country governments have consistently called for the WTO to acknowledge that public health should have primacy over incompatible market interests. In 2001, the Doha Declaration on TRIPS and Public Health was passed and includes the following language:

> We agree that the TRIPS Agreement does not and should not prevent members from taking measures to protect public health . . . We affirm that the Agreement can and should be interpreted and implemented in a manner supportive of a WTO member's right to protect public health and, in particular, to promote access to medicines for all.

The Doha Declaration was also used to interpret Article 31(f) of the TRIPS Agreement, which states that compulsory licensing shall be 'predominantly for the supply of the domestic market'. It helped emphasize the point that compulsory licensing is only useful for those countries that have the capacity locally to manufacture drugs.

Thus, pursuant to WTO rules, select countries with a public health crisis are able to forgo patent law and issue a compulsory license to a local manufacturer. However, given that the majority of developing countries lack the domestic capacity or technical expertise to manufacture on-patent pharmaceuticals, the interpretation of this terminology is crucial to ensuring access to medicine for the poor in many developing countries as well as the profit margins of the pharmaceutical industry. As such, the Doha Declaration includes the well-analyzed Paragraph 6, which recognizes the limitations of the terms of compulsory licensing, particularly for least-developed countries that cannot turn to local producers for the manufacture of medicines, and calls for an expeditious solution to the problem.

For three days the discussion over the interpretation of TRIPS with regard to public health and minimum standards of protection dominated the trade negotiations ('t Hoen 2002: 40). According to Article 8(1) of the TRIPS Agreement, members could 'adopt measures necessary to protect public health . . . provided that such measures are consistent with the provisions of this Agreement'. This afforded considerable discretion to governments implementing their intellectual property regimes. While developed countries stressed the importance of intellectual property protection in providing incentives for R&D into new drugs, developing states voiced concerns about the potential negative impact of drug price increases on access to essential medicines. Another issue that needed to be addressed involved the provision allowing WTO members to adopt safeguards such as compulsory licensing and parallel imports in pursuit of public health objectives. Article 31(f) of the TRIPS Agreement hindered effective use of the compulsory licensing provisions by developing countries lacking sufficient pharmaceutical manufacturing capabilities. It did so by requiring that generic drugs produced under a compulsory license 'shall be authorized predominantly for the supply of the domestic market of the Member authorizing such use'.

The long-negotiated Doha Declaration suggests a means for selective disengagement by permitting those countries that do not have the capacity to manufacture medicines to still use compulsory licensing by contracting out agreements with firms in other countries. This unleashes the potential for more competition in the pharmaceutical market, and a greater drug supply for those in need if developing countries can overcome certain barriers. For instance, there are a number of administrative procedures, such as requiring both the importing and exporting countries to issue compulsory licenses, ensuring that the WTO is involved in the overseeing of the procedures. There are also other stipulations contained in the Accord that could effectively limit its application in countries. In addition, many developing countries do not have the necessary administrative infrastructure and know-how to make use of the compulsory licensing provision. Still, irrespective of these potential constraints, the Accord sets an important precedent in ensuring that international trade law does not ignore the importance of public health necessities. Patients are taking precedence over patents. It provides, however imperfectly, the potential for countries to disengage from the exigencies of the TRIPS Agreement; or what we would call here an opportunity to 'opt out' or place contingencies on what are intended to be global standards of market civilization. Its true value will become evident as soon as countries begin to exercise their rights to invoke this provision.

In the end, the WTO Ministerial Conference adopted a Declaration that reaffirmed the sovereign right of countries to use the flexibilities built into the TRIPS Agreement to protect public health and promote access to medicines for all (WTO 2001: paragraph 4). WTO ministers also agreed to grant least-developed countries an extra ten-year extension on the implementation of pharmaceutical patent protection, extending the deadline to harmonize their regulations with international standards until 2016 (WTO 2001: paragraph 7). Paragraph 6 of the Doha Declaration recognized the difficulties faced by developing countries in invoking compulsory licensing under the TRIPS Agreement and instructed the Council for TRIPS to find an expeditious solution to this problem (Matthews 2004: 82).

The compulsory licensing problem was addressed in the Decision of the General Council of the WTO on 30 August 2003. The Decision clarifies the right of countries to take advantage of compulsory licensing for pharmaceutical products only in the case of a national emergency in order to address public health problems covered by Paragraph 1 of the Doha Declaration (Matthews 2004: 95). The Decision, importantly, reaffirms the right of governments to interpret the TRIPS Agreement in a manner supportive of their right to protect public health and highlights the need for the TRIPS Agreement to be interpreted in such a way as to protect public health and not for commercial policy objectives.

WTO dispute settlement and access to essential medicines

This section reviews the WTO's Dispute Settlement Mechanisms management of pharmaceutical issues; it is not intended to be an exhaustive review but a discussion of two cases to provide a suggestion of how the WTO is balancing trade and health issues. It also aims to point out that the WTO is not currently demonstrating sufficient regard for health concerns despite the safeguards for health that are expressed in the TRIPS Agreement.

By way of a brief background, the WTO Dispute Settlement Body (DSB) is a unified system for resolving disputes arising among its members and ensuring enforcement of WTO agreements by authorizing, as a last resort, trade sanctions against non-compliant members that deviate from their commitments. In essence, it serves as a global standard of market civilization that regulates the world of trade and disputes therein. The DSB provides a limited timeframe and an automatic mechanism for the settlement of disputes. It stipulates a 'negative consensus' rule for the establishment of dispute settlement panels, the adoption of their reports, and the authorization of retaliatory measures. This rule means that the panel process will be instituted if at least one state is in favor of it (Cohen 2002: 123). The dispute settlement system establishes a unique appellate procedure in the event a panel report is appealed by one of the parties to the dispute. Unlike previously, where rulings could only be adopted by consensus, the appellate report is adopted automatically and comes into force as a matter of institutional law unless there is a consensus against adoption. The latter would typically be more difficult to achieve. In many areas the WTO Agreements afford considerable discretion in how their obligations are implemented (WHO 2001).

The first dispute examined here shows how the WTO would not allow a government to make a limited exception to patent rights (stockpiling generic drugs in this case) to facilitate access to medicines. Although the example includes a developed country, Canada, the ruling is significant in its global ramifications. The second case, which involves Brazil and its local working requirements, demonstrates that the WTO is not consistently in favor of improving drug access.

The production and importation of generic copies of essential medicines help keep many drug prices affordable. Until a recent WTO dispute panel ruling involving Canada and the European Union, it was unclear whether the flexibility within the TRIPS Agreement allowed generic drug manufacturers to conduct tests and carry out preparations for regulatory approval for their generic products before patent expiry (the Bolar provision). Under Article 28.1 of the TRIPS Agreement, patent owners shall have the right to exclude others from making, using, selling, offering for sale, or importing the patented product during the term of the patent. According to Article 33, the term of protection available shall not end before the expiration of a period of twenty years from the filing date of the application against which the patent was granted. However, Section 55.2(1) concerning the 'regulatory review exception' and Section 55.2(2) dealing with the 'stockpiling exception' of Canada's *Patent Act* allows third parties to make, use, or sell the patented product during the term of the patent without the consent of

Table 13.1: Complaints discussed under the WTO Dispute Settlement Body

Dispute	*Core Issue*	*Findings*
Patent Protection of Pharmaceutical Patents WT/DS114 (1997-2000) *Complaining country:* European Communities *Target of complaint:* Canada	Complaint by the European Communities and their member states that Canada's Patent Act is not compatible with Articles 27.1, 28, and 33 of the TRIPS Agreement. The EC alleged that under Canadian patent legislation, a third party may, without the consent of the patent holder, use a patented product to conduct tests needed to obtain marketing approval of an innovative medicine before the expiry of a patent and stockpile generic drugs six months before the expiry of the patent term.	The panel found that the exception allowing generic drug makers to test patented drugs for the purposes of seeking marketing approval for their generic versions prior to the patent's expiry was not inconsistent with the TRIPS Agreement. The stockpiling exception was not permitted under TRIPS and that manufacturers must wait until patent expiry before starting commercial production.
Measures Affecting Patent Protection WT/DS199 (2000-2001) *Complaining country:* United States *Target of complaint:* Brazil	Complaint by the US that the provision in Brazil's 1996 industrial property law that allows a patent to be subject to compulsory licensing if the patented product is not 'worked' in Brazil is inconsistent with Brazil's obligations under Articles 27 and 28 of the TRIPS Agreement.	The US agreed to terminate the WTO panel proceeding based on the Brazilian government's commitment to hold prior talks with the US with sufficient advance notice in the event the Brazilian government deemed it necessary to grant a compulsory license on patents held by US companies (WT/DS199/4).

the patent owner in certain defined circumstances. The dispute panel ruled that TRIPS did allow governments to use the patented product to conduct tests for bioequivalence and that other tests needed to obtain marketing approval before the expiry of a patent.

This decision allows generic drugs to be on the market more quickly than if these tests could only be conducted after the patent actually expired. Generally, the regulatory review procedure is time consuming and can take one to two-and-a-half years to complete. While the ruling protects consumer interests by cutting time-to-market for generic drugs, it also recognizes the potential consequences of allowing generic competitors to manufacture and stockpile patented goods before the patent expiry. The dispute panel found that stockpiling or large-scale production of the generic drug before the patent expires violated the TRIPS Agreement because of the substantial curtailment of the exclusionary rights required to be granted to patent owners. This case represents an example whereby the WTO acknowledged the rights of governments to make limited exceptions to patent rights to facilitate access to medicines. What is most troubling about this ruling is that it still seems to favor commercial interests over health interests. The quick entry of generic drugs into the Canadian marketplace helps the consumer by providing alternative products, and, as a result of greater market choice, price competition in the market. Arguably, the disallowance of stockpiling slows down the entry of generic drugs into the market. Although Canada is clearly not a country in need, this is a case that sets a standard interpretation of the TRIPS Agreement globally.

Another dispute that illustrates the possible tension between health and trade policies is the dispute brought by the US against Brazil. The US alleged that the provision in Article 68 of Brazil's 1996 industrial property law (Law No. 9279 of 14 May 1996; effective May 1997) imposed a 'local working' requirement stipulating that a patent shall be subject to a compulsory license if the patented product is not manufactured in Brazil or if the patented process is not used in the territory of Brazil. According to the US, if the patent owner attempted to import the patent rather than 'work' the patent in Brazil, Article 68 would allow others to import either the patented product or product obtained from the patented process. The US felt Article 68 curtailed the exclusive rights of patent owners and discriminated against US owners of Brazilian patents whose products are imported but not produced in Brazil. In July 2001, the US agreed to terminate the WTO panel proceeding based on the Brazilian government's commitment to hold bilateral talks with the US prior to issuing a compulsory license on patents held by US companies. The flexibility of the TRIPS Agreement allows countries like Brazil to use the threat of compulsory licensing to secure more favorable terms in its negotiations for the supply of HIV/AIDS drugs with major pharmaceutical companies who continue to seek higher standards of protection (WTO 2002: 105). However, it should be noted that this dispute also reflects the difficulties and pressures that many developing countries face in using the public health safeguards provided for in the TRIPS Agreement.

Conclusions

This chapter has focused on the intersection between trade and health and where they fit in the system of global standards of market civilization; its focus is predominantly on the issue of pharmaceutical patent regimes and trade agreements. Health as a value and not just a commodity in international trade agreements has gained prominence with the establishment of the WTO. However, the chapter explicitly raises the question of how 'weighty' health concerns really are, even when there are written provisions for health in trade agreements, when trade interests are at stake (see also Geoffrey A. Pigman's chapter in this volume). The TRIPS Agreement includes provisions that protect health but these provisions have not had much real weight of force. This reality led health activists and developing-country governments to pressure the WTO for meaningful support for health concerns. This, in turn, led to the Doha Declaration of 2001 that then led to another lengthy process of negotiation that ended in August 2003 when governments were able to reach consensus on issues such as the use of compulsory licensing, particularly for those countries that lacked the manufacturing capacity to make use of it. The WTO is a global institution and as such it is a key player in the implementation and enforcement of global standards of market civilization; in this respect it is significant and of great concern that it does not include health as a priority in its mandate. I argue for meaningful change that would compel the WTO to incorporate the value of health (for an individual or a population), and not just as a commodity, into its decision-making processes and make health one of its key institutional concerns. This would involve a seismic shift in its institutional orientation and contribute to a more humanistic international patent regime that would lead ultimately to policies that do not exacerbate the present morally unsatisfactory and uncomfortable drug gap but rather contribute to its reduction.

14 Civilizing global trade

Alterglobalizers and the 'Double Movement'

Geoffrey A. Pigman

Upon first hearing 'civilizing world trade', at least two interpretations spring out. The notion of trade as civilizing the world, the *mission civilisatrice* preached by Richard Cobden and William Ewart Gladstone in the nineteenth century, is perhaps the first understanding that comes to mind: 'civilizing' as the descriptor that modifies 'world trade'. Yet another interpretation also commands acknowledgement: civilizing as an action, the idea of a project of making world trade somehow more civil. Civilizing world trade is at the core of what the alterglobalization movement of the late twentieth and early twenty-first century is trying to achieve.

But behind this apparent Janus face of trade, perhaps inadvertently exposed by its conjoining with notions of civilization, lies a deeper unity, as the work of Karl Polanyi and scholars writing in his tradition help us to understand. How individuals understand the relationship between trade and civilization plays an important role in shaping how trade functions in the global economy and in the global society in which global economic activity is situated. The relationship between trade and the societies between which it takes place changed significantly some two centuries ago: a time that was important also for the idea of civilization and how it was understood. Polanyi articulated a compelling critique of the process by which the self-regulating market disembedded itself from and progressively transformed human social relations in the nineteenth century. This movement of disembedding, according to Polanyi, in turn unleashed a second movement by the governments of nation states to mitigate the disastrous social effects of the first movement: to re-embed the market in human society. This second face of Polanyi's famed 'Double Movement' produced some extreme political results, including Adolf Hitler's Third Reich and Joseph Stalin's authoritarian distortion of utopian communism. But Polanyi and his followers, like the adherents of alterglobalization, suggest that 'another world is possible'.

Trade and civilization: transformations

In *The Great Transformation*, Polanyi (1957) explores in depth the key role of Britain in what he calls a great transformation in the relationship between markets – the practices of commerce, or trading, and of those who do the buying and selling – and human social relations. Polanyi takes an anthropological approach to understanding, and problematizing, this relationship. Notwithstanding the rhetoric of politicians extending from Gladstone to Baroness Margaret Thatcher, Polanyi argues that human society has not always been dominated by markets and trade. According to Polanyi, in the long sweep of history the market and trade-dominated society has been a relatively new invention. By studying the social and economic practices of tribes of Pacific Islanders that had remained relatively unaffected by outside influences, Polanyi and his colleagues found that the means of distribution of needs, and the social purposes of exchange of goods amongst the islanders differed markedly from any form of what economists might identify as 'primitive capitalism'. Purposes for exchange of goods across a distance, say between different islands, included showing respect (and related diplomatic rituals) and sharing the bounty of particular seasonal items. Profit and the accumulation of wealth did not feature significantly in the traditional societies studied (Polanyi 1957: 43–55).

Up until the time of the Industrial Revolution, Polanyi argues, markets, trade, and profit did not play a dominant role in human society in general. Production and commerce, which until then had been undertaken to serve other, broader human social purposes, became core human social activities. Trade across distance, which had been a marginal activity generally undertaken only to supply crucial needs entirely unavailable in a particular society, became an end in itself. Families moved from farms and villages into conurbations to supply labor for industrial factories (Polanyi 1957: 56–76).

Traditional social structures for caring for the poor, such as family, village, and church, were changed, moved, or swept aside by the progressive commoditization of labor, allowing for the emergence of real destitution amongst the poor for the first time in human history. The state was forced to become responsible for care of the poor (Polanyi 1957: 77–110, 135–50). Polanyi viewed this replacement of older social and economic relationships by market relationships as a process with its own internal dynamic: market relations, once they achieved enough of a critical mass to function independently, spread by themselves, seeking to replace older types of human socio-economic relations. One of the most important mechanisms by which markets have propagated themselves was through the creation of an ongoing ideological movement, founded by a coalition of beneficiaries of market relations and intellectuals who embraced markets as a perfection of Enlightenment rationalist ideals. Markets, in order to function best, are and must be self-regulating, their new advocates declaimed. In doing so, their advocates helped to make it so, in part by making the case for legislative and administrative reforms that facilitated the operation of the market economy (Polanyi 1957: 135–50). Joseph Stiglitz, in his foreword to the 2001 edition of *The Great Transformation*, identified this replication process with what we think of today as neo-liberal globalization.

The mammoth socio-economic impact of the rise of the self-regulating market occasioned an equally dramatic, twofold political transformation. The first part of this Double Movement is the attempt of the self-regulating market to disembed itself from human social relations. In politics this process revealed itself in constituencies and campaigns for Free Trade, the Gold Standard, and other mechanisms of freely convertible currencies, and limited government. The second part is the social and political reaction to the ravages occasioned by the first part. It is the attempt of society, using instruments of government and governance, to re-embed markets within the broader frame of human social relations. This process began spontaneously in reaction to the effects of the first part of the Double Movement, with the mid-nineteenth-century opposition movement to Free Trade in corn (grain) in Britain, and spread rapidly, appearing among other places in late nineteenth-century British municipal urban social movements to house and feed the poor and to provide public water and sewer facilities, state schools, and libraries, and in the German government's first steps to providing social insurance, including pensions, health care, and provision for unemployment (Polanyi 1957: 201–19). Polanyi argues that rising opposition to market society in the early twentieth century produced two much stronger political responses, each utopian in conception, both ultimately as dehumanizing and destructive of the fabric of human society as what they sought to supplant: communism and fascism. Each offered the promise of re-embedding markets, commerce, trade, and finance in a more coherent shared set of human social objectives, yet both fell short because of the difficulties they faced in securing and maintaining public consent to a centrally imposed and directed structure of social values and priorities (Polanyi 1957: 223–48).

Believing strongly that authoritarianism was not the only way to re-embed markets in society, Polanyi envisaged a socially desirable equilibrium point in which the conflicting aims of the Double Movement could be resolved, a type of social market global economy in which the positive forces of market relations could function, embedded in a democratically governed world that orders and protects human social relations (Polanyi 1957: 249–58). A version of this equilibrium could be said to have emerged in Western Europe, North America, and Japan in the post-war era: what John Ruggie (1982) dubbed 'embedded liberalism', the diffusion of disciplines of multilateral trade liberalization under the GATT–WTO (General Agreement on Tariffs and Trade–World Trade Organization) structure, the reduction of barriers to global capital flows, the continued integration of markets across the globe by means of advances in information and communications technologies, and indeed the continued spread (albeit on an increasingly unequal basis) of economic development. Some scholars regarded this process as culminating in the end of the Cold War, with the resulting reintegration of the former Warsaw Pact member states into the dominant neo-liberal global model of economic organization, a phenomenon Francis Fukuyama (1992) characterized as 'the end of history'. Yet as the post-Cold War era has already demonstrated, embedded liberalism has neither proved to be an equilibrium point, as Polanyi hoped, nor has it ended the production of poverty and destitution that triggered the second part of the Double Movement.

Mark Blyth (2002) argues that Polanyi's discussion of the Double Movement failed to capture its essentially cyclical character. Blyth periodizes the evolution of the industrial global political economy, arguing that each success of the first part of the Double Movement, disembedding of markets from society, has prompted a counter-push towards re-embedding, which once it has succeeded has in turn occasioned a repeat of the cycle. Blyth argues that ideas play a direct causal role in how the global economy actually functions, in the sense that how people think the economy works conditions their expectations and actions. According to Blyth, idea-influenced and idea-informed economic behavior produces subsequent economic conditions, which in turn generate ideas and understandings of its problems that shape the policy decisions of the next generation of policy-makers. For example, how US policy-makers understood the causes of the Great Depression of the 1930s shaped the policy decisions that created the global economic conditions of the post-Second World War period, in which policy-makers sought to understand economic problems and formulate responses thereto. For Blyth, the perceived failures of the global economic system of embedded liberalism by the 1970s generated an ideological movement to disembed markets once again from human social relations, a movement taken up by political leaders such as Ronald Reagan and Thatcher. The effects of that project at the turn of the twenty-first century are only just beginning to generate the ideas in which the next cycle of re-embedding is to be grounded.

Blyth's understanding of the causal role of ideas in producing economic policy and generating socio-economic conditions is reflected in the relationship between trade and civilization. As these ideas include civilization and how people understand it, how people have imagined the relationship between trade and civilization over the last two centuries is significant in affecting how trade functions in economy and society. Two very different examples serve to depict in sharp relief the contrasting ways of conceiving this relationship: the Free-Trade movement of the mid- and late nineteenth century, and the alter-globalization movement of the late twentieth and early twenty-first centuries. The movements have considerable similarities: each has been led by a coalition of intellectuals, political leaders, and economists. Each has succeeded in mobilizing substantial popular support across a range of metrics: location, occupation, class, wealth. Neither movement's support can be reduced to exogenously generated class or other economic 'interest' alone. Both movements have been able to capture the attention of global publics through the media and other cultural representations. Crucially, each movement has used a particular notion of civilization to validate or justify a particular policy approach towards trade. Yet a closer look at each movement reveals how their respective notions of civilization, and the policy approaches that those notions validate or justify, differ. Whereas for the nineteenth-century Free-Trade movement, trade was the vehicle for bringing civilization from Europe to the rest of the world, for the alterglobalization movement it is global trade itself that needs to become civilized.

Free trade and empire: *mission civilisatrice*

The coalition of supporters of nineteenth-century trade liberalization, first in Britain and eventually across Europe, North America, and the rest of the globe, is remarkable for the diversity of motives of its members. It was no surprise that the manufacturers of the new industrial heartland 'voted with their wallets', advocating Free Trade in order to secure lower tariffs on their products in as many export markets as possible, as well as cheaper industrial inputs where required (including food for their workers, if it meant wages could be kept lower). Yet core supporters of Corn Law repeal in Britain in the 1840s and the trade liberalization movement that grew from it had far more diverse motivations than a straight economic interest-based explanation would expect. Richard Cobden embraced Free Trade as the best mechanism to promote global peace, his own personal central political mission. He was later joined in his mission by a French peace activist of his day, Michel Chevalier, with whom he negotiated the 'Cobden–Chevalier' Anglo-French Commercial Treaty of 1860. John Bright and the Chartists saw Free Trade as a way to improve the dire conditions under which industrial workers labored, in that the importation of cheaper grain via Free Trade would lower food costs for the working class. Karl Marx favored Free Trade because he saw it as accelerating the development of capitalism, thereby bringing closer the point at which conditions would be right for socialist revolution. Gladstone embraced Free Trade for a constellation of political reasons (including the desire to curb government spending by cutting revenues), but not least because he regarded it as one of the principal means to transmit Britain's standard of living to the rest of the world: to export civilization itself (see John M. Hobson's and Leonard Seabrooke's chapters in this volume).

The *mission civilisatrice* of Free Trade as an idea attracted many supporters in the nineteenth century precisely because it cut across class and other interest groupings. It was a project intimately entangled with Britain's ideas of empire and with ways of understanding and justifying empire to itself as a society and to the rest of the world. The British Empire, according to Niall Ferguson (2003), spread a wealth of common goods to the parts of the globe with which it came in contact, including the rule of law, professional civil administration of government, institutions of higher education, the English language, and, importantly, a broadly liberal economic model characterized by open markets, convertible currencies, and relatively barrier-free domestic and international trade. The link between empire and trade as civilizing missions is captured in Norbert Elias's view of civilization as a process, of which the progressive specialization of human behaviors and increasing interdependence of individuals upon one another in society forms a natural sociological part (Elias 2000). According to Martin Wight, the rationale for the *mission civilisatrice* can be found in the Rationalist approach to colonial theory: that civilization is entitled to expand because it brings economic and social benefits to civilized society and barbarians alike (Wight 1991: 78–82). Sir F.D. Lugard (1923: frontispiece) quoted Joseph Chamberlain in this regard: 'We develop new territory as trustees for Civilisation, for the Commerce of the World.' In assessing the balance of gains and losses to native populations, Lugard acknowledged that 'civilisation facilitated the spread among native peoples of disease that previously had been confined to particular localities'. But against that he highlights gains from trade: 'Civilisation has decreased the sum of human misery inflicted by man upon man by tribal war, barbarous practices, and slave-trading. By promoting trade and increasing wealth it has raised the standard of life and comfort' (Lugard 1923: 92).

For Lugard, Free Trade and empire were quintessential and inseparable elements of being British: 'We hold these countries because it is the genius of our race to colonise, to trade, and to govern. The task in which England is engaged in the tropics – alike in Africa and the East – has become part of her tradition, and she has ever given of her best in the cause of liberty and civilisation' (Lugard 1923: 618–19; see also Barry Hindess's chapter in this volume). Despite the fact that Free Traders and imperialists did not often otherwise embrace compatible public policies, the civilizing mission was promoted discursively by advocates of Free Trade and advocates of empire alike. The work of David Livingstone and that of the Cobden Club are two contrasting examples of how the discursive relationship between Free Trade and civilization was produced and reproduced.

Livingstone, who began his illustrious career as a Christian missionary and ultimately became best known as an explorer of the African continent, drew together in his life work these intertwined notions of empire, civilization, and trade. From Livingstone's perspective, market relations remained embedded in human society. For Livingstone, commerce and empire were instruments that could be used to promote civilization, which, being infused by Christian ideas and values, was of the sort that subsumed, rather than being subsumed by, markets. Whilst engaging in missionary work in the interior of southern Africa in 1853, Livingstone first encountered the expanding operations of the slave trade, and he made it his life's work to end the African slave trade. Livingstone's vision was that only the establishment of British colonial settlements could bring protection to the indigenous African peoples from the predations of the slave traders (Huxley 1974: 55–6, 108; Ferguson 2003: 127–31). Livingstone aspired to replace the slave trade in the African interior with legitimate commerce, so his explorations sought to discover navigable waterways to facilitate trade between the peoples of the interior and the coasts. In 1858 Livingstone was appointed H.M. Consul in Quelimane and commissioned to undertake an exploration of central and eastern Africa 'for the promotion of Commerce and Civilisation with a view to the extinction of the slave-trade' (Huxley 1974: 97–8; Ferguson 2003: 154–7). Livingstone proposed to co-operate with Portugal to open the Zambesi River to the commerce of all nations, an undertaking that required convincing the Portuguese to abandon their tacit support of the slave trade (Huxley 1974: 101).

When Livingstone returned to Britain briefly in 1856, the British public embraced him and his mission with tremendous enthusiasm. He was perceived as leading a selfless crusade to bring to the interior of Africa Christianity, rule of law, legitimate trade, and the higher material standards of living it would bring: in short a global standard of civilization that mid-nineteenth-century Britain sought to promulgate throughout the world through commerce where possible, through empire as necessary. Her Majesty's Government may have had other less altruistic geopolitical objectives for backing Livingstone's mission, but its sense of helping those indigenous Africans perceived to be less fortunate was what won his project public support (Ferguson 2003: 132–3). In supporting Livingstone's efforts to end the slave trade by replacing it with 'legitimate' trade the British public were able to understand Britain's role in the world as a civilizing agent, whereas less than a century earlier the African slave trade had been viewed as legitimate commercial policy by British government and public alike.

The Cobden Club, by contrast, viewed trade as having the potential to lead civilization rather than to be its servant. A society of supporters of Free Trade that thrived for several decades following its establishment by Bright in 1866, the Cobden Club's membership was almost as diverse as the different range of reasons for supporting Free Trade: British businessmen, academics, members of parliament and their counterparts from a range of nations across Europe, North America, and the British Empire. The club held regular meetings, often in the format of a dinner followed by speeches, and published a steady stream of academic and political tracts supporting Free Trade. By doing so the Cobden Club and its members contributed to the social and economic dominance of Free Trade discourse in nineteenth-century Britain and in the policy decisions taken in Cabinet and in Parliament that underpinned it. The Cobden Club's publications and lobbying helped to normalize and reify Free Trade orthodoxy across Britain's rapidly evolving class structure and socio-economic demographics. One of the principal means by which they were able to accomplish this was through the use of discursive lines of justification that at least appeared to cut across class and other socio-economic cleavages (urban/rural, north/south, male/female). The club chairman, Thomas Milner Gibson, speaking at the 1873 Cobden Club annual dinner, made this point directly: 'Free Trade is neither democratic nor aristocratic. It is not a question of party. (*cheers*) We do not want to pull down one class and put up another; we found ourselves on that principle which we believe to be beneficial to all classes' (Cobden Club 1873: 84).

The mid-nineteenth-century notion of British 'civilization' met this normalizing objective better than most (see also Jacqueline Best's chapter in this volume). Amongst the many interconnected streams of justificatory argument that club members deployed, the relationship between Free Trade and civilization resurfaced repeatedly. The club's motto was 'Free Trade – Peace – Good-will Among Nations', a sort of Holy Trinity of seemingly incontestable public goods that formed an integral part of the nineteenth-century idea of civilization. At the 1873 dinner, club member T.B. Potter, MP, articulated clearly the relationship between the club itself and an idea of global civilization: 'There is scarcely a large town in the civilised world with which we (the Cobden Club) do not have communication, and I do trust that, humble as our efforts may be, they have been productive of some benefit for the cause we all have so much at heart' (Cobden Club 1873:

83). Potter went on to note that 'there are many around us, in various civilised countries in the world, who are honorary members of the Cobden Club' (Cobden Club 1873: 84).

Club chairman Milner Gibson invoked the Free Trade–civilization relationship in the section of his dinner speech in which he eulogized Cobden, the revered apostle of Free Trade and world peace:

> (Cobden's) was not a narrow and selfish patriotism. The blessings he desired for his own country he wished to extend to other nations. He believed in the pacific influence of commerce. He saw that it would at any rate tend to break down those barriers which separated nations, and behind which, to use his own expressive language, often nestled the feelings of revenge and jealousy and the love of conquest, which sometimes broke their bonds and deluged whole nations with blood. Now there is no name, I will venture to say, which is received with greater respect throughout the whole civilised world than the name of Richard Cobden.
>
> (Cobden Club 1873: 25–6)

Chevalier, Cobden's French counterpart, also invoked the Free Trade–civilization identity in a letter read at the 1873 club dinner:

> It is a convincing proof that civilisation, like an immense stream, carrying in its current science, power, and wealth, must advance more and more in that direction (Free Trade), and that any effort to oppose it must be defeated. In the future, if not in the present, Free Trade will be the pass-word of nations.
>
> (Cobden Club 1873: 32)

Another non-English member of the club, Moret y Prendergast, a Spaniard, identified qualities that made England a civilized nation, in a speech in which he argued against expanding the role of government in a socialist direction: 'England is strong, powerful, and civilised, because she is composed of free, independent, and energetic citizens, and, such being the case, she must always progress' (Cobden Club 1873: 79–80).

Two years later, in a Cobden Club publication entitled *Free Trade and the European Treaties of Commerce* (1875), leading Free-Trade campaigner Sir Louis Mallet articulated the discursive isomorphism between degree of trade liberalization and degree of civilization. Mallet's publication argued for renewal of Britain's bilateral treaties of commerce with the other major European powers, many of which were coming up for renewal in the mid- and late 1870s. Mallet regarded Free Trade in Europe as the core of the trade liberalization project, but he justified that viewpoint not because of the nature or importance of trade flows between Britain and the Continent, but because of the Continent's comparable level of civilization:

> the acquisition of new markets in Europe is far more essential to our national prosperity than the progress of our trade with distant and half-civilised

> countries, upon which we have been compelled to rely by the unnatural state of our relations with our nearest neighbours.
>
> (Cobden Club 1875: 7)

Mallet gives perhaps the most concise rendering of the ideological identity between Free Trade and the dominant nineteenth-century British view of what civilization was, and what it was not:

> that which is disguised under the specious name of 'protection' is, in reality, a mere tradition of primitive barbarism – a remnant of the bygone era when every foreigner was an enemy, and the rule of war – to take every advantage of the adversary and injure him as much as possible – entered into the spirit of all international dealings. The modern Treaty of Commerce is, on the contrary, a legible record of the dawning conviction that the good of each nation is the good of all.
>
> (Cobden Club 1875: 8)

For Mallet, as for many of his contemporaries, protectionism is equated with barbarism, and commercial trade liberalization treaties with the collective social realization of a common good for all. From Britain, the core nation state in the emerging nineteenth-century global market economy, the dominant relations of production, the self-regulating market, were reproduced across many regions of the globe. The reproduction of the dominance of liberal market relations of production took place by many means, ranging from 'gunboat diplomacy' to formal colonization to 'informal empire'. One of the most effective tools for this endeavor was the ability to effect the social construction of the self-regulating market by joining Free Trade, civilization, and empire discursively in ways that appeared altruistic, non-partisan, and incontestable. This was the heart of the Cobden Club's project, even as the very nature and content of their discourse revealed the extent of the contested nature of Free Trade and the urgent need to win over doubters and opponents in Continental Europe and North America. The civilization to which the Cobden Club members referred in their arguments was the civilization to which the government sponsors of Livingstone's mission to replace the slave trade in the upper Zambesi basin with 'legitimate' trade referred. Just as the role of markets in traditional nineteenth-century societies of the Zambesi would likely have been familiar to Polanyi given his anthropological research in the Pacific Islands, the civilization associated with 'legitimate' trade brought by Livingstone represented the disembedding of markets that Polanyi observed would provoke a strong response from civil society.

Alterglobalization: another world is possible

The end of the Cold War at the beginning of the 1990s heralded the ascendancy of what Mark Rupert (2000) has described as a 'muscular liberalism' that superseded the 'embedded liberalism' of the post-Second World War Western economies: 'a hard-edged liberalism which strives to focus the violence of market forces directly upon working people through policies which emphasize public fiscal retrenchment, containment of inflation, and "flexible labor markets" in a context of rigorous global competition' (Rupert 2000: 132). Stephen Gill (2003a, 2003b) argues that the discipline of global capital over social relations is being intensified through processes of 'new constitutionalism' that are reconstituting the state as a tool of neo-liberal globalization. John Gray (1998: 1-2) explicitly likens the transformative project of transnational institutions like the WTO, the International Monetary Fund, and Organization for Economic Co-operation and Development (OECD) to the first leg of Polanyi's Double Movement. Recalling Polanyi's description of the self-regulating market continually seeking to incorporate as much of the globe under its discipline as possible, the 1990s saw the former Soviet bloc countries become 'economies in transition' to neo-liberal market disciplines. The post-Second World War trade liberalization process, under the aegis of the GATT, sought both to accelerate and to expand its purchase on global society and global economy in several ways. The GATT Uruguay Round culminated in the 1994 Treaty of Marrakech, which created the WTO, a full-fledged international body with stepped up supra-national dispute settlement procedures and that expanded the reach of trade liberalization disciplines to areas such as intellectual property protection and agricultural trade (Williams 2003: 194, 197). Developing countries, many of which hitherto had continued to subordinate trade and other international economic policies to domestic social policies produced by political bargaining amongst social forces, joined the WTO and committed themselves to its trade liberalization obligations. Other trade barriers were reduced more rapidly at a regional level in bodies such as the expanding European Union (EU), Association of Southeast Asian Nations (ASEAN), Mercado Común del Sur (Mercosur), and through the North American Free Trade Agreement (NAFTA). Even more ambitiously, a drive spearheaded by the OECD, with the support of numerous industrial-country governments and managements of large multinational firms, was launched to subordinate to neo-liberal market disciplines domestic labor, health, and environmental legislation that affected the interests of large global investors adversely, under the auspices of a Multilateral Agreement on Investment (MAI) (Rugman 2002).

These processes have generally been grouped under the great and contested rubric of globalization, by supporters and detractors alike. As with Free Trade in the nineteenth century, neo-liberal globalization is constructed discursively by supporters as inevitable and having no legitimate counter-arguments, even when they are compelled to make arguments in its defense. As Ferguson (2003: xx–xxii) points out, neo-liberal globalization is the heritor of the value-laden notion of empire bequeathed to the world by Britain in the twentieth century and thereby linked ideationally to Free Trade and civilization in the nineteenth. Hence the isomorphism between neo-liberal globalization and Western civilization was legible even before subsequent events articulated the linkage more explicitly. And yet just as post-Cold War, disembedded neo-liberal globalization seemed to be within striking distance of achieving its objective of subsuming all the world's polities and economies, it summoned forth an opposition: a diverse and sometimes fractious coalition of global civil society who envisioned that another world was possible, a global economy re-embedded in human society (Ramonet 2004), 'a world driven less by economic exchange and more concerned with values, rights, and norms' (Sullivan 2003: 1).

The 'alterglobalizers' do not necessarily agree about what that world might look like, only that it should look different from what dominates today (Williams 2003: 200). In the US, the push to ratify NAFTA and the GATT Treaty of Marrakech elicited serious opposition both from a nationalist, protectionist right and a progressive, labor-environmentalist left (Rupert 2000: 54–118). In Europe, opposition to the WTO is shared between agriculturalists of the right and alterglobalizers of the left. Across Asia, the opposition ranges from Islamist movements, Hindu nationalist factions in India such as the RSS (Rashtriya Swayamsevak Sangh), right-wing nationalists in Japan, to Marxist and Maoist agriculturalist and artisanal producer movements from Nepal to the Philippines. Opposition to the MAI in 1998 spread amongst this heterogeneous patchwork of civil society largely by means of the Internet, with such speed and force that its political and corporate backers were forced to withdraw the initiative indefinitely. The 1999 WTO Ministerial meeting in Seattle became a site for protest by global civil society organizations challenging and questioning the priorities of a proposed new global trade liberalization negotiating round. Global social movements were troubled by the apparent supra-nationalism, permanence, and opacity of decision-making that characterized the WTO, which they perceived as taking the neo-liberal model of global governance to a new level beyond that of the previous GATT (Williams 2003: 197–9). Both left and right demanded greater institutional transparency, accountability, and participation in the governance of the WTO (Payne and Samhat 2004: 100). They criticized the WTO's intergovernmental institutional structure for privileging nation state governments and those interests that lobby governments most effectively, such as transnational firms, at the expense of broader civil society interests (Williams 2003: 200–1). The same organizations and others protested at the World Economic Forum's (WEF) 2000 Davos summit, and from that opposition was spawned the World Social Forum, a sort of alter-WEF with different social priorities, in Porto Allegre, Brazil. In effect, ever since the Seattle protests, it has become a feature of the global economic landscape that every major meeting of the political and corporate organizers of neo-liberal globalization will face publicly articulated opposition from civil society.

The alterglobalization movement of the left criticizes the global trade architecture generated by neo-liberal globalization in terms that Polanyi would understand, as a few examples make clear. Global Trade Watch, an arm of the US non-governmental organization (NGO) Public Citizen, describe themselves on their website as

> promot(ing) democracy by challenging corporate globalization, arguing that the current globalization model is neither a random inevitability nor 'Free

> Trade'. Our work seeks to make the measurable outcomes of this model available to the public, press, and policy-makers, while emphasizing that if the results are not acceptable, then the model can and must be changed.
>
> (Global Trade Watch 2004)

Another network of alterglobalization organizations, Our World is Not For Sale, describes itself as 'fighting against the current model of corporate globalization embodied in the global trading systems' and 'committed to a sustainable, socially just, democratic and accountable multilateral trading system' (Our World is Not For Sale 2004). On their web page 'WTO: Shrink or Sink', Our World is Not For Sale call for trade policies that would re-embed global trade in a different, more democratically ordered web of human social relations:

> 'Free trade' puts corporate profits before people and the environment. We need fair trade. Fundamental human and workers' rights must be respected, promoted and realized, as must the environment, health and safety, indigenous peoples' rights, development, safety, food security, and animal welfare.
>
> (Our World is Not For Sale 2004)

Speaking during demonstrations against the WEF in Melbourne, Australia in September 2000, Walden Bello, Executive Director of Focus on the Global South, an NGO based in Bangkok, highlighted the non-democratic and disembedded character of the WTO:

> By setting up the WTO, countries and governments discovered that they had set up a legal system that enshrined the priority of Free Trade above every other good – above the environment, justice, equity, and community. . . . In joining the WTO, developing countries realized that they were not, in fact, joining a democratic organization but one where decisions were made, not in formal plenaries but in non-transparent backroom sessions.

Bello advocates what he calls 'deglobalization': not in the sense of aggressive economic nationalism, but rather in terms of reorienting production towards local markets rather than towards exports, shifting social priorities more towards equity at the expense of growth, and promoting local economic development based on community co-operatives, private and state enterprises at the expense of transnational firms. Bello favors 'enshrining the principle of subsidiarity in economic life by encouraging production of goods to take place in the community and national level if it can be done so at reasonable cost in order to preserve community'. Lest his listeners have missed the Polanyian thrust of his comments, Bello drives the point home: 'We are speaking, in short, about re-embedding the economy in society, rather than having society driven by the economy' (Bello 2004).

Proponents of neo-liberal globalization have attempted systematically to brand the opposition as 'anti-globalization'; by conflating discursively the transnational left-progressive-labor-environmentalist coalition with indigenous right-wing localist, nationalist, and 'protectionist' opposition movements, neo-liberal supporters have attempted to construct an image of their opponents that is both Luddite and apparently inconsistent with an open, internationalist 'Free-Trade' spirit that purportedly seeks to create a rising tide that will lift all global economic boats (Rupert 2000: 54–62). In doing so, they have ignored what Polanyi's analysis explained so well: that both state-centric (Stalinism, fascism) and co-operative (embedded liberalism, social market economy) global idioms for re-embedding markets in human social relations were possible. Hence the core truth behind the naming of the alterglobalization (from the French, *altermondialisme*) movement: another world is possible, a civilization that is global but that structures its markets and other economic mechanisms to reflect different, shared social values and priorities (Sullivan 2003: 1–2).

The conflict between what are in effect radically different visions of civilization has been contested predominantly on the field of trade policy because, ever since the nineteenth century, trade has remained the most emotive, communicable discursive terrain on which to fight this kind of battle. In campaigns for the hearts, minds, and votes of publics across the world, it is easier to communicate about things one can touch, such as imported clothes and televisions, and to link them viscerally to things one depends on to survive every day, such as jobs, than it is to speak emotively about foreign investment rules, development funding, even environmental and health and safety standards. Hence both neo-liberal globalizers and alterglobalizers alike have sought to move other important issues for their respective projects onto the discursive terrain of trade: for neo-liberals, global investment rules and intellectual property protection, for alterglobalizers, health and safety standards, workers' rights, reproductive and women's rights, environmental protection. Moreover, the relentlessly expanding global tradability of goods and services and the globalization of production and marketing chains within firms and industrial sectors have resulted in trade politics increasingly becoming the site for the legal and political contestation of the economic practices of 'civilized' society (Williams 2003: 194).

So just as neo-liberals in the 1980s expanded the ambit of economic activity to be liberalized under the rubric of trade in the GATT Uruguay Round (such as services and agricultural trade, intellectual property and investment) at a time when they were winning the public debate (Pigman 1996), alterglobalizers in the late 1990s and early 2000s sought to re-embed neo-liberal markets in human social relations by introducing consideration of the impact of labor, environmental, health, and women's issues into the debate on trade liberalization. Alterglobalizers pressed for the WTO to incorporate global labor rights standards into WTO rules: an institutional re-embedding of the rights of workers into the neo-liberal global trade law and concomitant access to the powerful WTO supranational dispute resolution mechanism. In response the WTO ministerial declaration of 13 December 1996 at the Singapore ministerial meeting declared that the UN International Labor Organization, and not the WTO, was the appropriate venue for negotiating and enforcing labor standards (Klein 2000:

342). Alterglobalizers demanded that global firms adopt voluntary codes of corporate conduct committing firms to ethical trading practices that eschew the use of sweatshop, child, and prison labor (Klein 2000: 434–7). But their neo-liberal opponents pressed back: when the US state of Massachusetts passed legislation denying state contract work to firms doing business in Burma because of the repressive practices of the Burmese government, the European Union, acting on behalf of global firms wishing to trade in both Massachusetts and Burma, brought a complaint to the WTO seeking to have the Massachusetts law struck down (Klein 2000: 410–19).

The efforts of the alterglobalization movement in the 1990s initially did not meet with much success, as the battles over ratification of NAFTA and the Treaty of Marrakech yielded only token concessions to their agenda items. Yet the withdrawal of the MAI in 1998 and the delay of the launch of a new multilateral trade liberalization round following protests at the WTO Seattle ministerial meeting in 1999 can be seen as turning points, after which neo-liberals were forced to concede a position on the discursive field of global trade politics to those who contend that another world is possible (Sullivan 2003: 1). US President Bill Clinton in 1998 advocated greater participation by civil society organizations in the WTO, and after the Seattle protests WTO director-general Mike Moore launched a major public diplomacy undertaking to communicate the benefits of trade liberalization for each sector in the global economy (Williams 2003: 204–5; Moore 2003). The subsequent 'Kleptogate' financial scandals, involving firms such as Enron, WorldCom, HealthSouth, Adelphia, and Parmalat, triggered public perceptions of a crisis of market legitimacy in the US and Europe that generated popular pressure on global firms to adopt more rigorous and transparent corporate social responsibility strategies. Nike's adoption of a detailed, extensively self-critical 'corporate responsibility' policy and public communication strategy, which can be viewed on the Nike website, is indicative of how a major global firm has responded to public concerns about ethical trading practices in a changed global social environment by taking public diplomacy on corporate social responsibility to a new level (Nike 2005). At the WTO ministerial meeting at Cancun in September 2003, a coalition of developing country governments led by Brazil, China and India refused to discuss the 'Singapore questions', an agenda of liberalization measures involving investment rules, transparency of public markets, and customs facilitation, among other things, which had been proposed at the 1996 Singapore ministerial, and rejected a US–EU proposal on agricultural trade for failing to end government subventions to agricultural exports. In doing so governments of the global South indicated that they would no longer accept the defining of the global trade liberalization agenda by the North (Cassen 2004).

If the revolt against the MAI and the WTO Seattle ministerial meetings were turning points, another turning point was the 11 September 2001 al-Qa'eda attacks on New York and Washington, which abruptly returned the topic of civilization itself to public debate and, more significantly, reopened a space for the contestation of the contemporary understanding of civilization. In the months following the attacks, there was a surge in scholarly writing that referenced the latterly unfashionable notion of civilization, and many who sought to decode the import of the attacks from a range of academic and political perspectives invoked civilization in some way as a reference point. Ferguson posits the military removal of rogue regimes as part of the *mission civilisatrice* of Western civilization, likening Osama bin Laden's attack on the US to the killing of General Gordon by the Mahdi, an earlier Islamic 'renegade', in Khartoum in 1884 (Ferguson 2003: 268, 375). According to Ferguson, Bin Laden's strike resulted from 'the Middle East's distinctive civilization of clashes, a retarded political culture in which terrorism has long been a substitute for both peaceful politics and conventional warfare' (Ferguson 2004: 120). By contrast, Vandana Shiva (2001) contends that Western global economic power has destroyed its own civilization by annihilating the diverse cultures that comprised it, citing as examples the silencing of women in the Salem witch hunts and the genocide of Native Americans. Shiva cites Mahatma Gandhi's riposte when asked what he thought of Western civilization: 'It would be a good idea.' The al-Qa'eda attacks, according to Shiva, were a cultural backlash against neo-liberal globalization 'as alienated and angry young men of colonised societies and cultures react to the erosion of identity and security'. For Baudrillard (2004), Islam is cast as the principal enemy today because Islamists have been the most vehement in contesting Western values. Jean Baudrillard shares Shiva's view of Western civilization, arguing that neo-liberal globalization must by its nature be violent in its project of normalizing all spaces, physical or psychological, outside its realm of domination:

> The mission of the West (or rather of the ex-West, since it has not had for a long time any more values of its own) is to subject by all means the multiple cultures to the fierce law of equivalence. A culture that has lost its values can only be avenged on those of others. Even wars – thus that of Afghanistan – aim initially, beyond political or economic strategies, to standardize brutality, to strike alignment among all the territories. The objective is to reduce every refractory zone, to colonize and domesticate all wild spaces, whether it is in geographical space or in the mental universe.
>
> (Baudrillard 2004: 11, my translation from the French)

Michael Hardt and Antonio Negri (2000), writing prior to the attacks, also identify Islamic fundamentalism as a conservative response to the contemporary, post-modern global phenomenon that they call *Empire* and that encompasses the totality of the social, political, and economic manifestations of neo-liberal globalization (and is perhaps not as far from Ferguson's understanding of the contemporary legacy of Britain's empire or that of the US as it might initially appear). While Hardt and Negri flag Islamic fundamentalism as one of the more extreme right manifestations of opposition to empire as they conceptualize it, their work focuses on the possibility of a counter-hegemonic project: an individual and collective mode of 'being against' that seeks to resist and recreate empire from within its totalizing structure. Hardt and Negri give the name 'the multitude' to an alternate mode of all-inclusive, collective self-identification that cuts across class, ethnic, gender, and other social boundaries. The multitude, they argue, has the potential to go beyond 'being against' empire and, in doing so, to constitute itself the subject of a different civilization that would, among other things, subordinate trade policy to broader, shared human social objectives (Hardt and Negri 2000, 2004). Hardt and Negri in effect posit an incipient global civilization based on principles of equality, commonality in difference, and democratic self-governance (cf. Jacqueline Best's chapter in this volume). Such a civilization would look very different from the empire of neo-liberal globalization, but all the elements already exist for the multitude to actualize it (Hardt and Negri 2004).

Conclusions

As this brief tour of nineteenth- and twentieth-century debates over trade liberalization and civilization illustrates, trade practices and processes of civilization are intimately bound up with and inseparable from one another. As Blyth argues, in policy terms this relationship exists at an ideational level: how we understand economic policy debates and choices, particularly those concerning trade policy, depends upon how we understand ourselves as a human society, and from that same understanding of human society flows our conceptions of what civilization is and ought to be. The ongoing discursive contestation of trade policy exposes a real civilization of clashes: clashes between a disembedded, neo-liberal global market economy that dominates and marginalizes all other aspects of human social relations, on the one hand, and a global society in which market structures are embedded according to democratically negotiated and legislated social priorities, on the other. Perhaps, following Polanyi, we might wish collectively to move beyond trade as a metaphor or idiom for human interaction in civilized society. Yet whatever one's position on it, the genie of global trade is out of the bottle. The relationship between trade and civilization is relevant because how we understand civilization – what it is and what we want it to be – gives us the constitutive power to make civilization the master of trade rather than its servant. For the foreseeable future, trade is likely to remain the most contested battlefield in the struggle for the direction of civilization and the politics of globalization. At the end of the day, it may still be possible for trade to perform a *mission civilisatrice* in the sense of bringing social goods to a broader cross-section of global society. But this can only be possible once world trade has been 'civilized' itself, in the sense that the efficient forces of the market that trade engages have been subordinated to broadly shared global notions of what human social relations should be: democratically chosen values, norms, and objectives that serve the whole of the people who call them into being and empower them. 'Only a framework of global regulation – of currencies, capital movements, trade and environmental conservation – can enable the creativity of the world economy to be harnessed in the service of human needs' (Gray 1998: 199). Civilization can be constituted democratically to reflect global pluralism and diversity, but, given the nature of power politics, the task is bound to remain difficult (Hardt and Negri 2004). On a theoretical level, Hardt and Negri hint at the potential constitutive power of the multitude; at the applied level, the albeit modest successes of the as yet relatively young alterglobalization movement give some reason for optimism. The broad global support for the 2005 'Live 8' social movement seeking debt relief and more favorable trade conditions from the July 2005 G8 (Group of Eight) summit of industrial country leaders for the poorest African countries illustrates the potential for a global civilizing project of the multitude, but its uncertain outcome underscores how contingent the multitude's prospects remain.

Conclusion

15 Civilizing global market standards

Double-edged discourses and their policy implications

Leonard Seabrooke and Brett Bowden

Civilization is a dangerous concept. On this one point all of the contributors to this volume agree. The concept of civilization can be dangerous because of its ambiguities. At once it can call us to realize improvement within our own society while disparaging the legitimacy of other ways of organizing social, political, and economic life. It can provide us with a moral quest that can also justify imposing one's supposedly superior standard of institutions, values, and beliefs about socio-political organization onto so-called inferior and backward peoples who would do well to listen. If they refuse to take heed then a civilizing mission may be justified for their own good. Civilization is double-edged; it causes harm through the double standards it propagates.

When civilization is applied to markets similar problems abound. The notion of 'market civilization' too easily draws us into looking for standards in order to replicate how the economically powerful became so, rather than questioning the social and political foundations of dominance. We are too readily impelled to assess the notion of market civilization through economic measurements, asking how to technically build better systems for economic growth, or to unravel what cultural traits, even essences, underpin the favored economic model of the day. At the same time, however, the concept of market civilization can prompt the opposite, inviting us to investigate how the economically dominant provide, consciously or unconsciously, structures of discipline that keep subordinate actors, peoples, and cultures in their place (Gill 1995).

Such calls to inquiry, in our view, lead down the wrong track and reify the notion of civilization and market civilization. For us, the resurgence of interest in civilization in political theory, international relations, and studies of economic globalization makes it all the more important to scrutinize and understand how the concept is used rather than to explain how global standards of market civilization are employed. As variously discussed in this volume, all too often civilization is treated unproblematically as a gift that comes with cultural, political, or material preponderance (e.g. Mozaffari 2001; Fidler 2000). Alternatively, civilization is seen as fixed to cultural identities and ways of life that are incommensurable and sure to 'clash' in the struggle for world dominance, or even survival (e.g. Huntington 1996). However, it is too easy to straw man (or woman for that matter) entities such as 'Western' civilization, 'Islamic' civilization, or 'Confucian' civilization; these unhelpful conglomerations tell us little. Civilization too readily provides a cloak to mask power relations, and not only those imposed from above but also how civilizing processes can be resisted from below. With this volume our aim has been to problematize and contextualize the concept of civilization and its application to global markets rather than to reify and deify it.

We suggest that a more fruitful approach is to assess how articulations of standards of civilization are historically contingent, and how such standards are applied in various forms of globalization. As Norbert Elias tells us, there is no 'zero point of civilizing processes' from which to evolve from savage to barbarian to civilized (Elias 1992: 146). Contrary to long-held beliefs, there is no evolutionary historical trajectory against which states and economies can join. This is particularly the case when discussing how civilization relates to economic globalization. Indeed, much of the literature invoking civilization or an end point to history has posited economic globalization as providing the means for less developed states to attach themselves (Fukuyama 1989, 1992; Friedman 1999). But such path-dependent logic returns us to a problem that many authors in the volume have noted: that modernization theory and its contemporary equivalents in 'good governance', 'transparency', 'national integrity systems', and the like, provide a standard of civilization that is over-rationalized and deterministic. Such catch-calls demand technical capacity building when deeper social dynamics may make them redundant, inappropriate, or just plain pointless. All too often such thinking, as discussed in the previous chapters, is self-referential. The abstracted goals of the project are rationalized as the only object worthy of attention. This tendency encourages the assessment of the success of global standards on any policy issue to be made by checking formal implementation rather than the social change it engenders. Economic performance is measured by the standard indicators when social changes underlying or inhibiting growth are neglected and begging for attention. Such a view leads to policy-making that has no historical and no comparative sociological or cultural understanding (Kristensten 2005). It leads to policy-making in a fishbowl. As Elias relates through his critique of social planning, such attitudes can do great harm:

> The contemporary type of rapidly-growing institutionalized and technicized social planning is – in the poorer, less developed as in the richer, more developed countries – aligned towards future, further development. However, this more conscious, to a greater extent *socially planned* further development, which in some societies encompasses more and more sectors and, in many, all sectors of social practice, is characteristic of a more encompassing *unplanned* development and is constantly interwoven within this unplanned further development of human societies.
>
> (Elias 1997: 370, emphasis in original)

'Unplanned' development, as Elias puts it, provides the major constraint to any institution or power wishing to establish a global standard of market civilization. It also calls on us to provide a more sociological and nuanced understanding of the relationships between the civilizers and those they seek to civilize. Similarly, Reinhard Bendix once commented that while external powers – be they the International Monetary Fund (IMF), the World Trade Organization (WTO), the Organization for Economic Co-operation and Development (OECD), or others – may seek to install 'functional equivalents' of their preferred policies within states, first the state must be willing to adopt them (Bendix 1977: 416). For policies to work, they need legitimacy.

Gerrit Gong has argued that modernization is inextricably linked to civilization, and that investigating civilization calls us to recognize that there are no 'value-free models of development or economic and financial interaction' (Gong 1998, 2002). Indeed, questions of legitimacy in the willing adoption or imposition of global standards of market civilization inevitably raise questions of justice and values. The idea that there exist standards of market civilization brings to the fore questions of justifying various processes of globalization. The contributors to this volume have all taken a stance on how standards of civilization within processes of globalization can or should be justified and what values they should learn from or attempt to enforce. Their key point of convergence is that once civilizing standards are taken into account there is not an apolitical process of diffusion taking place under globalization. Nor can international institutions simply dictate a standard of civilization to their member states.

Conceptual reprise

Individually and collectively, the chapters in this volume bring together political theory and political economy in an endeavor to contribute to, and advance. both. While the contributors come from a variety of conceptual backgrounds, readers will have detected a common interest in the role of ideas in the creation of global standards of market civilization and the institutional changes they engender. Recognition of the need for analysis of identity and power is also frequent. as are analyses of the material conditions that market standards have an impact upon.

For the most part, this book will be of particular conceptual interest to those who study how ideas about policy options are diffused and adopted in the international political economy. One strand of increasingly prominent scholarship here is constructivist work in international political economy and international relations more generally (Finnemore 1996; McNamara 1998; Keck and Sikkink 1998; Reus-Smit 1999; Blyth 2002; Parsons 2003). As signaled in the introductory chapter, constructivist literature has maintained a long-running interest in the concept of civilization as a social construct, just as it has placed emphasis on studying the social processes through which ideas and norms are transmitted. We stress caution in relation to how ideas and norms can be studied with respect to civilization, particularly given the general disposition within constructivist literature to study normative change towards the building of something 'bigger and better' (for a contrast on 'bad' norms see Rae 2002). Once more Elias provides sound counsel in arguing against a view of norms as 'benevolent, socially wholesome and integrating facts' (Elias 1996: 159). Rather, for Elias there is an 'inherently doubled-edged character of social norms, to the fact that they bind people to each other and at the same time turn people so bound against others. Their integrating tendency is, one might say, a disintegrating tendency' (Elias 1996: 159).

Constructivists should be aware that when playing with civilization they are playing with fire. This is particularly the case with constructivists who focus on how 'ideational entrepreneurs' carry and transmit ideas and norms. Much of this work concentrates on how ideas and norms are generated within international institutions and then diffused or disseminated to states – especially developing states – who wish to be considered civilized full members of an international society of states (Finnemore 1996). Caution is required here in interrogating contingencies behind the creation of such standards of civilization rather than replicating their normative agenda. Furthermore, despite drawing on the rubric of 'social' constructivism, there is nothing very sociological about top-down assumptions as to how norms are diffused. The interaction of ideational and material resources that back persuasion, including getting actors to morally inculcate or at least obey a global standard, has not been sufficiently explored (Payne 2001). More attention needs to be paid to how the creation of standards creates not only a rationalization of appropriate behavior but also a moral authority that must be specified historically (Hall 1997).

Similarly, recent Gramscian literature has also taken special interest in the concept of civilization and the transmission of norms and ideas (Cox 2001; Gill 1995; Morton 2005). Robert W. Cox, for example, has recently put forward the notion of civilization as '*a fit or correspondence between material conditions or existence and intersubjective meanings*' (Cox 2001: 110, italics in original). From this point of view civilization represents '*continuities* in human thought and practices' that have been created not within one particular state, but from 'civil society' (Cox 2001: 106, our emphasis). For Cox, this conception of civilization allows a comparative historical investigation of how people have dealt with economic phenomena, like globalization, and what futures they have imagined. However, the problem here is that such a focus asks us to look for *continuities* in thought across time. For us this appears too large an aim and too big a target. The histories of standards of civilization presented in this volume have emphasized discontinuities and contingencies that call attention to the double-edged nature of civilization within economic globalization. Despite Cox's emphasis on civil society and ground-up processes, we feel that any search for grand continuities, even if civil society is a focus, will inevitably smooth over history and overlook the traumas of civilizing processes and practices.

This book has sought to not only explore how global standards of market civilization have been created and imposed, but also how they are being contested. To that end, the agency of the recipients of standards of market civilization is important (see also Hobson and Seabrooke 2006). The case material in Part II of the book provides a number of studies that will be of interest to students of institutional theory and comparative and international political economy. Much of the literature in institutional theory (particularly that which informs the constructivist work mentioned above) focuses on how standards were imposed from above through the 'logic of appropriateness' that defined roles for actors to play, as opposed to ends to be acquired, the 'logic of instrumentality' (March and Olsen 1989, 1998). Like standards of civilization, logics of appropriateness call for orderly conduct, requiring actors to be on their best behavior in order to play well with others. Studies of such phenomena that only look from the top down effectively remove the agency of those on the receiving end of civilizing standards by concentrating on normative consensus (Sending 2002). However, as John L. Campbell has asserted, we should not see actors as 'institutional dopes blindly following the institutionalized scripts and cues around them' (Campbell 1998: 383). Rather, a focus on actions and practices dispels us of this notion of engineered conformity. Moreover, it reminds us that institutional change is an intersubjective phenomenon that must provide room for contestation for any policy change to have a chance of being effective. As many of the chapters in Part II have argued, while actors may signal that they conform to the global standard, the 'institutional script', their actions and practices are somewhat different. Indeed, these chapters also demonstrate that 'institutional isomorphism' is not simply a matter of copying the structures of the dominant in a local setting but, rather, engaging in processes of 'translation' and 'bricolage' to fuse local practices, norms, and values onto introduced global standards (Campbell 2004: 28–9; Jacobsson *et al.* 2004). Such processes produce institutional pluralism rather than institutional isomorphism.

Detailing such processes takes us into 'everyday' life and away from dealing with top-down power structures. As discussed in many of the chapters above, particularly in Part I, standards of civilization impact on how people regard themselves, who they look to for salvation, and who they look to for survival. Here civilization is deeper than an external structure being imposed; rather, it is the internalization of orderly behavior. As Emile Durkheim noted, civilization 'imposes upon man monotonous and continuous labor, [which] implies an absolute regularity of habits' (see Hamilton 1994). More recently, Ted Hopf has sought to unravel the 'thinkability' and 'logicability' of what is possible in the construction of identity and one's interests (Hopf 2002b: 13–15). As discussed in this book, the effective implementation of global standards of market civilization requires some degree of internalization. Expecting policy outcomes without such internalization of civilizing standards has led to a great deal of frustration among international institutions and prompted their calls for 'transparency', 'ownership', and 'political will'. An insufficient understanding of how macro-incorporation of a civilizing standard is not possible without micro-level inculcation is undoubtedly one source of this frustration and a topic for further conceptual and empirical development.

Five themes recapped

As stated in the introductory chapter, five themes run through this book: normalization; contestation; market mechanisms; self-inculcation; and the ranking of peoples. These themes are concerned with outlining the processes or mechanisms by which global standards of market civilization are produced, implemented, and contested. Importantly, these themes also ask us where the source of the adoption/ rejection of civilizing standards lies, as well as differing views on whether the state or the market should take a civilizing role over the economy. We recap these themes here briefly.

Normalization

One key process in the fostering of global standards of market civilization in the contemporary capitalist international political economy is the normalization of liberal positivism. As discussed by Jacqueline Best and Peter Larmour, liberal positivism has found institutional expression through the emphasis on 'transparency' within, respectively, the IMF and Transparency International. Mlada Bukovansky and Barry Hindess highlight how the attempted stripping of morality from civilizing standards on, respectively, corruption and citizenship is strongly associated with the encouragement of a form of neo-liberalism within developing states that posits an instrumental rationality destructive to local values. Our focus on normalization seeks to challenge the oft-espoused view that, as stated by David Fidler, 'standards of civilization and globalization share the central objective of improving the conditions of economic interaction between the West and the rest' (Fidler 2000: 400).

Contestation

As argued in a number of places in this book, the implementation of global standards of market civilization is not a simple top-down process but, to be successful, must be adopted from those on the receiving end of the civilizing standard. Even so, such global standards can be contested, including the rejection of the standard or, more likely, the translation of a standard in ways that are more congruent with social norms and political dynamics within the recipient states. The chapters by André Broome, Jillian Cohen, Gemma Kyle, and Leonard Seabrooke all stress this point to differing extents. For Broome, World Bank labor reforms fail to budge long-established practices related to non-wage benefits. Cohen shows how the tension in the double-meaning of civilization in global markets – potentially for human betterment and potentially for orderly conduct and the enforcement of property rights – led to a skewed drugs policy under the WTO that was effectively contested by developing states through recourse to moral arguments for human flourishing. As such, the WTO's institutional space permitted room not only for the promulgators of civilizing standards but also those seeking to contest them. In Kyle's chapter the OECD's harmful tax practices initiative is a global standard based on sovereignty, which itself provides the sovereign tax havens it targets with the rhetorical ammunition to defend their rights. For Seabrooke, emerging market economies' (EMEs) access to global capital markets must comply with contemporary standards of international creditworthiness. However, these standards are rationalized around financial data to the extent that EMEs have some capacity to provide the formal institutions and financial data to 'talk the talk' while also contesting the policy direction by not implementing changes on the ground. In sum, contestation reminds us that global standards can be shaped as well as received by those who are not dominant.

Market mechanisms

All contributors to this book agree that free capitalist markets do not *necessarily* contribute to a state's capacity for socio-political self-organization. However, there are some important differences here. Michael Oliver's chapter, for example, takes a clear position in arguing that states would do best to leave international monetary stability to the market and not to rely on state intervention. Here the pre-eminence of the market is justified in that it serves as the key civilizer. Kyle and Seabrooke also put forward pragmatic assessments of how developing states may engage capitalist markets. In both cases the global standard that has been created to economically benefit Western powers may also benefit developing states if they can shape and contest the standard's implementation.

Self-inculcation

One essential element in the implementation of global standards of market civilization is a moral realigning of the self that suggests a deeper process of normalization than that outlined above. Self-inculcation suggests a process whereby one's ideas about, values towards, and usage of the market economy is fundamentally reshaped. Particularly important in the contemporary period is the growth of a discourse on self-responsibility of the individual and, by extension, of the state. Broome, Matthew Watson, and Hindess provide evidence to suggest that such processes are occurring. For Broome the World Bank's propagation of self-responsible labor markets seeks to morally realign the self. Watson's historical survey outlines how the moral self is associated with notions of civility within the international political economy, including ideas about fairness. Hindess outlines how, through the extension of democratic citizenship, a neo-liberal standard of civilization seeks to instill the view that if you fail in the international political economy, as an individual or as a state, it is your fault. Understanding self-inculcation is vital to understanding civilizing processes as it provides a window into what meaning and weight people give to the introduction of any given global standard.

Ranking of peoples

While the ranking of peoples was an essential part of the nineteenth-century explicit standard of civilization, it is still present today. This theme is taken up by Brett Bowden, John M. Hobson, and Geoffrey A. Pigman. Bowden outlines the origins and evolution of the concept of civilization in different linguistic and cultural contexts, and how it is intimately tied to claims of national superiority that provided a justification for embarking upon 'civilizing missions'. Hobson's chapter discusses the European construction of racist standards in the late eighteenth century to explicitly rank Eastern people as lower on a 'civilizational league table' despite the East's material and technological edge in previous centuries. This explicit ordering of peoples directly informed imperialism and 'civilizing missions', and is still with us today, albeit implicitly, in relations between the US and East Asia. Pigman investigates the civilizing ideas that accompanied the development of world trade over the previous two centuries. Particularly important here is the juxtaposition that while Free Traders in the nineteenth century used the civilizing-mission discourse to open up markets, in the contemporary period 'alterglobalizers' are now using the benefits of open markets to reject civilizing missions. In sum, the ranking of peoples calls us to investigate changes in social attitudes that assist and challenge civilizing standards.

Policy implications and future research

What policy implications may be drawn from this study of global standards of market civilization? As noted above, the first is that we must turn our attention away from discussions of building technical capacity through implementing international institutions' global standards, or tracing idea and norm diffusion of ideational entrepreneurs, to provide a more thorough sociological understanding of what states and their peoples want in order to manage their political and economic lives – while not forgetting their social and cultural lives. There is little point in an international institution providing a common template for socio-political self-organization, a standard of civilization, if its policies within an economic reform program carry no meaning for the people involved. All too often policy-makers and scholars of the various international institutions assume that the problem is administrative or technical capacity, and that given sufficient training the developing state would comply. But this is hardly the case. For example, the high failure rate of the IMF's taxation reform programs is not a problem of training or technical capacity; which is readily available to most of its member states. Rather, the problem is the significance to which people within the state, its citizens, view taxation as morally justifiable and, if so, what types of taxation and at what kinds of rates, etc. Any aim to normalize a taxation system without addressing this problem of the relationship between the desired policy and the moral self will surely be contested, either publicly or in more silent forms of resistance (Kerkvliet 2005). So while the IMF might plan with the Philippines to implement a new socially planned taxation system, much informal community-based taxation takes place in the 'unplanned' economy (Seabrooke 2005a). Opening the door to more sociological analysis of what conduct is considered appropriate would undoubtedly permit greater tailoring and customization of policy with greater social legitimacy and implementation outcomes. On the flipside, a further danger is to avoid cultural stereotyping: for instance, that certain peoples or cultures do not have the capacity to engage with 'modern' forms of capitalism at a productive level (Landes 1998), or that cultural traits determine a certain path towards development (Harrison and Huntington 2000). Such an implicit ranking of peoples is unacceptable.

Policy-making that concerns the creation and implementation of market mechanisms can learn from comparative historical investigations of former systems (North 1990) as well as work in economic sociology (such as Elias and Weber) on civilizing processes of rationalization. Understanding the rationalization of markets, including motives for control and profit, is particularly important in identifying influences on market behavior that are outside of the self-referential performance criteria. Furthermore, the logic that markets work best when everyone has the same system, permitting a greater chance of perfect information, should be questioned when one considers that modern corporations tend to prefer stable profits and control over fair and free market competition (Fligstein 1990, 2001). So, instead of homogeneity among market actors, by knowing what civilizing standards are being rejected and contested, market differentiation and specialization rather than market exclusion might just be possible, preferable, and profitable. As we have seen above, the introduction of market capitalism into many societies is being shaped by domestic pressures through translation and bricolage. A greater understanding and acceptance of what civilizing standards are viewed as legitimate and those that are not would both accelerate and improve this process.

There are a number of topics that could not be included in this volume but provide fruitful avenues for future research. Here we mention but a few. One significant gap in political economy that begs for attention is studies of consumption within markets. If a civilization is thought by many to be determined in large part by the consumer culture, then we need to know the political and social dynamics that surround it. The growth of conspicuous consumption in some societies and the fast-paced expansion of global branding are both in need of treatment. Further research on the WTO is necessary, particularly in relation to food technology and the meaning and significance people give to certain food products. Work also needs to be done on the spread of technological standards into big producer and consumer markets with different standards of civilized conduct in respect to property rights, such as the wrangle between Microsoft and LINUX in China. The implications of this battle will transform not only the Chinese market but also global trends. Finally, if civilization is held to be both a concept that enables human betterment but also provides orderly conduct according to rules established by a community, then labor migration within regional trading blocs is an important topic for examination. Particularly attractive here is research on migration from the newly joined states of the European Union (EU), which has sparked the term 'welfare tourist' and debates over what rights newly minted EU citizens from 'backward' states should have compared to the more 'civilized' states in Northwestern Europe.

In conclusion

This book began by stating that it is primarily concerned with how global standards of market civilization are variously conceptualized and the process by which they are developed and evolve, and how they are in turn applied and enforced in an era of economic globalization. Using historical and contemporary case studies and noting the continuities, parallels, and divergences between past and present, the authors have demonstrated how international institutions have enthusiastically embraced and applied global standards to deal with the challenges and potential windfalls presented by globalization. Part I of the collection provides a solid conceptual foundation with which to tackle and in turn understand the issues dealt with in a series of select case studies expounded in Part II. Collectively we have shown how the application of global standards of market civilization can have both positive and deleterious effects on a number of crucial issue-areas, many of which are either directly or indirectly related: from financial crises to issues of endemic poverty to personal health and well-being. Not all of the authors herein necessarily agree on the most appropriate means to tackle the problems that these issues pose. The cases we have addressed here are particularly topical issues and important arenas of concern, but, as mentioned earlier, further significant arenas of study are endlessly appearing.

As we also stated at the outset of this book, we have endeavored to open up new insights into the issues explored here through a concerted and conscientious union of political theory and political economy. While the insertion of political theory into disciplines such as international relations has opened up new avenues of contestation and arenas for debate in the workings of world politics, it has not caught on so readily in the study of international political economy. With this book we hope to have made the beginnings of a small inroad into what we believe is a more than worthwhile venture. We think this has proved a profitable coming together of political theory and political economy that has enhanced our capacity to explore and address some of the key issues facing our world in a time of greater interdependence and heightened globalization. But more than just an exercise in academic adventurism, we have also endeavored to demonstrate tangible 'real-world' relevance by providing well-researched empirical material.

Finally, if the concept of civilization must be used at all, and recent trends in and beyond academic scholarship suggest it will be in vogue for some time yet, we urge that it is used in a more nuanced and contextualized manner than it has been thus far. As Elias suggests, civilizing processes always contain violence as those who claim superiority claim their dominance (Linklater 2004). However, Elias also outlines a positive conception of civilization that we embrace as the capacity to think 'from the standpoint of the multiplicity of people' (Elias 1994: 140). Following Elias, while we have sought to demonstrate that appropriate use of the concept can prove fruitful, we also urge that it be used cautiously; that appeals to civilization serve to neither reify nor deify the ideal, for as this book has also sought to demonstrate, both come with considerable risks attached.

Bibliography

Abernethy, D.B. (2000) *The Dynamics of Global Dominance*, London: Yale University Press.

Ades, A. and R. Di Tella (1997) 'The New Economics of Corruption: A Survey and Some New Results', *Political Studies* 45: 496–515.

Ahluwalia, M.S. (1999) 'The IMF and the World Bank in the New Financial Architecture', in M.S. Ahluwalia, *International Monetary and Financial Issues for the 1990s*, Vol. XI, New York: United Nations, pp. 1–45.

Alam, A. and A. Banerji (2000) 'Uzbekistan and Kazakhstan: A Tale of Two Transition Paths', Policy Research Working Paper No. 2472, Washington, DC: World Bank.

Aldcroft, D.H. and M.J. Oliver (1998) *Exchange Rate Regimes in the Twentieth Century*, Cheltenham: Edward Elgar.

Alexandrowicz, C.H. (1973) *The European–African Confrontation*, Leiden: A.W. Sijthoff.

Alkire, S. and L. Chen (2004) 'Global Health and Moral Values', *The Lancet* 364: 1074.

Andritzky, J.R., G.J. Bannister, and N.T. Tamirisa (2005) 'The Impact of Macroeconomic Announcements on Emerging Market Bonds', IMF Working Paper WP/05/83, Washington, DC: International Monetary Fund.

Anghie, A. (1996) 'Francisco de Vitoria and the Colonial Origins of International Law', *Social and Legal Studies* 5: 321–36.

Arendt, H. (1958) *The Human Condition*, Chicago: University of Chicago Press.

Armijo, L.E. (1999) 'Mixed Blessing: Foreign Capital Flows and Democracy in Emerging Markets', in L.E. Armijo (ed.) *Financial Globalization and Democracy in Emerging Markets*, Basingstoke: Macmillan, pp. 17–50.

——(2001) 'The Political Geography of World Financial Reform: Who Wants What and Why?', *Global Governance* 7: 379–96.

——(ed.) (2002) *Debating the Global Financial Architecture*, Albany: SUNY Press.

Armitage, D. (2004) 'John Locke, Carolina and the *Two Treatises of Government*', *Political Theory* 32: 1–26.

Ashcroft, J. (2003) 'Prepared remarks' at the Conference for signing the UN Convention against Corruption, Merida, Mexico, 9 December, www.state.gov/g/inl/rls/rm/27072.htm.

ATO (Australian Taxation Office) (2004) 'Tax Havens and Tax Administration', www.ato.gov.au/content/46908.htm.

Baldwin, R.E. and P. Martin, (1999) 'Two Waves of Globalization: Superficial Similarities, Fundamental Differences', NBER Working Paper No. 6904, Cambridge, MA: National Bureau of Economic Research.

Barnett, M. and M. Finnemore (2004) *Rules for the World: International Organizations in Global Politics*, Ithaca: Cornell University Press.

Barry, A., T. Osborne, and N. Rose (eds) (1996) *Foucault and Political Reason*, Chicago: University of Chicago Press.

Baudrillard, J. (2004) 'La violence de la mondialisation', *Manière de voir* 75: 10–12.

Baum, G. (1996) *Karl Polanyi on Ethics and Economics*, London: McGill–Queen's University Press.

Bello, W. (1994) *Dark Victory*, London: Pluto Press.

——(2004 [2000]) 'The Struggle for a Deglobalized World', Focus on the Global South, September 2000, www.nadir.org.

Bendix, R. (1977) *Nation-Building and Citizenship*, London: University of California Press.

Benveniste, E. (1971) *Problems in General Linguistics*, Coral Gables: University of Miami Press.

Bernabè, S. and A. Kolev (2003) 'Identifying Vulnerable Groups in the Kyrgyz Labour Market: Some Implications for the National Poverty Reduction Strategy', Centre for Analysis of Social Exclusion Discussion Paper No. 71, London: Centre for Analysis of Social Exclusion.

Best, J. (2003a) 'From the Top Down: The New Financial Architecture and the Re-embedding of Global Finance', *New Political Economy* 8: 363–84.

——(2003b) 'Moralizing Finance: The New Financial Architecture as Ethical Discourse', *Review of International Political Economy* 10: 579–603.

——(2005) *The Limits of Transparency*, Ithaca: Cornell University Press.

Bhabha, H.K. (1994) *The Location of Culture*, London: Routledge.

Biersteker, T.J. and C. Weber (eds) (1995) *State Sovereignty as Social Construct*, Cambridge: Cambridge University Press.

Blaut, J.M. (1993) *The Colonizer's Model of the World*, London: Guilford Press.

Blyth, M. (2002) *Great Transformations: Economic Ideas and Institutional Change in the Twentieth Century*, Cambridge: Cambridge University Press.

Bordo, M.D. (1981) 'The Classical Gold Standard, Some Lessons for Today', *Federal Reserve Bank of St Louis Review* May: 2–17.

——(2003) 'Market Discipline and Financial Crisis Policy: A Historical Perspective', paper prepared for the Contemporary Economic Policy Session: Market Discipline in Banking: Theory and Evidence, Western Economic Association International Meeting, Denver, Colorado, 13 July.

Bordo, M.D., B. Eichengreen, and D.A. Irwin (1999) 'Is Globalization Today Really Different than Globalization a Hundred Years Ago?', NBER Working Paper No. 7195, Cambridge, MA: National Bureau of Economic Research.

Bordo, M.D., B. Eichengreen, and J. Kim (1998) 'Was There Really an Earlier Period of International Financial Integration Comparable to Today?', NBER Working Paper No. 6738, Cambridge, MA: National Bureau of Economic Research.

Bordo, M.D., B. Eichengreen, D. Klingebiel, and M.S. Martinez-Peri (2001) 'Is the Crisis Problem Growing More Severe?', *Economic Policy* 16: 53–82.

Bordo, M.D., A. Mody, and N. Oomes (2004) 'Keeping Capital Flowing: The Role of the IMF', *International Finance* 7: 421–50.

Bordo, M.D. and H. Rockoff (1996) 'The Gold Standard as a "Good Housekeeping Seal of Approval"', *Journal of Economic History* 56: 389–428.

Boughton, J.M. (2001) *Silent Revolution: The International Monetary Fund, 1979–1989*, Washington, DC: International Monetary Fund.

Boughton, J.M. and K.S. Lateef (ed.) (1995) *Fifty Years after Bretton Woods: The Future of the IMF and the World Bank*, Washington, DC: International Monetary Fund and World Bank.

Bowden, B. (2002) 'Reinventing Imperialism in the Wake of September 11', *Alternatives: Turkish Journal of International Relations* 1: 28–46.

——(2004a) 'In the Name of Progress and Peace: The "Standard of Civilization" and the Universalizing Project', *Alternatives: Global, Local, Political* 29: 43–68.

——(2004b) 'The Ideal of Civilisation: Its Origins and Socio-Political Character', *Critical Review of International Social and Political Philosophy* 7: 25–50.

——(2004c) 'Expanding the Empire of Civilization: Uniform, Not Universal', doctoral dissertation, Political Science Program, Research School of Social Sciences, Australian National University.

——(2005) 'The Colonial Origins of International Law: European Expansion and the Classical Standard of Civilisation', *Journal of the History of International Law* 7: 1–23.

Brandt Commission (1983) *Common Crisis, North South*, London: Pan Books.

Braudel, F. (1980) 'The History of Civilizations: The Past Explains the Present', in F. Braudel, *On History*, trans. Sarah Matthews, London: Weidenfeld & Nicolson, pp. 177–218.

Brooks, S.M. (2005) 'Interdependent and Domestic Foundations of Policy Change: The Diffusion of Pension Privatization around the World', *International Studies Quarterly* 49: 273–94.

Brown, K. (1999) 'Harmful Tax Competition: The OECD View', *George Washington Journal of International Law and Economics* 32: 311–23.

Broz, J.L. (2005) 'Congressional Politics of International Financial Rescues', *American Journal of Political Science* 49: 479–96.

Bukovansky, M. (2006) 'The Hollowness of Anti-Corruption Discourse', *Review of International Political Economy*, 13: 181–209.

Bull, H. (1977) *The Anarchical Society*, London: Macmillan.

Bulmer, M. and A.M. Rees (eds) (1996) *Citizenship Today*, London: UCL Press.

Burchell, G., C. Gordon, and P. Miller (eds) (1991) *The Foucault Effect*, Chicago: University of Chicago Press.

Burchell, S. and A. Linklater (1996) *Theories of International Relations*, Basingstoke: Macmillan.

Burstein, D. (1988) *Yen! The Threat of Japan's Financial Empire*, Moorebank: Bantam.

Bush, G.W. (2001) '"No Nation Can be Neutral in this Conflict." Remarks by the President to the Warsaw Conference on Combatting Terrorism', United States White House, 6 November, www.whitehouse.gov/news/releases/2001/11/20011106-2.html.

——(2002) 'President Thanks World Coalition for Anti-Terrorism Efforts: Remarks by the President on the Six-Month Anniversary of the September 11th Attacks', United States White House, 11 March, www.whitehouse.gove/news/releases/2002/03/2002 0311-1.html.

Camdessus, M. (1998) 'Press Briefing by IMF Managing Director Michel Camdessus', International Monetary Fund, 1 October, www.imf.org/external/np/tr/1998/tr981001.htm.

——(1999a) 'Economic and Financial Situation in Asia: Latest Developments', background paper prepared for presentation to the Asia-Europe Finance Ministers Meeting, Frankfurt: International Monetary Fund.

——(1999b) 'From the Crises of the 1990s to the New Millennium: Remarks to the International Graduate School of Management', International Monetary Fund, 27 November, www.imf.org/external/np/speeches/1999/112799.htm.

——(1999c) 'Governments and Economic Development in a Globalized World: Remarks at the 32nd International General Meeting of the Pacific Basin Economic Council', International Monetary Fund, 17 May, www.imf.org/external/np/speeches/1999/051799.htm.

Cammack, P. (2004) 'What the World Bank Means by Poverty Reduction, and Why it Matters', *New Political Economy* 9: 189–211.

Campbell, D. (1992) *Writing Security*, Manchester: Manchester University Press.

Campbell, J.L. (1998) 'Institutional Analysis and the Role of Ideas in Political Economy', *Theory and Society* 27: 377–409.

——(2004) *Institutional Change and Globalization*, Princeton: Princeton University Press.

——and O.K. Pedersen (1996) 'The Evolutionary Nature of Revolutionary Change in Postcommunist Europe', in J.L. Campbell and O.K. Pedersen (eds) *Legacies of Change: Transformations of Post-Communist Europe*, New York: Aldine de Gruyter, pp. 207–51.

Campbell, R.H. and A. Skinner (1982) *Adam Smith*, London: Croom Helm.

Carruthers, B.G. and W.N. Espeland (1991) 'Accounting for Rationality: Double-Entry Bookkeeping and the Rhetoric of Economic Rationality', *American Journal of Sociology* 97: 31–69.

Cartapanis, A. and M. Herland (2002) 'The Reconstruction of the International Financial Architecture: Keynes' Revenge?', *Review of International Political Economy* 9: 271–97.

Cassen, B. (2004) 'Le libre-échange, c'est aussi la guerre . . . ', *Manière de voir* 75: 26–8.

Cazes, S. (2002) 'Do Labour Market Institutions Matter in Transition Economies? An Analysis of Labour Market Flexibility in the Late Nineties', International Institute for Labour Studies Discussion Paper DP/140/2002, Geneva: International Institute for Labour Studies.

Chang, H.-J. (2002) *Kicking Away the Ladder*, London: Anthem Press.

Cheung, S.N.S. (1996) 'A Simplistic General Equilibrium Theory of Corruption', *Contemporary Economic Policy* 14: 1–5.

Christopher, A.J. (1984) *Colonial Africa*, Totowa: Barnes & Noble.

Chwieroth, J.M. (2005) 'Neoliberal Norms and Capital Account Liberalization in Emerging Markets: The Role of Domestic-Level Knowledge-Based Experts', unpublished manuscript, London School of Economics, November.

Clark, I. (1989) *The Hierarchy of States*, Cambridge: Cambridge University Press.

Clavin, P. (1991) 'The World Economic Conference 1933: The Failure of British Internationalism', *Journal of European Economic History* 20: 489–527.

——(1992) 'The Fetishes of So-Called International Bankers: Central Bank Cooperation for the World Economic Conference, 1932–3', *Contemporary European History* 1: 281–311.

Cobden Club (1873) 'Free Trade and Free Enterprise', Report of the Proceedings at the Dinner of the Cobden Club, 28 June, London, Paris, and New York: Castell, Petter & Galpin.

——(1875) *Free Trade and the European Treaties of Commerce*, London, Paris, and New York: Castell, Petter & Galpin.

Cohen, B.J. (1981) *Banks and the Balance of Payments: Private Lending in the International Adjustment Process*, in collaboration with Fabio Basagni, London: Croom Helm.

——(1986) *In Whose Interest? International Banking and American Foreign Policy*, New Haven: Yale University Press.

Cohen, J.C. (2002) 'Developing States' Responses to the Pharmaceutical Imperatives of the TRIPS Agreement', in B. Granville (ed.) *The Economics of Essential Medicines*, London: The Royal Institute of International Affairs, pp. 113–47.

Colley, L. (1992) *Britons: Forging the Nation 1707–1837*, New Haven: Yale University Press.

Collingwood, R. G. (1992) *The New Leviathan*, Oxford: Clarendon Press.

Collins, K. (2004) 'The Logic of Clan Politics: Evidence from the Central Asian Trajectories', *World Politics* 56: 244–61.

Conklin, A.L. (1997) *A Mission to Civilize*, Stanford: Stanford University Press.

Cooley, A. (2000) 'International Aid to the Former Soviet States: Agent of Change or Guardian of the Status Quo?', *Problems of Post-Communism* 47: 34–44.

Cox, R.W. (1987) *Production, Power and World Order*, New York: Columbia University Press.

——(2001) 'Civilizations and the Twenty-First Century: Some Theoretical Considerations', *International Relations of the Asia-Pacific* 1: 105–30.

——(2002) *Political Economy of a Plural World: Critical Reflections on Power, Morals and Civilization*, with M.G. Schecter, London: Routledge/RIPE series in Global Political Economy 77.

Crouch, C. and H. Farrell (2004) 'Breaking the Path of Institutional Development? Alternatives to the New Determinism', *Rationality and Society* 16: 5–43.

Cullet, P. (2003) 'Patents and Medicines: The Relationship Between TRIPS and the Human Right to Health', *International Affairs* 79: 139–60.

Curtin, P.D. (1964) *The Image of Africa*, Madison: University of Wisconsin Press.

Dam, K.W. (1982) *The Rules of the Game: Reform and Evolution in the International Monetary System*, Chicago: University of Chicago Press.

Dar, A. and Z. Tzannatos (1999) 'World Bank Lending for Labor Markets: 1991 to 1998', World Bank Social Protection Discussion Paper No. 9902, Washington, DC: World Bank.

Darwin, J. (2000) 'Civility and Empire', in P. Burke, B. Harrison, and P. Slack (eds) *Civil Histories*, Oxford: Oxford University Press, pp. 321–36.

Davis, K. and M.J. Trebilcock (1999) 'What Role Do Legal Institutions Play in Development?', Draft prepared for the International Monetary Fund's Conference on Second Generation Reforms, Washington, DC, 8–9 November, www.imf.org/external/pubs/ft/seminar/1999/reforms/index.htm#agenda.

Davis, L.E. and R.E. Gallman (2001) *Evolving Financial Markets and International Capital Flows: Britain, the Americas, and Australia, 1865–1914*, Cambridge: Cambridge University Press.

De Sousa, L. (forthcoming) 'TI in Search of a Constituency: The Franchising of the Global Anti Corruption Movement (an Overview of the National Chapters' Formation, Nature and Quality)', unpublished working paper, Canberra: Research School of Social Sciences, Australian National University.

De Vries, M.G. (1985a) *The International Monetary Fund, 1972–1978: Cooperation on Trial, Volume 2: Narrative and Analysis*, Washington, DC: International Monetary Fund.

——(1985b) *The International Monetary Fund, 1972–1978: Cooperation on Trial, Volume 3: Documents*, Washington, DC: International Monetary Fund.

Dean, M. (1999) *Governmentality*, London: Sage.

Desrosieres, A. (1998) *The Politics of Large Numbers: A History of Statistical Reasoning*, Cambridge, MA: Harvard University Press.

DiMaggio, P. and W. Powell (1983) 'The Iron Cage Revisited: Institutional Isomorphism and Collective Rationality in Organizational Fields', *American Sociological Review* 48: 147–60.

——(1991) *The New Institutionalism in Organizational Analysis*, Chicago: University of Chicago Press.

Doig, A. and S. McIvor (2003) 'The National Integrity System: Assessing Corruption and Reform', *Public Administration and Development* 23: 317–32.

Dolowitz, D. and D. Marsh (2000) 'Learning from Abroad: The Role of Policy Transfer in Contemporary Policy-Making', *Governance* 13: 5–23.

Donnelly, J. (1998) 'Human Rights: A New Standard of Civilization?', *International Affairs* 74: 1–24.

Dow, A., S. Dow, and A. Hutton (1997) 'The Scottish Political Economy Tradition and Modern Economics', *Scottish Journal of Political Economy* 44: 368–83.

Drinnon, R. (1980) *Facing West*, Minneapolis: University of Minnesota Press.

Dutt, R.P. (1943) *The Problem of India*, New York: International Publishers.

Easson, A. (2004) 'Harmful Tax Competition: An Evaluation of the OECD Initiative', *Tax Notes International* 7 June: 1037–77.

Eatwell, J. (1997) *International Financial Liberalization*, New York: Office of Development Studies, United Nations Development Programme.

Eatwell, J. and L. Taylor (2000) *Global Finance at Risk*, New York: The New Press.

EC (European Commission) (1998) (DG1) Note on the WHO's Revised Drug Strategy, Doc. No. 1/D/3/BW D (98), www.cptech.org/ip/health/who/eurds98.html.

Economist (1998) 'Complaints by High-Tax European Union Countries about "Harmful" Tax Competition from Low Tax Ones Should be Given Short Shrift', 30 July.

Edwardes, M. (1971) *East–West Passage*, New York: Taplinger.

Eichengreen, B. (1989) 'Hegemonic Stability Theories of the International Monetary System', in R.N. Cooper, B. Eichengreen, C.R. Henning, G. Holtham, and R. Putnum (eds) *Can Nations Agree? Issues in International Economic Cooperation*, Washington, DC: The Brookings Institution, pp. 255–98.

——(1992) *Golden Fetters: The Gold Standard and the Great Depression, 1919–1939*, Oxford: Oxford University Press.

——(1996) *Globalizing Capital: A History of the International Monetary System*, Princeton: Princeton University Press.

——(1999) *Toward a New International Financial Architecture*, Washington, DC: Institute for International Economics.

——(2004) 'Viewpoint: Understanding the Great Depression', *Canadian Journal of Economics* 37: 1–27.

——(2005) 'Chinese Currency Controversies', *Asian Economic Papers* 4.

——and M. Bordo (2003) 'Crises Now and Then: What Lessons from the Last Era of Financial Globalization?', in P. Mizen (ed.) *Monetary History, Exchange Rates and Financial Markets, Essays in Honour of Charles Goodhart*, Vol. 2, Cheltenham: Edward Elgar, pp. 52–91.

Eichengreen, B. and B. Park (2002) 'Hedge Fund Leverage Before and After the Crisis', *Journal of Economic Integration* 17: 1–20.

Eisenstadt, S.N. (2000) 'Multiple Modernities', *Daedalus* 129: 1–29.

Elias, N. (1988) 'Violence and Civilization: The State Monopoly of Physical Violence and its Infringement', in J. Keane (ed.) *Civil Society and the State: New European Perspectives*, London: Verso, pp. 177–98.

——(1992) *Time: An Essay*, Oxford: Basil Blackwell.

——(1994) *Reflections on a Life*, Cambridge: Polity Press.

——(1996) *The Germans: Power Struggles and the Development of Habitus in the Nineteenth and Twentieth Centuries*, New York: Columbia University Press.

——(1997) 'Towards a Theory of Social Processes: A Translation', trans. R. van Krieken and E. Dunning, *The British Journal of Sociology* 48: 355–83.

——(2000) *The Civilizing Process*, Oxford: Blackwell.

Eschle, C. and N. Stammers (2004) 'Taking Part: Social Movements, INGOs and Global Change', *Alternatives* 29: 333–72.

Euben, J.P. (1989) 'Corruption', in T. Ball, J. Farr, and R.L. Hanson (eds) *Political Innovation and Conceptual Change*, Cambridge: Cambridge University Press, pp. 220–46.

Evans, P. (1989) 'Predatory, Developmental and Other State Apparatuses', *Sociological Forum* 4: 561–84.

Febvre, L. (1973) 'Civilization: Evolution of a Word and a Group of Ideas', in P. Burke (ed.) *A New Kind of History: From the Writings of Febvre*, London: Routledge & Kegan Paul, pp. 219–57.

Ferguson, A. (1966) *An Essay on the History of Civil Society* [1767], Edinburgh: Edinburgh University Press.

——(1975), *Principles of Moral and Political Science* [1792], 2 vols, Hildesheim: Georg Olms Verlag.

Ferguson, N. (2003) *Empire: How Britain Made the Modern World*, London: Penguin Books.

——(2004) *Colossus: The Price of American Empire*, New York: The Penguin Press.

Fidler, D.P. (2000) 'A Kinder, Gentler System of Capitulation? International Law, Structural Adjustment Policies, and the Standard of Liberal, Globalized Civilization', *Texas International Law Journal* 35: 387–413.

Financial Action Task Force on Money Laundering (2003) 'The Forty Recommendations', www1.oecd.org/fatf/40Recs_en.htm.

Finnemore, M. (1996) *National Interests in International Society*, Ithaca: Cornell University Press.

Finnemore, M. and K. Sikkink (1998) 'International Norms Dynamics and Political Change', *International Organization* 52: 887–917.

Fiore, P. (1918) *International Law Codified and Its Legal Sanction*, New York: Baker, Voorhis & Company.

Fishlow, A. (1985) 'The Political Economy of Debt: Lessons from the Past: Capital Markets During the 19th Century and the Interwar Period', *International Organization* 39: 383–439.

Fitzgibbons, A. (1995) *Adam Smith's System of Liberty, Wealth and Virtue*, Oxford: Clarendon Press.

Fligstein, N. (1990) *The Transformation of Corporate Control*, Cambridge: Cambridge University Press.

——(2001) *The Architecture of Markets: An Economic Sociology of Twenty-First-Century Capitalist Societies*, Princeton: Princeton University Press.

Forbes, D. (1966) 'Introduction', in A. Ferguson, *An Essay on the History of Civil Society 1767*, Edinburgh: Edinburgh University Press, pp. xii–xli.

Fossedal, G.A. (1989) *The Democratic Imperative*, New York: Basic Books.

Foucault, M. (1970) *The Order of Things*, New York: Vintage Books.

——(1977) *Discipline and Punish: The Birth of the Prison*, London: Penguin Books.

——(1997) *Ethics: Subjectivity and Truth*, New York: The New Press.

Frieden, J.A. (1987) *Banking on the World: The Politics of American International Finance*, New York: Harper & Row Publishers.

Friedman, T.L. (1999) *The Lexus and the Olive Tree: Understanding Globalization*, New York: Farrar, Strauss & Giroux.

Fryer, P. (1988) *Black People in the British Empire*, London: Pluto.

Fukuyama, F. (1989) 'The End of History?', *The National Interest* 16: 3–18.

——(1992) *The End of History and the Last Man*, London: Hamish Hamilton.

Fusfeld, D. (2002) *The Age of the Economist*, 9th edn, London: Addison Wesley.

Gaffney, M. (1998/99) 'Competition: More Harm than Good?', *International Tax Review* 10: 46–8.

Galtung, F. (2006) 'Measuring the Immeasurable: Boundaries and Functions of (Macro) Corruption Indices', in F. Galtung and C. Sampford (eds) *Measuring Corruption*, Aldershot: Ashgate, 101–130.

Gardner, R.N. (1980) *Sterling–Dollar Diplomacy in Current Perspective*, New York: Columbia University Press.

GATT (General Agreement on Tariffs and Trade) (1947) Article XX(b).
——(1989a) Document, C/M/232, May.
——(1989b) Document, C/M/236, October.
Germain, R.D. (1997) *The International Organization of Credit*, Cambridge: Cambridge University Press.
——(ed.) (2000) *Globalization and its Critics*, Basingstoke: Macmillan.
——(2001) 'Global Financial Governance and the Problem of Inclusion', *Global Governance* 7: 411–26.
Gerschenkron, A. (1962) *Economic Backwardness in Historical Perspective*, Cambridge, MA: Harvard University Press.
Giddens, A. (1991) *The Consequences of Modernity*, Cambridge: Polity Press.
Gill, S. (1995) 'Globalisation, Market Civilisation and Disciplinary Neoliberalism', *Millennium: Journal of International Studies* 24: 399–423.
——(1998) 'New Constitutionalism, Democratisation and Global Political Economy', *Pacifica Review* 10: 23–38.
——(2003a) *Power and Resistance in the New World Order*, Basingstoke: Palgrave.
——(2003b) 'Towards a Stark Utopia? New Constitutionalism and the Politics of Globalization', in L. Benería and S. Bisnath (eds) *Global Tensions: Challenges and Opportunities in the World Economy*, New York: Routledge, pp. 13–26.
Gilpin, R. (1987) *The Political Economy of International Relations*, Princeton: Princeton University Press.
Global Trade Watch (2004) www.citizen.org/trade, accessed 2 August.
Gold, J. (1988) *Exchange Rates in International Law and Organization*, Washington, DC: American Bar Association.
Goldstein, M. (1999) 'Safeguarding Prosperity in a Global Financial System: The Future International Financial Architecture', Report of an Independent Task Force Sponsored by the Council on Foreign Relations, Washington, DC: Institute for International Economics.
Goldthwaite, R.A. (1998) 'Banking in Florence at the End of the Sixteenth Century', *Journal of European Economic History* 27: 471–536.
Gong. G.W. (1984) *The Standard of 'Civilization' in International Society*, Oxford: Clarendon.
——(1998) 'Asian Financial Crisis: Culture and Strategy'. ICAS Fall Symposium, University of Pennsylvania, 29 September, www.icasinc.org/f1998/gwgf1998.html.
——(2002) 'Standards of Civilization Today', in M. Mozaffari (ed.) *Globalization and Civilizations*, London: Routledge, pp. 77–96.
Grabel, I. (2000) 'The Political Economy of "Policy Credibility": The New-Classical Macroeconomics and the Remaking of Emerging Economies', *Cambridge Journal of Economics* 24: 1–19.
Gray, J. (1998) *False Dawn: The Delusions of Global Capitalism*, London: Granta.
Greenberg, M. (1969) *British Trade and the Opening of China 1800–42*, Cambridge: Cambridge University Press.
Greenspan, A. (1998) Testimony of Chairman of the Reserve Board. Paper read at Committee on Banking and Financial Services, US House of Representatives, at Washington, DC, 30 January.
Greif, A. (2006) *Institutions: Theory and History*, Cambridge: Cambridge University Press.
Gross, J. (2003) 'OECD Defensive Measures against Harmful Tax Competition Legality under WTO', *International Tax* 31: P390–400.
Guha, R. (1997) 'Not at Home in Empire', *Critical Inquiry* 23: 482–93.
Guillén, M.F. (2001) *The Limits of Convergence: Globalization and Organizational Changes to Argentina, South Korea, and Spain*, Princeton: Princeton University Press.

Habermas, J. (1989) *The Structural Transformation of the Public Sphere: An Inquiry into a Category of Bourgeois Society*, Cambridge, MA: MIT Press.

Haley, M.A. (2001) *Freedom and Finance: Democratization and Institutional Investors*, Basingstoke: Palgrave.

Hall, P.A. and D. Soskice (eds) (2001) *Varieties of Capitalism: The Institutional Foundations of Comparative Advantage*, Oxford: Oxford University Press.

Hall, R.B. (1997) 'Moral Authority as a Power Resource', *International Organization* 51: 591–622.

——(2003) 'The Discursive Demolition of the Asian Development Model', *International Studies Quarterly* 47: 71–99.

Hall, W.E. (1924) *A Treatise on International Law*, 8th edn, Oxford: Clarendon Press.

Hamilton, A. and M.J. Oliver (2006) 'The Evolution of an External Paradigm: Sterling in the Bretton Woods System, 1944–1979', *Review of International Political Economy*, forthcoming.

Hamilton, G.G. (1994) 'Civilization and the Organization of Economies', in N. Smelser and R. Swedberg (eds) *Handbook of Economic Sociology*, Princeton: Princeton University Press, pp. 183–205.

Hampton, M. (2002) 'Offshore Pariahs? Small Island Economies, Tax Havens and the Reconfiguration of Global Finance', *World Development* 30: 1657–73.

Hardt, M. and A. Negri (2000) *Empire*, Cambridge, MA: Harvard University Press.

——(2004) *Multitude: War and Democracy in the Age of Empire*, New York: The Penguin Press.

Hargreaves, A. (1982) 'European Identity and the Colonial Frontier', *Journal of European Studies* 12: 167–79.

Harrell, S. (1995) 'Introduction: Civilizing Projects and the Reaction to them', in S. Harrell (ed.) *Cultural Encounters on China's Ethnic Frontier*, Washington, DC: University of Washington Press, pp. 3–36.

Harrison, L.E. and S.P. Huntington (eds) (2000) *Culture Matters: How Values Shape Human Progress*, New York: Basic Books.

Held, D. (1995) *Democracy and the Global Order*, Cambridge: Polity.

Helleiner, E. (1994) *States and the Re-emergence of Global Finance: From Bretton Woods to the 1990s*, Ithaca: Cornell University Press.

——(2003) 'Denationalizing Money? Economic Liberalism and the "National Question" in Currency Affairs', in M. Flandreau, C.-L. Holtfrerich, and H. James (eds) *International Financial History in the Twentieth Century: System and Anarchy*, Cambridge: Cambridge University Press, pp. 213–37.

Hertz, N. (2001) *The Silent Takeover*, London: Heinemann.

Hill, L. (2001) 'The Hidden Theology of Adam Smith', *European Journal of the History of Economic Thought* 8: 1–29.

Hindess, B. (2000) 'Representation Ingrafted upon Democracy', *Democratization* 7: 1–18.

——(2001) 'The Liberal Government of Unfreedom', *Alternatives* 26: 93–111.

——(2004a) 'Liberalism: What's in a Name', in W. Larner and W. Walters (eds) *Global Governmentality: Governing International Spaces*, London: Routledge, pp. 23–39.

——(2004b) 'International Anti-Corruption as a Program of Normalisation', Paper presented to a workshop on 'Corruption: Expanding the Focus', Research School of Social Sciences and Asia Pacific School of Economics and Government, Australian National University, Canberra, 30–31 July.

Hirschman, A. O. (1978) *The Passions and the Interests*, Princeton: Princeton University Press.

Hobbes, T. (1968) *Leviathan*, London: Penguin.

Hobson, J.A. (1901) *The Social Problem*, London: James Nisbet.

——(1902) *Imperialism: A Study*, London: George Allen & Unwin.

——(1909) *The Crisis of Liberalism: New Issues of Democracy*, London: P.S. King & Son.

——(1919) *Taxation in the New State*, London: Methuen.

——(1936) *Veblen*, London: Chapman & Hall.

Hobson, J.M. (2002) 'Two Hegemonies or One? A Historical-Sociological Critique of Hegemonic Stability Theory', in P.K. O'Brien and A. Clesse (eds) *Two Hegemonies*, Aldershot: Ashgate, pp. 305–25.

——(2004) *The Eastern Origins of Western Civilisation*, Cambridge: Cambridge University Press.

Hobson, J.M. and L. Seabrooke (eds) (2007) *Everyday International Political Economy: How Small Actors Transform the World Economy*, Cambridge: Cambridge University Press.

Holmes, S. (1995) *Passions and Constraints*, Chicago: University of Chicago Press.

Hont, I. and M. Ignatieff (eds) (1983) *Wealth and Virtue: The Shaping of Political Economy in the Scottish Enlightenment*, Cambridge: Cambridge University Press.

Hopf, T. (2002a) 'Making the Future Inevitable: Legitimizing, Naturalizing and Stabilizing. The Transition in Estonia, Ukraine and Uzbekistan', *European Journal of International Relations* 8: 403–36.

——(2002b) *Social Construction of International Politics: Identities and Foreign Policies, Moscow, 1955 and 1999*, Ithaca: Cornell University Press.

Hopkin, J. (2002) 'States, Markets, and Corruption: A Review of Some Recent Literature', *Review of International Political Economy* 9: 574–90.

Horsman, R. (1981) *Race and Manifest Destiny*, Cambridge, MA: Harvard University Press.

Howard, M. (1978) *War and the Liberal Conscience*, London: Temple Smith.

Hudson, A. (2000) 'Offshoreness, Globalization and Sovereignty: A Postmodern Geopolitical Economy', *Royal Geographical Society* NS 25: 269–83.

Hume, D. (1985 [1777]) *Essays: Moral, Political, and Literary*, Indianapolis: Liberty Classics.

Huntington, S.P. (1987) 'Modernization and Corruption', in A. J. Heidenheimer, M. Johnston, and V.T. LeVine (eds) *Political Corruption: A Handbook*, New Brunswick: Transaction, pp. 59–63.

——(1993) 'The Clash of Civilizations?', *Foreign Affairs* 72: 22–49.

——(1996) *The Clash of Civilizations*, New York: Simon & Schuster.

Husted, B.W. (1999) 'Wealth, Culture, and Corruption', *Journal of International Business Studies* 30: 339–60.

Huxley, E. (1974) *Livingstone and His African Journeys*, New York: Saturday Review Press.

Hyam, R. (1976) *Britain's Imperial Century*, London: Batsford.

Iggers, G. (1982) 'The Idea of Progress in Historiography and Social Thought since the Enlightenment', in G. Almond, M. Chodorow, and R. Pearce (eds) *Progress and its Discontents*, Berkeley: University of California Press, pp. 41–66.

IMF (International Monetary Fund) (1998) 'Republic of Uzbekistan: Recent Economic Developments', IMF Staff Country Report No. 98/116, Washington, DC: IMF.

——(1999) *International Capital Markets: Developments, Prospects, and Key Policy Issues*, Washington, DC: IMF.

——(2000) 'Code of Good Practices on Transparency in Monetary and Financial Policies', International Monetary Fund, 3 August, www.imf.org/external/np/mae/mft/index.htm.

——(2001) 'Code of Good Practices on Fiscal Transparency', International Monetary Fund, 23 March, www.imf.org/external/np/fad/trans/code.htm.

——(2005) 'Financial Market Update – June 2005', International Capital Markets Department, Global Markets Analysis Division, Washington, DC: IMF.

Inayatullah, N. and D.L. Blaney (2004) *International Relations and the Problem of Difference*, London: Routledge.

Ingham, G.K. (1984) *Capitalism Divided? The City and Industry in British Social Development*, Basingstoke: Macmillan.

International Financial Institution Advisory Commission (2000) *Report of the International Financial Institution Advisory Commission*, Washington, DC: International Financial Institution Advisory Commission.

International Organization for Standardization (2005) 'New Work Item Proposal – Social Responsibility', www.iso.ch.

Isaacson, M. (2004) 'United States', *Offshore-fox.com*, www.offshore-fox.com/offshore-corporations/offshore_corporations_0402.html.

Ishihara, S. (1991) *The Japan That Can Say No*, New York: Simon & Schuster.

Jacobsson, B., P. Lægreid, and O.K. Pedersen (2004) *Europeanization and Transnational States*, London: Routledge.

Jacobzone, S. (2000) 'Pharmaceutical Policies in OECD Countries: Reconciling Social and Industrial Goals', Paris: OECD Publications.

James, H. (1995) 'The Historical Development of the Principle of Surveillance', *IMF Staff Papers* 42: 762–91.

——(1996) *International Monetary Cooperation since Bretton Woods*, Oxford: Oxford University Press.

Jayasuriya, K. (2000) 'Authoritarian Liberalism, Governance and the Emergence of the Regulatory State in Post-Crisis East Asia', in R. Robison (ed.) *Politics and Markets in the Wake of the Asian Crisis*, London: Routledge, pp. 315–29.

Jeck, A. (1994) 'The Macrostructure of Adam Smith's Theoretical System: A Reconstruction', *European Journal of the History of Economic Thought* 1: 551–76.

Justman, S. (1993) *The Autonomous Male of Adam Smith*, Norman: University of Oklahoma Press.

Kant, I. (1963 [1795]) 'Perpetual Peace', in L.W. Beck (ed.) *Kant on History*, Indianapolis: Bobbs-Merrill, pp. 85–135.

Kapstein, E.B. (2002) 'Virtuous Circles? Human Capital Formation, Economic Development and the Multinational Enterprise', OECD Development Centre Technical Papers 191, Paris: OECD.

Katzenstein, P.J. (1996) *The Culture of National Security: Norms and Identity in World Politics*, New York: Columbia University Press.

Kaufmann, D. (1997) 'Corruption: The Facts', *Foreign Policy* 107: 114–31.

Keck, M. and K. Sikkink (1998) *Activists beyond Borders: Transnational Advocacy Groups in International Politics*, Ithaca: Cornell University Press.

Keefer, P. (2004) 'A Review of the Political Economy of Governance: From Property Rights to Voice', World Bank Policy Research Working Paper 3315, Washington, DC: World Bank.

Keene, E. (2002) *Beyond the Anarchical Society*, Cambridge: Cambridge University Press.

Kelly, T. (1998) 'Ability and Willingness to Pay in the Age of Pax Britannica, 1890–1914', *Explorations in Economic History* 35: 31–58.

Kenen, P.B. (2001) *The International Financial Architecture*, Washington, DC: Institute for International Economics.

Kerkvliet, B.J.T. (2005) *The Power of Everyday Politics: How Vietnamese Peasants Changed National Policy*, Ithaca: Cornell University Press.

Keynes, J.M. (1980) *The Collected Writings of John Maynard Keynes*, Vol. 26, London: Macmillan.

Khan, M.H. (2002) 'Corruption and Governance in Early Capitalism', in J.R. Pincus and J.A. Winters (eds) *Reinventing the World Bank*, Ithaca: Cornell University Press, pp. 164–84.

Kimmis, J. (2000) 'Tax Havens: Releasing the Hidden Billions for Poverty Eradication', Oxfam GB Policy Paper, Oxford: Oxfam.

Kindleberger, C.P. (1973) *The World in Depression 1929–1939*, London: Allen Lane.

Kjær, P. and O.K. Pedersen (2001) 'Translating Liberalization: Neoliberalism in the Danish Negotiated Economy', in J.L. Campbell and O.K. Pedersen (eds) *The Rise of Neoliberalism and Institutional Analysis*, Princeton: Princeton University Press, pp. 219–48.

Klein, N. (2000) *No Logo*, New York: Picador.

Klitgaard, R. (1988) *Controlling Corruption*, Berkeley: University of California Press.

Köhler, H. (2001) 'The Challenges of Globalization and the Role of the IMF: Remarks by IMF Managing Director to a Meeting with Members of the Deutsche Bundestag', International Monetary Fund, 2 April, www.imf.org/external/np/speeches/2001/040201.htm.

——(2002) 'Strengthening the Framework for the Global Economy: A Speech Given on the Occasion of the Award Ceremony of the Konrad Adenauer Foundation Social Market Economy Prize', International Monetary Fund, 15 November, www.imf.org/external/np/speeches/2002/111502.htm.

——(2003a) 'The Challenges of Globalization and the Role of the IMF: Address at the Annual Meeting of the Society for Economics and Management', International Monetary Fund, 15 May.

——(2003b) 'Implementing the Monterrey Consensus: Address at the High-Level Segment of the ECOSOC', International Monetary Fund, 30 June, www.imf.org/external/np/speeches/2003/061803.htm.

——(2003c) 'Transcript of Remarks at the Fourth Annual Conference of the Parliamentary Network on the World Bank', International Monetary Fund, 9 March, www.imf.org/external/np/tr/2003/tr030309.htm.

Komiya, R. and M. Itoh (1988) 'Japan's International Trade and Trade Policy, 1955–1984', in T. Inoguchi and D. Okimoto (eds) *The Political Economy of Japan*, Vol. II, Stanford: Stanford University Press, pp. 173–224.

Kotsonis, Y. (1998) *Making Peasants Backward: Managing Populations in Russian Agricultural Cooperatives, 1861–1914*, Basingstoke: Macmillan.

Krastev, I. (2004) *Shifting Obsessions: Three Essays on the Politics of Anti-corruption*, Budapest and New York: Central European University Press.

Kratochwil, F. and J.G. Ruggie (1986) 'International Organization: A State of the Art on an Art of the State', *International Organization* 40: 753–75.

Kristensen, P.H. (2005) 'Modelling National Business Systems and the Civilizing Process', in G. Morgan, R. Whitely, and E. Moen (eds) *Changing Capitalism: Internationalism, Institutional Change and Systems of Economic Organization*, Oxford: Oxford University Press, pp. 383–414.

Krueger, A.O. (2001) 'Transcript of a Briefing with Journalists', International Monetary Fund, 24 September, www.imf.org/external/np/tr/2001/tr010924.htm.

Lambsdorff, J. (2004) 'Background Paper to the 2004 Corruption Perceptions Index', www.transparency.org/cpi/2004/dnld/framework_en.pdf.

Landa, L. (1980) *Essays in Eighteenth-Century English Literature*, Princeton: Princeton University Press.

Landes, D.S. (1998) *The Wealth of Nations*, London: Little, Brown & Co.

Langley, P. (2002) *World Financial Orders*, London: Routledge.

Larmour, P. (2003) 'Transparency International and Policy Transfer in Papua New Guinea', *Pacific Economic Bulletin* 18: 115–20.

——(2005) *Foreign Flowers: Institutional Transfer and Good Governance in the Pacific Islands*. Honolulu: Hawai'i University Press.

Larmour, P. and M. Barcham (2004) 'National Integrity Systems Pacific Islands Overview Report', www.transparency.org.au/documents/NISPACoverview04.pdf.

Larsen, F. (2002) 'How to Govern (Better) the World Economy', Helsinki: Helsinki Conference: Searching for Global Partnerships.

Lauterpacht, H. (1947) *Recognition in International Law*, Cambridge: Cambridge University Press.

Lawson, N. (1992) *The View from No 11*, London: Bantam Press.

League of Nations (1944) *International Currency Experience: Lessons of the Inter-war Period*, Geneva: League of Nations.

Levine, D. (1998) 'The Self and Its Interests in Classical Political Economy', *European Journal of the History of Economic Thought* 5: 36–59.

Levy, D. (1995) 'The Partial Spectator in the *Wealth of Nations*: A Robust Utilitarianism', *European Journal of the History of Economic Thought* 2: 299–326.

Lindgren, R. (1973) *The Social Philosophy of Adam Smith*, The Hague: Martinus Nijhoff.

Linklater, A. (2004) 'Norbert Elias, the "Civilizing Process" and the Sociology of International Relations', *International Politics* 41: 3–35.

Lipson, C. (1985), *Standing Guard: Protecting Foreign Capital in the Nineteenth and Twentieth Centuries*, Berkeley: University of California Press.

List, F. (1885) *The National System of Political Economy*, London: Longmans, Green.

Liu, M.Y. (2003) 'Detours from Utopia on the Silk Road: Ethical Dilemmas of Neoliberal Triumphalism', *Central Eurasian Studies Review* 2: 2–10.

Locke, J. (1988 [1698]) *Two Treatises of Government*, Cambridge: Cambridge University Press.

Lorimer, J. (1883) *Institutes of the Law of Nations*, Vol. 1, Edinburgh: William Blackwood & Sons.

Low, D.A. (1996) *The Egalitarian Moment*, Cambridge: Cambridge University Press.

Lugard, F.D. (1923) *The Dual Mandate in British Tropical Africa*, Edinburgh: W. Blackwood.

Lui, F.T. (1996) 'Three Aspects of Corruption', *Contemporary Economic Policy* 14: 26–9.

Lukes, S. (1974) *Power: A Radical View*, London: Macmillan.

Lundberg, K. (2002) 'High Road or Low? Transparency International and the Corruption Perceptions Index', Kennedy School of Government Case Program C15-02-1658.0.

Luong, P.J. (2001) *Institutional Change and Political Continuity in Post-Soviet Central Asia: Power, Perception, and Pacts*, Cambridge: Cambridge University Press.

——(2004) 'Politics in the Periphery: Competing Views of Central Asian States and Societies', in P.J. Luong (ed.) *The Transformation of Central Asia: States and Societies from Soviet Rule to Independence*, Ithaca: Cornell University Press, pp. 1–28.

Machiavelli, N. (1950) *The Prince and the Discourses*, New York: Modern Library, Macmillan.

MacKenzie, D. (2003) 'An Equation and its Worlds: *Bricolage*, Exemplars, Disunity and Performativity in Financial Economics', *Social Studies of Science* 33: 831–68.

McKinnon, R.I. (1993) 'The Rules of the Game: International Money in Historical Perspective', *Journal of Economic Literature* 31: 1–44.

McLure, C. (2005) 'Will the OECD Initiative on Harmful Tax Competition Help Developing and Transition Countries?', *Bulletin for International Fiscal Documentation* 59: 90–8.

McNamara, K.R. (1998) *The Currency of Ideas: Monetary Politics in the European Union*, Ithaca: Cornell University Press.

Malinowski, B. (1929) 'Practical Anthropology', *Africa* 2: 22–39.

Mamdani, M. (1996) *Citizen and Subject*, Princeton: Princeton University Press.

Mann, M. (1993) *The Sources of Social Power, Vol. II: The Rise of Classes and Nation-States, 1760–1914*, Cambridge: Cambridge University Press.

March, J.G. and J.P. Olsen (1989) *Rediscovering Institutions: The Organizational Basis of Politics*, New York: Free Press.

——(1998) 'The Institutional Dynamics of International Political Orders', *International Organization* 52: 943–69.

Marshall, T. (1950) *Citizenship and Social Class*, Cambridge: Cambridge University Press.

Matthews, D. (2004) 'WTO Decision on Implementation of Paragraph 6 of the Doha Declaration on the TRIPS Agreement and Public Health: A Solution to the Access to Essential Medicines Problem?', *Journal of International Economic Law* 7: 73–107.

Mauro, P. (1995) 'Corruption and Growth', *Quarterly Journal of Economics* 110: 681–712.

——(1997) *Why Worry about Corruption?*, Economic Issues Series #6, Washington, DC: International Monetary Fund.

——(2004) 'The Persistence of Corruption and Slow Economic Growth', IMF Staff Papers 51.

Mauro, P. and Y. Yafeh (2003) 'The Corporation of Foreign Bondholders', IMF Working Paper WP/03/107, Washington, DC: International Monetary Fund.

Mehmet, O. (1999) *Westernizing the Third World*, 2nd edn, London: Routledge.

Michael, B. (2004) 'Explaining Organizational Change in International Development: The Role of Complexity in Anti Corruption Work', *Journal of International Development* 16: 1067–88

Michie, J. and J.G. Smith (eds) (1999) *Global Instability*, London: Routledge.

Mill, J. (1975) *History of British India*, Chicago: Chicago University Press.

Mill, J.S. (1962) 'Civilization [1836]', in G. Himmelfarb (ed.) *Essays on Politics and Culture*, Garden City: Doubleday & Company, 51–84.

——(1977 [1865]) *Collected Works of John Stuart Mill*, Toronto: University of Toronto Press.

Millikin, J. (1999) 'The Study of Discourse in International Relations: A Critique of Research Methods', *European Journal of International Relations* 5: 225–54.

Mitchell, D. (2001) 'The OECD Pulls a Bait-and-Switch on the US Treasury', *The Wall Street Journal Europe* 11 July: 7.

Moggridge, D. (ed.) (1972) *The Collected Writings of John Maynard Keynes, volume 9: Essays in Persuasion*, London: Macmillan Press for the Royal Economic Society.

Montesquieu, C. (1949 [1748]) *The Spirit of the Laws*, New York: Hafner Publishing Company.

Moody Stuart, G. (1997) *Grand Corruption: How Business Bribes Damage Developing Countries*, Oxford: WorldView Publications.

Moore, M. (2003) *A World without Walls: Freedom, Development, Free Trade and Global Governance*, Cambridge: Cambridge University Press.

Morgan, L.H. (1964 [1877]) *Ancient Society*, Cambridge, MA: The Belknap Press.

Morton, A.D. (2005) *Unravelling Gramsci: Hegemony, Imperialism and Resistance in the Global Political Economy*, London: Pluto Press.

Mosley, L. (2000) 'Room to Move: International Financial Markets and National Welfare States', *International Organization* 54: 737–73.

——(2003a) 'Attempting Global Standards: National Governments, International Finance, and the IMF's Data Regime', *Review of International Political Economy* 10: 331–62.

——(2003b) *Global Capital and National Governments*, Cambridge: Cambridge University Press.

Mosseau, M. (2000) 'Market Prosperity, Democratic Consolidation, and Democratic Peace', *Journal of Conflict Resolution* 44: 472–507.

Mozaffari, M. (2001) 'The Transformationalist Perspective and the Rise of a Global Standard of Civilization', *International Relations of the Asia-Pacific* 1: 247–64.

——(ed.) (2002) *Globalization and Civilizations*, London: Routledge.

MSF (Médecins Sans Frontières) (2001) 'Fatal Imbalance: The Crisis in Research Development for Drugs for Neglected Diseases', Geneva: MSF Access to Essential Medicines Campaign.

——(2003) 'Doha Derailed: A Progress Report on TRIPS and Access to Medicines', www.accessmed-msf.org/documents/cancunbriefing.pdf.

Muldrew, C. (1998) *The Economy of Obligation: The Culture of Credit and Social Relations in Early Modern England*, New York: St Martin's Press.

Namazie, C.Z. (2003a) 'Why Labour Hoarding May be Rational: A Model of Firm Behaviour during Transition', Centre for Analysis of Social Exclusion Discussion Paper No. 69, London: Centre for Analysis of Social Exclusion.

——(2003b) 'The Effect of Unobservables on Labour Supply Decisions: The Formal and Informal Sector During Transition', Centre for Analysis of Social Exclusion Discussion Paper No. 72, London: Centre for Analysis of Social Exclusion.

Nike (2005) Nikebiz.com, Responsibility, Overview, www.nike.com/nikebiz/nikebiz.jhtml?page = 54.

Nisbet, R. (1980) *History of the Idea of Progress*, London: Heinemann.

Noonan Jr, J.T. (1984) *Bribes*, New York: Macmillan.

Norgaard, R. (1994) *Development Betrayed: The End of Progress and a Coevolutionary Revisioning of the Future*, London: Routledge.

North, D.C. (1990) *Institutions, Institutional Change and Economic Performance*, Cambridge: Cambridge University Press.

Nye, J.S. (1967) 'Corruption and Political Development: A Cost–Benefit Analysis', *American Political Science Review* 61: 417–27.

Obstfeld, M. (1998) 'The Global Capital Market: Benefactor or Menace?', *Journal of Economic Perspectives* 12: 9–30.

OECD (Organization for Economic Co-operation and Development) (1997) OECD Convention on Combating Bribery of Foreign Public Officials in International Business Transactions, OECD, 21 November, www.oecd.org/document/21/0,2340,en_2649_37447_2017813_1_1_1_37447,00.html.

——(1998) 'Harmful Tax Competition: An Emerging Global Issue', Paris: OECD.

——(2000) 'Towards Global Tax Co-operation: Report to the 2000 Ministerial Council Meeting and Recommendations by the Committee on Fiscal Affairs. Progress in Identifying and Eliminating Harmful Tax Practices', Paris: OECD.

——(2001) 'The OECD's Project on Harmful Tax Practices: The 2001 Progress Report', OECD Forum on Harmful Tax Practices, Paris: OECD.

——(2002) 'Agreement on Exchange of Information on Tax Matters', www.oecd.org/dataoecd/15/43/2082215.pdf.

——(2004a) 'A Process for Achieving a Global Level Playing Field', OECD Global Forum on Taxation, Berlin, 3–4 June, www.oecd.org/dataoecd/13/0/31967501.pdf.

——(2004b) 'The OECD's Project on Harmful Tax Practices: The 2004 Progress Report', Paris: OECD.

Offer, A. (1997) 'Between the Gift and the Market: The Economy of Regard', *The Economic History Review* 50: 450–76.

Oliver, M.J. (1997) 'Whatever Happened to Monetarism? A Review of British Exchange Rate Policy in the 1980s', *Twentieth Century British History* 8: 49–73.

——(2006) 'Financial Crises', in M.J. Oliver and D.H. Aldcroft (eds) *Economic Disasters of the Twentieth Century*, Cheltenham: Edward Elgar, forthcoming.

Oliver, M.J., A. Hamilton and T. Miller (2006) 'Downhill from Devaluation: The Battle for Sterling, 1967–1972', *Economic History Review*, forthcoming.

O'Neill, P. (2001) 'Confronting OECD's Notions of Taxation', *Washington Times*, 10 May.

Onuf, P. and N. Onuf (1993) *Federal Union, Modern World: The Law of Nations in an Age of Revolutions, 1776–1814*, Madison: Madison House.

O'Rourke, K. and J. Williamson (1999) *Globalization and History: The Evolution of the Nineteenth-Century Atlantic Economy*, Cambridge, MA: MIT Press.

Our World Is Not For Sale (2004) www.ourworldisnotforsale.org.

Pagden, A. (1998) 'The Genesis of "Governance" and Enlightenment Conceptions of the Cosmopolitan World Order', *International Social Science Journal* 50: 7–15.

——(2000) 'Stoicism, Cosmopolitanism, and the Legacy of European Imperialism', *Constellations* 7: 3–22.

——(2001) *Peoples and Empires*, New York: The Modern Library.

Palan, R. (1998) 'Trying to Have Your Cake and Eating It: How and Why the State System has Created Offshore', *International Studies Quarterly* 42: 625–44.

Parsons, C. (2003) *A Certain Idea of Europe*, Ithaca: Cornell University Press.

Parsons, T. (1967) *Sociological Theory and Modern Society*, New York: Free Press.

Pauly, L.W. (1997) *Who Elected the Bankers? Surveillance and Control in the World Economy*, Ithaca: Cornell University Press.

Payne, R.A. (2001) 'Persuasion, Frames and Norm Construction', *European Journal of International Relations* 7: 37–61.

Payne, R.A. and N.H. Samhat (2004) *Democratizing Global Politics*, Albany: SUNY Press.

Peil, J. (1999) *Adam Smith and Economic Science*, Cheltenham: Edward Elgar.

Persaud, B. (2001) 'OECD Curbs on Offshore Financial Centres: A Major Issue For Small States', *The Round Table* 359: 199–212.

Pettit, P. (1997) *Republicanism: A Theory of Freedom and Government*, Oxford: Oxford University Press.

Pigman, G.A. (1996) 'United States Trade Policies at Loggerheads: Super 301, the Uruguay Round and Indian Services Trade Liberalization', *Review of International Political Economy* 3: 728–62.

Pocock, J.G.A. (1975) *The Machiavellian Moment: Florentine Political Thought and the Atlantic Republican Tradition*, Princeton: Princeton University Press.

Polanyi, K. (1957 [1944]) *The Great Transformation*, Boston: Beacon Press.

Pomeranz, K. (2005) 'Empire and "Civilizing" Missions, Past and Present', *Daedalus* 134: 34–44.

Pomfret, R. (1995) *The Economies of Central Asia*, Princeton: Princeton University Press.

Pomfret, R. and K. Anderson (2001) 'Economic Development Strategies in Central Asia Since 1991', *Asian Studies Review* 25: 185–200.

Pope, J. (1996) *National Integrity Systems: The TI Source Book*, Berlin: Transparency International.

Prah Ruger, J. (2004) 'Health and Social Justice', *The Lancet* 364: 1075–81.

Price, R. (1997) *The Chemical Weapons Taboo*, Ithaca: Cornell University Press.

Quinn, S. (1997), 'Goldsmith-Banking: Mutual Acceptance and Interbanker Clearing in Restoration London', *Explorations in Economic History* 34: 411–32.

Rae, H. (2002) *State Identities and the Homogenisation of Peoples*, Cambridge: Cambridge University Press.

Rahn, R. (2004) 'Halting French Economic Thrust', *Washington Times*, 4 November.

Ramonet, I. (2004) 'Protestataires, unissez-vous!', *Manière de voir* 75: 6–7.

Rato, de, R. (2004) 'The IMF at 60: Evolving Challenges, Evolving Role, Opening Remarks at the Conference on "Dollars, Debts and Deficits: 60 Years after Bretton Woods"', International Monetary Fund, 14 June.

Rawls, J. (1972) *A Theory of Justice*, Oxford: Oxford University Press.
——(1993) *Political Liberalism*, New York: Columbia University Press.
——(1999) *The Law of Peoples*, Cambridge, MA: Harvard University Press.
Redmond, J. (1992) 'The Gold Standard between the Wars', in S.N. Broadberry and N.F.R. Crafts (eds) *Britain in the International Economy*, Cambridge: Cambridge University Press, pp. 346–68.
Redwood, H. (1995) *Brazil: The Future Impact of Pharmaceutical Patents*, Felixstowe, Suffolk: Oldwicks Press.
Reinicke, W.H. (1995), *Banking, Politics and Global Finance: American Commercial Banks and Regulatory Change, 1980–1990*, Aldershot: Edward Elgar.
Reus-Smit, C. (1999) *The Moral Purpose of the State: Culture, Social Identity, and Institutional Rationality in International Relations*, Princeton: Princeton University Press.
Ricardo, D. (1891) *Principles of Political Economy and Taxation*, London: George Bell & Sons.
Ricoeur, P. (1965) *History and Truth*, Evanston: Northwestern University Press.
Rizvi, S.A.T. (2002) 'Adam Smith's Sympathy: Towards a Normative Economics', in E. Fulbrook (ed.) *Intersubjectivity in Economics*, London: Routledge, pp. 241–53.
Robinson, R. and J. Gallagher (1981) *Africa and the Victorians*, 2nd edn, London: Macmillan.
Robinson, W. (1996) *Promoting Polyarchy*, Cambridge: Cambridge University Press.
Rodrik, D. (1997) 'Has Globalization Gone Too Far?', Washington, DC: Institute for International Economics.
Rojas-Suarez, L. (2001) 'Can International Capital Standards Strengthen Banks in Emerging Markets?', Institute for International Economics Working Paper 01-10, Washington, DC: Institute for International Economics.
Rose, N. (1999) *Powers of Freedom*, Cambridge: Cambridge University Press.
Rose-Ackerman, S. (1978) *Corruption: A Study in Political Economy*, New York: Academic Press.
——(1999) *Corruption and Government: Causes, Consequences, and Reform*, Cambridge: Cambridge University Press.
Rostow, W.W. (1961) *The Stages of Economic Growth*, Cambridge: Cambridge University Press.
Rousseau, J.-J. (1968) *The Social Contract*, Harmondsworth: Penguin.
Ruggie, J.G. (1982) 'International Regimes, Transactions, and Change: Embedded Liberalism in the Postwar Economic Order', *International Organization* 35: 379–415.
——(1993) 'Territory and Beyond: Problematizing Modernity in International Relations', *International Organization* 47: 139–74.
——(1998) '"What Makes the World Hang Together?" Neo-Utilitarianism and the Social Constructivist Challenge', *International Organization* 52: 855–85.
Rugman, A.M. (2002) 'New Rules for International Investment: The Case for a Multilateral Agreement on Investment (MAI) at the WTO', in C. Milner and R. Read (eds) *Trade Liberalization, Competition and the WTO*, Cheltenham: Edward Elgar, pp. 176–89.
Rupert, M. (2000) *Ideologies of Globalization*, London: Routledge.
Sachs, J.D. (1994) 'Understanding Shock Therapy', Social Market Foundation Occasional Paper 7, London: Social Market Foundation.
Sachsenmaier, D. (2002) 'Multiple Modernities – The Concept and its Potential', in D. Sachsenmaier and J. Riedel with S.N. Eisenstadt (eds) *Reflections on Multiple Modernities: European, Chinese and Other Interpretations*, Leiden: Brill, pp. 43-67.
Said, E. (1991) *Orientalism*, London: Penguin.
Said, E.W. (1992) 'Nationalism, Human Rights, and Interpretation', in B. Johnson (ed.) *Freedom and Interpretation*, New York: Basic Books, pp. 175–205.

Sampson, S. (in press) 'Integrity Warriors: Global Morality and the Anticorruption Movement in the Balkans', in C. Shore and D. Haller (eds) *Understanding Corruption*, London: Routledge.

Sanders, R. (2002) 'The Fight against Fiscal Colonialism: The OECD and Small Jurisdictions', *The Round Table* 365: 325–48.

Santiso, J. (1999) 'Analysts Analyzed: A Socio-economic Approach to Financial and Emerging Markets', *International Political Science Review* 20: 307–30.

——(2003) *The Political Economy of Emerging Markets: Actors, Institutions and Crisis in Latin America*, Basingstoke: Palgrave.

Sartori, G. (1987) *The Theory of Democracy Revisited*, Chatham: Chatham House.

Schäfer, W. (2001) 'Global Civilization and Local Cultures: A Crude Look at the Whole'. *International Sociology* 16: 301–19.

Scherer, F.M. (2000) 'The Pharmaceutical Industry', in A.L Culyer and J.P Newhouse (eds) *Handbook of Health Economics*, Vol. 1, New York: Elsevier Science B.V, pp. 1298–336.

Schmitt, C. (1996) 'The Land Appropriation of a New World', *Telos* 109: 29–80.

Schneider, B. (ed.) (2003) *The Road to International Financial Stability*, Basingstoke: Palgrave.

Schneider, L. (1979) 'Adam Smith on Human Nature and Social Circumstance', in G. O'Driscoll (ed.) *Adam Smith and Modern Political Economy: Bicentennial Essays on The Wealth of Nations*, Ames: Iowa State University Press, pp. 44–67.

Scholte, J.A. (2000) *Globalization: A Critical Introduction*, Basingstoke: Palgrave.

Scholte, J.A. and A. Schnabel (eds) (2002) *Civil Society and Global Finance*, London: Routledge.

Schumpeter, J.A. (1942) *Capitalism, Socialism and Democracy*, New York: Harper & Row.

——(1976) *Capitalism, Socialism, and Democracy*, London: Allen & Unwin.

Schwarzenberger, G. (1955) 'The Standard of Civilisation in International Law', in G.W. Keeton and G. Schwarzenberger (eds) *Current Legal Problems*, London: Stevens & Sons, pp. 212–34.

Seabrooke, L. (2001) *US Power in International Finance: The Victory of Dividends*, London: Palgrave.

——(2004) 'The Economic Taproot of US Imperialism: The Bush Rentier Shift', *International Politics* 41: 293–318.

——(2005a) 'Civilizing Tax Regimes: The International Monetary Fund and Tax Reform in East Asia', paper presented at the International Studies Association annual conference, Hawai'i, 1–5 March.

——(2005b) 'Disintermediation', in M. Griffiths (ed.) *Routledge Encyclopaedia of International Relations and Global Politics*, London: Routledge, pp. 192–96.

——(2006) *The Social Sources of Financial Power: Domestic Legitimacy and International Financial Orders*, Ithaca: Cornell University Press.

Sending, O.J. (2002) 'Constitution, Choice and Change', *European Journal of International Relations* 8: 443–70.

Seth, S. (2000) 'A Postcolonial World?', in G. Fry and J. O'Hagan (eds) *Contending Images of World Politics*, London: Macmillan, pp. 214–26.

Sharman, J. (2004) 'International Organisations, Blacklisting and Tax Haven Regulation', paper presented at the International Studies Association annual conference, Montreal, 1–4 March.

——(2005) 'South Pacific Tax Havens: From Leaders in the Race to the Bottom to Laggards in the Race to the Top?', unpublished paper, Government and International Relations, University of Sydney.

Shiva, V. (2001) 'Globalization and Talibanization', *Outlook India*, 30 October, www.outlookindia.com.

Shklar, J.N. (1990) 'Montesquieu and the New Republicanism', in G. Bock, Q. Skinner, and M. Viroli (eds) *Machiavelli and Republicanism*, Cambridge: Cambridge University Press, pp. 265–79.

Shleifer, A. and R.W. Vishny (1993) 'Corruption', *Quarterly Journal of Economics* 108: 599–617.

Shumer, S.M. (1979) 'Machiavelli: Republican Politics and its Corruption', *Political Theory* 7: 5–34.

Sik, E. (2002) 'The Bad, the Worse and the Worst: Guesstimating the Level of Corruption', in S. Kotkin and A. Sajo (eds) *Political Corruption: A Skeptic's Handbook*, Budapest: Central European University Press, pp. 91–115.

Simmel, G. (1978) *The Philosophy of Money*, London: Routledge & Kegan Paul.

Simmons, B.A. (2000) 'The Legalization of International Monetary Affairs', *International Organization* 54: 573–602.

——(2001) 'The International Politics of Harmonization: The Case of Capital Market Regulation', *International Organization* 55: 589–620.

Simmons, B. and Z. Elkins (2004) 'The Globalization of Liberalization: Policy Diffusion in the International Political Economy', *American Political Science Review* 98: 171–89.

Sinclair, T.J. (2005) *The New Masters of Capital: American Bond Ratings Agencies and the Politics of Creditworthiness*, Ithaca: Cornell University Press.

Singh, A. (1999) '"Asian Capitalism" and the Financial Crisis', in J. Michie and J.G. Smith (eds) *Global Instability*, London: Routledge, pp. 9–36.

Skinner, A. (1979) *A System of Social Science*, Oxford: Clarendon Press.

——(1993) 'Adam Smith: The Origins of the Exchange Economy', *European Journal of the History of Economic Thought* 1: 21–46.

Skinner, Q. (1978) *The Foundations of Modern Political Thought*, Vol. 1, *The Renaissance*, Cambridge: Cambridge University Press.

——(1990) 'The Republican Ideal of Political Liberty', in G. Bock, Q. Skinner, and M. Viroli (eds) *Machiavelli and Republicanism*, Cambridge: Cambridge University Press, pp. 293–309.

Slaughter, A.-M. (1997) 'The Real New World Order', *Foreign Affairs* 76: 183–97.

Slotkin, R. (1973) *Regeneration through Violence*, Middleton: Wesleyan University Press.

Smith. A. (1910) *The Wealth of Nations*, London: J.M. Dent & Sons.

——(1982 [1759]) *The Theory of Moral Sentiments*, Indianapolis: Liberty Fund.

——(1998 [1776]) *An Inquiry into the Nature and Causes of the Wealth of Nations*, Oxford: Oxford University Press.

Solomon, R. (1982) *The International Monetary System, 1945–1981*, New York: Harper & Row.

Song, H.-H. (1997) 'Adam Smith's Conception of the Social Relations of Production', *European Journal of the History of Economic Thought* 4: 23–42.

Starobinski, J. (1993) *Blessings in Disguise; or The Morality of Evil*, Cambridge, MA: Harvard University Press.

Steffeck, J. (2003) 'The Legitimation of International Governance: A Discourse Approach', *European Journal of International Relations* 9: 249–75.

Stiglitz, J. (1998) 'Towards a New Paradigm for Development: Strategies, Policies, and Processes', Prebisch Lecture at UNCTAD, Geneva, 19 October.

——(1999) *Participation and Development*, Seoul: World Bank.

——(2002) *Globalization and Its Discontents*, New York: W.W. Norton.

Strang, D. (1995) 'Contested Sovereignty: The Social Construction of Colonial Imperialism', in T.J. Biersteker and C. Weber (eds) *State Sovereignty as Social Construct*, Cambridge: Cambridge University Press, pp. 22–49.

Strange, S. (1988) *States and Markets*, London: Pinter.

——(1996) *The Retreat of the State*, Cambridge: Cambridge University Press.

——(1998) 'The New World of Debt', *New Left Review* 230: 91–114.

Sullivan, J.S. (2003) *The Future of Corporate Globalization: From the Extended Order to the Global Village*, Westport: Quorum Books.

Surowiecki, J. (2002) 'Bush's Buddy Economy', *The New Yorker*, 2 September.

Suzuki, S. (2005) 'Japan's Socialization into Janus-Faced European International Society', *European Journal of International Relations* 11: 137–64.

Taddei, A. (1999) 'London Clubs in the Late Nineteenth Century', Discussion Papers in Economic and Social History, Number 28, University of Oxford, April.

Tanzi, V. (2000) 'Globalization, Technological Developments, and the Work of Fiscal Termites', International Monetary Fund Working Paper WP/00/181, Washington, DC: IMF.

Tanzi, V. and H. Davoodi (1998) *Roads to Nowhere: How Corruption in Public Investment Hurts Growth*, Economic Issues Series #12, Washington, DC: International Monetary Fund.

Taube, G. and J. Zettelmeyer (1998) 'Output Decline and Recovery in Uzbekistan: Past Performance and Future Prospects', IMF Working Paper WP/98/132, Washington, DC: IMF.

't Hoen, E. (2002) 'TRIPS, Pharmaceutical Patents, and Access to Essential Medicines: A Long Way From Seattle to Doha', *Chicago Journal of International Law* 3: 27–48.

Thomas, G.M., J.W. Meyer, F.O. Ramirez, and J.Boli (eds) (1987) *Institutional Structure*, Beverly Hills: Sage.

Thornton, A.P. (1966) *The Imperial Idea and Its Enemies*, New York: St Martin's Press.

Tilly, C. (1992) *Coercion, Capital and European States, AD* 990–1992, Oxford: Blackwell.

Tisne, M. and D. Smilov (2004) 'From the Ground Up: Assessing the Record of Anticorruption Assistance in Southeastern Europe', Policy Studies Series, Budapest: Centre for Policy Studies, Central European University.

Transparency International (2005) 'TI History', www.transparency.org.

Trouiller, P. *et al.* (2002) 'Neglected Diseases and Pharmaceuticals: Between Deficient Market and Public Health Failure', *The Lancet* 359: 2188–94.

US Department of State (1948) *Proceedings and Documents of United Nations Monetary and Financial Conference, Bretton Woods, New Hampshire, 1–22 July 1944*, Department of State Publications 2866, International Organization and Conference Series 1, 3. Washington, DC.

Verburg, R. (2000) 'Adam Smith's Growing Concern on the Issue of Distributive Justice', *European Journal of the History of Economic Thought* 7: 23–44.

Verme, P. (1998) 'Unemployment, Labour Policies and Health in Transition: Evidence from Kazakhstan', WIDER Working Paper 151, Helsinki: UNU/WIDER.

——(2000) 'The Choice of the Working Sector in Transition: Income and Non-income Determinants of Sector Participation in Kazakhstan', *Economics of Transition* 8: 691–731.

Vitoria, F. d. (1995 [1559]) *De Indis et de Ivre Belli Relectiones*, Buffalo: William S. Hein & Co.

Vladimir, M. and G. Heinrich (1999) 'Kyrgyzstan: A Case Study of Social Stratification', UNU/WIDER Working Papers No. 164, Helsinki: UNU/WIDER.

Vlcek, W. (2004) 'The OECD and Offshore Financial Centres: Rearguard Action against Globalisation?', *Global Change, Peace and Security* 16: 227–42.

Vogel, E.F. (1979) *Japan as Number One: Lessons for America*, Cambridge, MA: Harvard University Press.

Volcker, P. and T. Gyohten (1992) *Changing Fortunes: The World's Money and the Threat to American Leadership*, New York: Times Books.

Wade, R.H. (2003) 'What Strategies Are Viable for Developing Countries Today?', *Review of International Political Economy* 10: 621–44.

Wade, R.H. and F. Veneroso (1998) 'The Asian Crisis: The High Debt Model Versus the Wall Street-Treasury–IMF Complex', *New Left Review* 228: 3–22.

Walker, R.B.J. (1993) *Inside/Outside*, Cambridge: Cambridge University Press.

Wallerstein, I. (1984) *The Politics of the World Economy*, Cambridge: Cambridge University Press.

Walter, A. (1991) *World Power and World Money: The Role of Hegemony and International Monetary Order*, Hemel Hempstead: Harvester Wheatsheaf.

Watson, A. (1974) *Legal Transplants: An Approach to Comparative Law*, Edinburgh: Scottish Academic Press.

Webb, M. (2004) 'Defining the Boundaries of Legitimate State Practice: Norms, Transnational Actors and the OECD's Project on Harmful Tax Competition', *Review of International Political Economy* 11: 787–827.

Weber, M. (1976) *The Protestant Ethic and the Spirit of Capitalism*, London: George Allen & Unwin.

——(1988) *Gesammelte Aufsätze zur Wissenschaftslehre*, Tübingen: J.C.B. Mohr.

——(1998) *The Agrarian Sociology of Ancient Civilizations*, London: Verso.

Wechsler, W.F. (2001) 'Follow the Money', *Foreign Affairs* 80: 40.

West, E.G. (1976) *Adam Smith*, Indianapolis: Liberty Fund.

Westney, E. (1987) *Imitation and Innovation: The Transfer of Western Organizational Patterns to Meiji Japan*, Cambridge, MA: Harvard University Press.

WHO (World Health Organization) (1996) 'Revised Drug Strategy. World Health Assembly Resolution', WHA 49.14, Geneva: WHO.

——(2001). 'Globalization, TRIPS and Access to Pharmaceuticals', *WHO Policy Perspectives on Medicines* 3, March (WHO/EDM/2001.2).

——(2004) 'Equitable Access to Essential Medicines: A Framework for Collective Action', *WHO Policy Perspectives on Medicine* 8, March (WHO/EDM/2004.4).

Wiener, A. (2004) 'Contested Compliance: Interventions on the Normative Structure of World Politics', *European Journal of International Relations* 10: 189–234.

Wight, M. (1977) *Systems of States*, Leicester: Leicester University Press.

——(1991) *International Theory: The Three Traditions*, (eds) G. Wight and M. Porter. Leicester: Leicester University Press, for the Royal Institute of International Affairs.

Wilde, O. (1993) *An Ideal Husband*, London: A. & C. Black.

Williams, D. (1998) 'Economic Development and the Limits of Institutionalism', *SAIS Review* 18: 1–17.

——(1999) 'Constructing the Economic Space: The World Bank and the Making of Homo Oeconomicus', *Millennium* 28: 79–99.

Williams, M. (2003) 'Contesting Global Trade Rules', in L. Benería and S. Bisnath (eds) *Global Tensions: Challenges and Opportunities in the World Economy*, New York: Routledge, pp. 193–206.

Williams, W.A. (1972) *The Tragedy of American Diplomacy*, New York: W.W. Norton.

Williamson, J. (1977) *The Failure of World Monetary Reform, 1971–74*, London: Thomas Nelson.

Williamson, J. and M. Mahar (1998) 'A Survey of Financial Liberalization', *Essays in International Finance*, Princeton: International Finance Section, Princeton University.

Wood, J.C. (1983) *British Economists and the Empire*, London: Croom Helm.

World Bank (1993a) 'Uzbekistan: An Agenda for Economic Reform', World Bank Country Study, Washington, DC: World Bank.

——(1993b) 'Kyrgyzstan: The Transition to a Market Economy', World Bank Country Study, Washington, DC: World Bank.

——(1993c) 'Kazakhstan: The Transition to a Market Economy', World Bank Country Study, Washington, DC: World Bank.

——(1994a) 'Uzbekistan: Adjusting Social Protection', Report No. 13023-UZ, Washington, DC: World Bank.

——(1994b) 'Staff Appraisal Report, Kyrgyz Republic: Social Safety Net Project', Report No. 12986-KG, Washington, DC: World Bank.

——(1994c) 'Kazakhstan: Economic Report Volume One', Report No. 12856-KZ, Washington, DC: World Bank.

——(1994d) 'Uzbekistan: Economic Memorandum, Subsidies and Transfers', Report No. 12934-UZ Volume 1, Washington, DC: World Bank.

——(1995a) *World Development Report 1995: Workers in an Integrating World*, Washington, DC: World Bank/Oxford University Press.

——(1995b) 'Staff Appraisal Report, Republic of Kazakhstan: Social Protection Project', Report No. 13690-KZ, Volume 1, Washington, DC: World Bank.

——(1995c) 'Staff Appraisal Report, Republic of Kazakhstan: Social Protection Project', Report No. 13690-KZ, Volume 2, Washington, DC: World Bank.

——(1998) 'Kazakhstan: Living Standards during the Transition', Report No. 17520-KZ, Washington, DC: World Bank.

——(1999) 'Uzbekistan: Social and Structural Policy Review', Report No. 19626, Washington, DC: World Bank.

——(2004) 'The New Pensions in Kazakhstan: Challenges in Making the Transition', Report No. 30873-KZ, Washington, DC: World Bank.

World Bank, Operations Evaluation Department (2001) 'Kyrgyz Republic: Country Assistance Evaluation', Report No. 23278-KY, Washington, DC: World Bank.

Wright, R. and G.A. Paul (1987) *The Second-Wave: Japan's Global Assault on Financial Services*, Exeter: A. Wheaton & Co.

WTO (World Trade Organization) (2001) 'Declaration on the TRIPS Agreement and Public Health', WT/MIN(01)/DEC/2, www.thunderlake.com/ministerials/DOHA_TRIPSFINAL.pdf.

——(2002) 'WTO Agreements and Public Health: A Joint Study by the WHO and the WTO Secretariat', Geneva: WTO and WHO.

Zagaris, B. (2001a) 'Issues Low Tax Regimes Should Raise When Negotiating with the OECD', *Tax Notes International* 29 January: 523–32.

——(2001b) 'News Analysis: Initiatives by OECD, Financial Action Task Force on Money Laundering at Critical Junctures', *Tax Notes International* 18 June: 3087–97.

——(2001c) 'Development in International Tax Enforcement: A Brave New World at the Millennium', *Tax Notes International* 20 August: 991–7.

Zuckerman, E.W. (1999) 'The Categorical Imperative: Securities Analysts and the Illegitimacy Discount', *American Journal of Sociology* 104: 1398–438.

——(2004) 'Structural Incoherence and Stock Market Activity', *American Sociological Review* 69: 405–32.

Zuckerman, M. (1987) 'Identity in British America: Unease in Eden', in N. Canny and A. Pagden (eds) *Colonial Identity in the Atlantic World 1500–1800*, Princeton: Princeton University Press, pp. 115–57.

Index

For Product Safety Concerns and Information please contact our EU representative GPSR@taylorandfrancis.com
Taylor & Francis Verlag GmbH, Kaufingerstraße 24, 80331 München, Germany

www.ingramcontent.com/pod-product-compliance
Ingram Content Group UK Ltd.
Pitfield, Milton Keynes, MK11 3LW, UK
UKHW010959180926
475701UK00004B/460
* 9 7 8 0 4 1 5 4 5 9 8 5 3 *